WHO PACKS PISTOLS?

Cybill Shepherd, Betty Thomas (from "Hill Street Blues"), Susan Howard (of "Dallas") and Nancy Reagan are licensed to carry handguns. Joan Rivers has applied for a permit. Even Eleanor Roosevelt packed a .25 caliber pocket Colt.

Should you?

"The 'gentler sex' is fed up with being raped, mugged and murdered. Today millions of women are packing pistols. And they shoot very well."

—*Philadelphia Inquirer*

ARMED & FEMALE

"A must for all American women . . . a job well done and long overdue."

—Helen L. Grieco,
Executive Director,
National Organization for
Women, San Francisco
Chapter

"Self-defense is not merely our legal right but our moral duty; because women are more vulnerable than men, their need and obligation to defend themselves is even greater than that of men. This is an important and timely book."

—Dr. Thomas S. Szasz,
Professor of Psychiatry,
Syracuse University

"[The] interviews here with rapists and victims reinforce her argument—and may convince additional numbers of women to acquire weapons."

—*Publishers Weekly*

ABOUT THE AUTHOR

Paxton Quigley was once an anti-gun activist—a member of the National Committee for Handgun Control—who helped pass the Handgun Control Act of 1968. But over twenty years have passed, during which violent crime in America has escalated . . . and Paxton Quigley has changed her mind about gun ownership.

Today she is a recognized handgun expert, trained by the top authorities in the field, including Massad Ayoob, Jeff Cooper, and Ray Chapman. She is an award-winning competition shootist, an expert security consultant, and she has worked as a bodyguard to many high-level executives and celebrities, including Yoko Ono.

Her unique perspective, intensive research and thorough treatment of the issues make *Armed & Female* indispensable for any woman who cares about her own safety.

ARMED

&

Female

PAXTON QUIGLEY

— *smp* —
ST. MARTIN'S PAPERBACKS

Published by arrangement with E. P. Dutton

ARMED & FEMALE

Copyright © 1989 by Paxton Quigley Productions.
Illustrations by Allen Baron.

Library of Congress Catalog Card Number: 88-28533

ISBN: 0-312-95150-7

Printed in the United Stares of America

E. P. Dutton hardcover edition published 1989
St. Martin's Paperbacks edition/November 1990

10 9 8 7 6 5 4

To my grandmother,
Paula Spencer, a woman of revolutionary spirit,
who has been an inspiration to me.
1889–1988

Acknowledgments

NO BOOK PUBLISHED is ever solely the work of the author. Numerous people make it happen. If it weren't for the early suggestions of Michael Korda in leading me to the important scholars and lawyers in the handgun debate, it would have taken me much longer to research the book.

I am profoundly grateful to criminologist and constitutional lawyer Don B. Kates, Jr., America's foremost scholar of gun-control issues, who spent hours of his time providing me with a wealth of information and contacts as well as reading manuscript drafts.

My gratitude extends to New York attorney Mark Benenson, who specializes in firearms law; Dr. Martin Reiser of the Los Angeles Police Department; Model Mugging founder, Matthew Thomas; Model Mugging of Los Angeles instructors Lisa Gaeta and Dr. Al Potash; actress Lee Purcell and film producer Gary Lowe; Second Amendment Foundation founder, Alan Gottlieb; gun instructress Wendy Allen; Dr. John Brinkley of Harborview Medical Center, Seattle; New York City attorney Sue Wimmershoff Caplan; Marjolgn Bijlefeld, National Coalition to Ban Handguns; Jane Clarenbach, Handgun Information Center; Susan Whitmore, Handgun Control, Inc.; Professor Franklin Zimring, University of California, Berkeley; Caroline Crawshaw, National Rifle Association; Dr. Paul

Blackman, National Rifle Association; Sue Osthoff, Women Against Abuse; Silver Creek Outfitters, Ketchum, Idaho; and to the staff of the Ketchum Community Library.

I wish to thank the following combat gun masters, who so patiently taught me how to shoot and spent their time assisting me in the project: Massed Ayoob, director of Lethal Force Institute; Ray Chapman, director of Chapman Academy Practical Shooting; Jeff Cooper, director of The American Pistol Institute; John Farnam, director of Defensive Training, Inc.; and Mike Dalton and Mickey Fowler, directors of International Shootists Inc.

My appreciation extends to Bob Duggan, Martha Braunig, Lance Weber, Jack McGeorge, Skip Batley, Bruce Carlton, Clay Owen, Paul Dallenbach, and Flint Smith for their caring and outstanding training at Executive Security International, Aspen, Colorado.

Thanks go to G. Gordon Liddy, Moshe Alon, Steven Goldrat, Lynton Jordahl, and Jack Sague at the G. Gordon Liddy Academy of Corporate Security and Private Investigation, Miami, Florida.

I am grateful to the following manufacturers, who graciously lent me their firearms: Beretta USA Corp; Charter Arms Corporation; Detonics Firearms Industries; Gun South/Steyr; Heckler & Koch Inc.; Interarms; Sigarms Inc.; Smith & Wesson; Springfield Armory, Strum Ruger and Company, Inc.; and Taurus International Manufacturing.

Thanks to Bianchi International and Safariland for equipping me with their leather accessories as well as to Craig Spegel, Competition Electronics Inc.; Ohler Research Inc.; Cannon Safe; Cold Steel, Inc.; Crosman; and Daisy Manufacturing Company.

An important acknowledgment goes to Federal Cartridge Company, who kindly provided thousands of rounds of ammunition for my gun training.

To my sons, David and Jon, and my parents, a special

1117192225272931333537394143454749525456586062646668707274767880828486889092949698100

thanks for their understanding, love, and support. And to friends Barbara Cohn, Kip Morrison, Marie Yates, John Sack, Phil Simms, Kenyon Kramer, and David Columbia for their encouragement and friendship.

My heartfelt appreciation goes to Allen Baron, who graciously volunteered hours of his time to draw the illustrations for the book.

I would like to thank my editor, Joyce Engelson, who had the courage to take on the subject of women and guns and then helped me gain a clearer understanding of many important gun-related issues. And also warm thanks go to my agent, Susan Protter, who believed in the project right from the beginning.

Most of all, I want to thank Jeffrey Mannix. Without him, this book would never have been written. He gave me encouragement, ideas, strength, love, and a wonderful humor to help me overcome huge obstacles in preparing the book. He also was instrumental in my becoming a stronger, wiser woman.

Finally, I want to thank the women who shared traumatic and personal details of their lives with me and who inspired the writing of this book.

CONTENTS

PREFACE

IN THE WAKE of the assassination of Robert Kennedy in 1968, I campaigned vociferously for handgun controls. I was on Senator Kennedy's presidential campaign staff in Washington, D.C., and along with other staff members and astronaut John Glenn founded the first anti-gun political-action committee—the National Committee for Handgun Control—which contributed significantly to the first federal law policy on handguns, known as the Handgun Control Act of 1968.

This was banner legislation, I thought; for the first time in America's violent history, law-abiding citizens would witness the beginning of the end of senseless murder and terrorism, as we pursued peaceful social solutions to our growing domestic troubles.

Our vision was simple enough: Crime was the result of an unwatchful, uncaring, uninvolved society, and criminals were the victims of the system. If guns were made harder or impossible for everyone to acquire, we thought violent crimes in the street and crimes of passion at home would subside, even though, as we knew, guns could be easily purchased on the black market.

We waited for change. We demanded judicial change that afforded respect to the criminal-victim, and we put trust in our peers to restore a modicum of order in our increasingly complex society.

Something inside of me said, We're losing. Or was it just going to take more time? The wheels of reform move cog over cog, after all, I told myself. But crime continued to escalate the next year, and the next, and the next. And during the twenty years that followed, crime reached proportions considered epidemic. At first, there were stories in the newspapers and on television of violent crime, but they were about people we didn't know. Soon, however, we began to hear of friends and acquaintances who were robbed, raped, or mugged. In some cases, we ourselves were the victims. We bolted doors, installed alarm systems, and expanded our police departments. Yet we grew more frightened, until some of us wouldn't even go out alone at night. Had we finally become a nation of victims?

It was only last year that I came to realize that our gun-control laws did not work and the police could not realistically help in life-threatening situations.

It was like a light being switched on. I was accompanying a friend to pick up a gun that had been repaired by a gunsmith in the little Western town of Hailey, Idaho. While I was waiting, I became curious about all the old rifles and six-shooters displayed there, and I said to Mr. Clayton, the gun-shop owner, "Do you have a gun that's good for me to keep for self-defense?"

Huh? What did I say? Had I gone mad?

The next thing I knew, I was holding a compact, stainless-steel revolver and Mr. Clayton was commending me on having the good sense to recognize the need for a woman to protect herself these days—his wife and daughter, he said, both had handguns and knew how to shoot them well—because a woman should never depend on any man to always be there to protect her. Mr. Clayton wasn't much of a women's libber, he said, but he had taught his daughter early on that she shouldn't ever trust men to do anything she should be able to do herself.

His words "These days" echoed in my ears. He was right: *these days* were far more dangerous than those days. For more than ten years, I had been living on my own in Los Angeles. My house had been burglarized twice in two years, my car stolen from in front of my house while I watched from the kitchen window, and two of my friends raped—one in her own bed. I had even found myself sitting in my car in my garage a number of times after returning from evening engagements, afraid to exchange the safety of my car for the uncertainty of my unattended house. With each evening's newscast, the things that went bump in the night began to evoke more and more fear and sleeplessness in me. I didn't know it until that day in Hailey, but I frequently felt threatened, and I was often scared.

I gave the gun back to Mr. Clayton and told him I'd think about it. He gently touched my shoulder and carefully reminded me that, once I had thought about buying a handgun, continued deliberation was like putting off buying a fire extinguisher for my kitchen.

I left the store. I now realize I began writing *Armed & Female* at the same moment. And after intense research—interviewing hundreds of women who own handguns, learning about violent crime against women and being privileged to hear the stories and thoughts and emotions of women who had been assaulted and raped, conversing with law-enforcement officers and criminologists, listening to the advice of hardened criminals behind bars in some of our country's most intense prisons, and studying the issues burning the tongues of the pro-gun and anti-gun champions—my attitude toward guns has changed. I have come to understand that my views on the nature of nonviolence do not conflict with defending myself or my family.

I began forming new opinions after talking to many women who had been victims of crime and who might have had a better chance if they had had guns and had known how to use them. I was most impressed and influenced by the growing number of responsible women with whom I spoke who have owned guns for years and just refuse to be victimized. And I was equally affected by the many women who unequivocally rejected guns and, in some cases, the whole idea of learning self-defense or practicing it.

I have tried to remain true to the manner in which stories and accounts were told to me, and to ensure privacy I have altered names, dates, and locations, except in the cases of Randi McGinn and Elyse Singer, who agreed to let their names be used.

If this trend of gun ownership by women continues, and if it becomes an actual movement, there seems to be every indication that fewer and fewer people will try to rape or assault women.

It is apparent to me that the arming of American women needs to be brought out into the open, discussed, and advanced—a rueful awakening, without a doubt, but perhaps the last frontier needed to be won by women on the road to equality.

SUN VALLEY, IDAHO, 1988

1

Women with Guns

"ALL THE TIME I was locked in the trunk, I could hear him yelling from the driver's seat about what he was going to do to me."

Kate Petit's car sputtered to a stop on the interstate highway between Lake Kissimmee and Tampa, where she lives alone in a nicely groomed but older condominium development on the established side of town.

"You know, I have never made that drive to the lake without worrying somewhere along the way about the risk of having a flat tire or breaking down and being stranded on the side of the road, alone."

Kate was stranded, all right. What looked to her like a mixture of smoke and steam was pouring out the top, bottom, and sides of the engine compartment. She knew it was safer to stay in the car with the windows and doors secured, but sitting in a burning car, to her thinking, was by far the most dangerous thing she could do, so she grabbed her purse and took up a position at the side of the road at a conservative distance from the car's gas tank.

"I didn't know what to expect next. You just hear so many stranded-women-on-the-highway stories that I became short of breath and nervous as soon as the car took its final gasp and I pulled to a stop on the shoulder of the road. Just being stopped on the highway after going sixty miles an hour for the last half-hour is unnerving enough, but with the car burning and all those cars whizzing by shaking the ground, I just hoped—well, maybe prayed— that a state highway-patrol car would pull up and some yes-ma'am-type trooper would tell me not to worry and take me home."

The car that stopped was not a highway-patrol car, and Kate tried to reason with herself that anyone stopping, short of an actual policeman, could be more of a problem than her stalled car, but she knew she couldn't stand there all day. So she greeted the well-dressed, middle-aged good samaritan with enthusiasm for his assistance, and grinned a big hello with an audible sigh of relief.

"I had to size up the situation in a hurry," said Kate. "Here was this respectable-looking gentleman who stopped an expensive-looking car on the highway and backed all the way up in front of me and my burning car. I didn't have much choice except to ask him for help."

Kate was right. She had no choice. After being polite and sympathetic, the man took a knife from the inside pocket of his suit coat and pressed it sharply into Kate's ribs, telling her that if she didn't cooperate he would push the knife into her heart.

"He slit a tear in my blouse and I felt the knife cut me. I was absolutely numb. All of a sudden there was no more traffic noise, or even a fear of being stuck on the highway, or any concern for my car," explained Kate. "I was this man's prisoner."

Kate was ordered into the trunk of the man's car. She had no choice. She got in the trunk. The man drove with Kate in the trunk for what Kate guessed to be a half-hour. The last few minutes were on an unpaved road; then the car stopped and the engine was turned off. During the entire time, the man yelled back obscenities to Kate in the trunk. She wouldn't respond when he demanded to know if she could hear him, so he yelled louder and got more obscene. When the car stopped, Kate recalls vividly the sound of the key in the trunk lock.

By the time she heard that sound, Kate had repositioned herself so that she was lying on her back, her feet tucked up under her, and her knees pushing hard up against the inside of the license-plate wall. Kate's head was jammed up against the back seat, and she hoped the overhang wouldn't obstruct a clear view of him when he opened the trunk. She knew he would have his knife out—that was the only thing she was really sure of.

Kate doesn't remember when the man stopped yelling at her in the trunk, and doesn't remember what he said as he opened the trunk. All she remembers is the flood of daylight momentarily blinding her when the trunk lid popped open and an almost slow-motion sight of the bullet holes being made in the man's chest by the .38-caliber revolver she took out of her purse.

She had planned to shoot every bullet in her gun at the man when the trunk opened, but after three shots he slumped into the trunk on top of her, dead.

"The nightmare was over, but when he fell on me, bleeding, I became so frightened I thought I was suffocating. I gashed my head on the lid as I got out of the trunk. It was so horrible having him lie on top of me, dead like that. When I got out of the trunk, I forced his legs in beside him and slammed the lid. I went over to a tree and threw up.

"You know, I have carried that gun for years in my purse when I drive alone or have to go into areas of town I think are unsafe. It's funny, but all those years I never really thought about actually shooting someone, much less killing anyone. But I frequently recognized a feeling of being safe or being less vulnerable when I had my gun with me. And when this horrible thing happened, my only fear was about not having the opportunity to get to it. You're not going to believe this, but when he put me in the trunk with my purse I was very relieved," Kate firmly said.

The police investigation revealed that the dead man was

a twice-convicted felon who had previously been found guilty of eleven counts of sexual assault, including sodomy, child molestation, and rape. He had served prison sentences in another state at various times for a number of convictions. At the time he picked up Kate on the highway, he was out on parole for good prison behavior after having served only twenty-two months for raping a woman and her twelve-year-old daughter.

If you are over the age of twelve and female, be prepared to be criminally assaulted some time in your life. If you are about thirty years old now, there's a fifty-fifty chance of your being raped, robbed, or attacked.

The odds are reduced as you get older, and are different in various parts of our country. Chances of being raped at any age in New York are one in eight; Los Angeles, one in seven; Atlanta, one in five; Detroit, one in four. Across our nation, one out of every four families will be victims of serious crimes like burglary, rape, robbery, or murder. Our cities are citadels of crime. And there is no such thing anymore as safe rural America.

The statistics are more than frightening. Only four criminals go to prison for every hundred reported crimes. And the FBI estimates that 60 percent of all crimes are not even reported.

For every hundred prisoners with life sentences, twenty-five are freed before their third year; forty-two are out by their seventh year; and people acquitted of murder by reason of insanity spend an average of only five hundred days in mental hospitals before being released.

The nation's prison population increases at a breathtaking pace each year. There are now more than 550,000 behind bars. Nearly six out of ten have been there before, and more than half have been there four or more times.

If you are concerned, fearful about your safety, you are not alone. A Gallup poll finds that six out of ten women in this country are afraid to walk at night in their own neighborhoods.

America is experiencing an epidemic of crime and criminal violence with no immediate or long-range cure in sight. Many people continue to ignore the far-reaching threat and deny their vulnerability, betting that violence will not reach them. For some, it is not truth but hope that matters most.

If crime happens, however, know beforehand that in almost every instance no one will be there to protect you but yourself. Police will not be there unless officers are accidentally nearby, and witnesses can be counted on not to interfere.

One example among thousands occurred on the Thursday evening of July 22, 1988. A woman was severely beaten and raped in the parking lot of her apartment in suburban Los Angeles. Not an uncommon event these days certainly, but the story illustrates how the war on women has escalated, and how the victimized are beginning to try to change the odds.

Suzanne MacDonnell is a young attractive professional woman. She works out four times a week and takes a karate class on Tuesday nights. On July 22 Suzanne was walking from her car to her apartment when she heard moaning coming from the garbage bin in her parking lot.

"It was dark, and at first I couldn't see who was there." She approached the container cautiously and suddenly noticed a woman lying on the ground, crying and pleading for help. "Please, someone, help me, I've been raped, I'm hurt," the woman's voice whispered.

Instinctively Suzanne went to the woman's aid, kneeling beside her, trying to comfort her as best she could. Then the woman smashed her in the face.

"I saw a flash and felt a burning sensation across my nose and eyes. I fell backward and my head hit the pavement. It wasn't a woman at all, it was a man who had set a trap. He hit me again." Her eyes blazing with anger, she continued, "I must have been out for a few seconds, because the next thing I remember was my skirt over my head and his hand pushed against my blood-filled mouth. I never really got a good look at his face."

All Suzanne remembers is that the man wore a red dress and had long blond hair, probably a wig. He raped her and then dumped her in the trash bin. In the darkness, Suzanne cried for help. No one came. She didn't have the strength to lift the lid, so she waited, and moaned for help with the little energy she had. Found almost unconscious six hours later, Suzanne was taken to the hospital and treated for injuries that would heal in time. Treatment of her anger, fear, and distrust of men is ongoing, and to counter her fright and to feel safe again, Suzanne now owns a gun.

"What happened to me is bizarre, there is no question about that. But even though it is not an ordinary kind of crime, it made me extremely aware of my vulnerability. If this could happen to me—to me!—then I have to be on guard about the everyday dangers that we all know exist but ignore as happening to someone else. Now I fasten my seat belt in the car, replace batteries in my smoke detectors, have a fire extinguisher in the kitchen, and carry a handgun. I may be dumb, but I'm not stupid."

Another incident that was told to me involved two young women who avoided assault and rape. Meg Stoddard and Gretchen Winters met during their first week of residency at a hospital in Boston. They quickly discovered many coincidences: both were born in neighboring states in the Northwest, were raised on a farm, played tennis and golf, and each attended a medical school that the other had been rejected from. And so they decided to share a small flat in the Brookline section of Boston.

One cold snowy night in December, after a long and arduous shift at the hospital, they decided to call out for a pizza delivery and spend the evening watching television. As Gretchen was putting on her "couch potato" clothes, the outer door bell rang. Meg buzzed the front door and yelled to Gretchen that the pizza had arrived.

The young delivery man greeted Meg with an affable smile, but as she paid him something about him disturbed her, and she deliberately kept him from entering the apartment. When she started to shut the door, he suddenly seized her arm and pressed a six-inch hunting knife to her throat. He slapped his hand over her mouth when she attempted to cry out. He forced her into the apartment and kicked the door shut. In the kitchen, Gretchen was listening to the seven o'clock news and putting the final touches on the salad. Impatient for the pizza, she walked into the living room and saw the attacker holding Meg at knife point. She screamed.

"Shut up, bitch. You want me to cut her throat?" he growled. "Sit down."

The crazed look in his eyes warned Gretchen that he was on drugs and clearly capable of hurting them. She purposely sat down on the left side of the sofa. The attacker rambled on, threatening to have "real fun" with both of them. Meg and Gretchen looked at each other for a moment, aware that a woman in the neighborhood had recently been murdered under similar circumstances.

Breathing hard, the man grabbed Meg's long blond hair and sliced open her nightgown. Gretchen nervously slid her shaking hand toward a hollowed-out book that sat on an end table. The book contained her loaded gun.

"Stop, you bitch!" She froze. "Watch what I'm doing because you're next," he said, laughing.

Gripping Meg's hair with his left hand, he pulled the knife away from her throat and began unzipping his fly. He turned away briefly, and Gretchen reached for the revolver, stood up, and said firmly, "Let go of her." The man swirled and faced a .357 Magnum revolver aimed at the center of his chest.

"He was absolutely paralyzed," Gretchen recounted, "just like a deer caught in the beam of headlights. Meg was screaming and crying as I cursed at him to drop the knife.

He obeyed and I kicked the knife out of his reach. He pleaded with me not to shoot him."

She ordered the assailant to lie flat on his stomach with his hands behind his back and told Meg to call the police. As she stood over him, he shouted obscenities at her and an odd thought struck her. If she had to shoot him, would she doctor him?

Although it seemed like an eternity, eight minutes later the police arrived, took the attacker away, spent some time taking a report, and left.

Meg and Gretchen's story was told to me years after it occurred. Each is now married and living in separate cities, but both women own handguns and, needless to say, they hope they will never have to use them. They lived through a nightmare, but Gretchen is proud that she was able to defend her friend and herself against an incident that she never thought would happen.

There are many other women who, like Meg and Gretchen, are armed. They represent a growing movement. In fact, it is a quiet drive that began in the late 1960s, with more women living alone and working outside of the home and having more disposable income. In turn, women have become accessible targets, not only for rape, but for robbery and assault, and the need for personal protection has become more acute.

The inner cities have always been rife with violence, and black women were one of the first groups of females to purchase guns for self-defense. As crime extended to the suburbs and small towns, white middle-class women began owning guns, and now a large cross section of women are learning to shoot.

No one really knows how many women own guns, or have access to guns and know how to shoot them. According to a 1988 Gallup poll commissioned by gun maker Smith & Wesson, between 1983 and 1986 gun ownership among women jumped 53 percent, to more than twelve million. The poll also found that the number of women who were considering buying a weapon quadrupled to nearly two million. And a 1986 survey done by the Department of Sociology at Louisiana State University finds a handgun in 40 percent of Louisiana *female-headed households*. The National Research Opinion Center claims that 44 percent of adult women own or have access to firearms. That's forty-two million, and of those, Dr. Paul H. Blackman, research coordinator for the Institute for Legislative Action of the National Rifle Association, estimates that twenty-two million own their own guns.

More than 50 percent of the 104,000 women who responded to a March 1987 *Ladies' Home Journal* survey say they have guns in their homes, with 40 percent of them reporting that the firearms are owned strictly for protection. Forty-two percent of the respondents also report that they have been victims of crime when they answered the magazine's special survey, "The Private Life of the American Woman."

That same month *McCall's* did a similar but less extensive survey, with one-third of the respondents saying they or a member of their household owned a handgun for protection. Of those, more than two-thirds said they would use the weapons to defend themselves at home.

Owning a gun for self-defense is the focus of this book. The pros and cons of using lethal force will be thoroughly discussed. Choosing the proper weapon will be explored. And the training necessary to make that gun useful will be stressed.

Gun defense in the home is the primary focus, not gun defense outside. Although a large percentage of violent crimes do occur in the streets and, as you will read, some women carry guns out of fear of being attacked in the streets, I do not recommend it—not unless you have acquired a license to *carry* a concealed weapon in those states that require it, are very well trained in street defense, and practice frequently on a combat course. There are too many women (as well as men) who carry guns without knowing combat shooting. Competency with a gun is extremely important and especially crucial in a public place where bystanders may be present.

A woman who carries a gun on the street should not think that its mere possession will dispel the dangers that made her buy it. She may feel less fearful and more confident, but just because she carries a gun doesn't mean it is safer for her to walk the streets.

If a woman chooses to carry a gun after being thoroughly trained in shooting, she should carry it discreetly, neither displaying nor mentioning it to friends or associates. As gun-defense expert Massad Ayoob says in his book *In the Gravest Extreme,* "The license to carry concealed deadly weapons in public is not a right but a privilege. To be worthy of this privilege, one must be both discreet and competent with the weapon."

Owning a weapon is a private matter; before beginning research on this subject, I thought I knew no women gun owners. To my surprise, I learned that some of my associates and acquaintances have guns and practice shooting regularly.

One such woman was Judy Miller, who was seated next to me at a university alumni luncheon. After the introductions and the fund-raising appeals were over, we naturally talked to each other. It's funny that after a few minutes you can learn so much about a person. Judy is divorced, lives with her sixteen-year-old son, and is a professor of business management at a Chicago-area university. When I told her I was doing research on women and crime, this mild-mannered, very attractive, slight woman who looks far younger than her forty-nine years astounded me by saying that she owned not one but two guns, and has for the last twenty years.

She then confided in me that she keeps a loaded pistol by her bedside and always carries a gun in her briefcase. Moreover, she will take out the pistol and hold it if she walks alone in a subterranean parking lot or unaccompanied at night on a deserted street. She knows it is against the law in Chicago to carry a concealed weapon without a permit, but she chooses to disobey the law. She spoke seriously and with a firmness and confidence I have not heard from many women.

For Judy, the immediate concern in everyday existence is being prepared to face a city that is filled with so much danger. Questioned whether she is overly distrustful, she replied that she feels neither paranoid nor especially fearful.

Rather, at an early age Judy developed a philosophy of what she calls self-sufficiency. A very thoughtful woman, Judy explained that, when she was young, her father always enjoyed going to the lake and walking on the beach. Then one day he was threatened by a couple of kids, and some months later he was mugged. The police came to the house to ask her father questions about his assailants, but the family never knew if the boys were apprehended. Although her father continued walking on the beach, he became suspicious and untrusting. "He really didn't enjoy himself anymore, because he became fearful. From then on, when my sister and I wanted to go to the beach, he insisted that he come with us. I grew angrier and angrier at what they had done to him."

It was in her early twenties that Judy worked through the concept of protecting herself and taking charge of her life, and not relying on anyone else, like the police, a boyfriend, or friends of the family. Her solution was a gun. When she was twenty-five, she went by herself to a gun range, tried a number of different handguns, and learned how to shoot. To this day, Judy practices once or twice a month.

"For me, the concept of self-sufficiency comes from within, and physically protecting myself is part of it," Judy explained. "Am I willing to commit myself totally? Yes—a hundred percent, absolutely. In other words, the issue of carrying a weapon, be it a knitting needle, a hat pin, a concealed knife, a gun, or even a hand grenade—I would rather go to jail than have to see my loved ones, including myself, killed or injured unnecessarily."

Judy does not like carrying a gun illegally, but it is almost impossible to obtain a permit to carry a concealed weapon of any kind in Chicago. She, like so many other women I spoke to, realizes that the police cannot be expected to protect everyone. "So, you use your head and work out the problem of doing something that's illegal," she quietly said. "Then you work through your head, as well as your stomach, the fact that you may hurt or kill someone. I have worked this all through. I am willing to use my weapon, ready to kill, rather than be a victim. There is no argument. This is how I feel, and I have felt this way for more than twenty years. I don't care what anybody thinks of it."

Unlike many other women, Judy has never been victimized, although she has been in a situation where she was prepared to use her gun. It was ten o'clock one cold winter evening in 1984, when she and her son, Mark, were watching television in the living room and heard someone trying to force open a locked kitchen window. The window wouldn't open, and the person quickly moved to pry open the lock on a side door.

Judy and her son didn't say a word to each other; they each knew what to do. Judy went to get her gun, Mark to call the police. Judy stood on the side of the door and yelled, "Go away, don't try and get in." They didn't hear a thing, but whoever it was went away. The police arrived twenty minutes later, asked them some questions, and left, presumably to scour the neighborhood.

Would she have shot? She quickly answered yes. "The gun was loaded, but I didn't say that I had a loaded gun, for the simple reason that I'm afraid of the person who is crazy enough to take that as a challenge. I tried to sound very forceful and I felt confident, but my adrenaline was pumping a mile a minute!" She laughed for an instant to ease the tension, but then was serious again. "He wasn't going to hurt us. I don't intend for that to ever happen," she said adamantly.

Judy cannot understand why it has taken women so long to turn to guns for self-defense.

"Speculation tells me that the classic reason is that too many women think that an assault would not happen to them. They're dependent upon a man to lead them or to protect them, or they haven't thought through the risks thoroughly," she said. "There are a lot of women who think that, if they don't think about the possibility of being attacked, they won't be attacked. That's statistically ignorant, and I believe that attitude is changing."

"Again," Judy reiterated to me, "the base issue goes back to self-worth, and whether or not you're totally committed to leading a good strong life and taking charge of your own destiny."

Is a gun a good deterrent against a crime? Judy thinks so. Deterrence refers not to the actual firing of guns in stopping crimes, but to the nonoccurrence of crimes when those who contemplate them are deterred by the potential victims' actual or assumed possession of arms.

The newest statistics indicate that a gun is a formidable deterrent. Gary Kleck, a distinguished scholar of criminology and a professor at Florida State University, produced a study based exclusively on surveys by anti-gun groups that concluded that guns are used in defending against 645,000 crimes every year, with only one-third of the guns actually being fired.

Don B. Kates, Jr., a leading constitutional attorney and criminologist, studied 150 cases of armed resistance by citizens against criminal attackers. His findings are similar to Kleck's overall results. Criminals were captured or driven off without a shot's being fired in 50 percent of the instances, and wounded or killed in 43 percent of the instances. In the remaining 7 percent, assailants, wounded or not, escaped.

FBI statistics for 1981 show that, nationwide, citizens justifiably killed 30 percent more criminals than did police. In California, 1981 statistics show citizens justifiably killing twice as many felons as did the police; in Chicago and Cleveland it was three times as many.

Based on U.S. Department of Justice national victims' surveys and Gary Kleck's research, victims who resisted with guns were not only much less likely to lose their possessions to robbers than those who resisted with any other kind of weapons, but were also less likely to be injured than victims who did not resist at all. In contrast, knife-armed resisters were six times more likely to be injured than gun-armed resisters, and about twice as likely to suffer injury as victims who did nothing.

The notion of deterrence must also be viewed from the criminal's point of view. Professors James D. Wright and Peter H. Rossi, sociologists from the University of Massachusetts, conducted an extensive gun-issue study commissioned by the National Institute of Justice that involved in-depth interviews with 1,874 imprisoned felons in ten states. The Wright/Rossi work provides us with detailed information for the first time about the behavior patterns and criminal thinking of professional bad guys.

More than half of the felons in the Wright/Rossi study agreed that "a criminal is not going to mess around with a victim he knows is armed with a gun," and "most criminals are more worried about meeting an armed victim than they are about running into the police." Nearly 40 percent responded that there had been at least one time when they decided not to commit a crime because they knew or believed that the victim was armed.

Clearly, armed citizens are a real threat to criminals. One of the most convincing cases illustrating the deterrent effect of gun ownership comes from a highly publicized effort to train women in firearms use, cosponsored by the Orlando, Florida, Police Department and the *Orlando Sentinel Star.*

There had been a series of very brutal rapes in Orlando in 1966, and during that time, according to police captain Jack Stacey, residents, mostly women, were buying two hundred to three hundred guns per week. Most had no idea of basic gun safety or operation, or how and when to use a gun for protection. The *Orlando Sentinel Star* had an anti-gun editorial policy and vehemently disapproved of these gun purchases. Martin Andersen, publisher of the newspaper, and Emily Bavar, editor of the newspaper's magazine supplement, went to the chief of police, Carlisle "Stoney" Johnstone, and insisted that he do something to stop the sale of handguns to women. Chief Johnstone said that he could not stop the sale of guns, because the law permitted the purchase of handguns in Orlando. As discussion continued, it was decided that, since it wasn't possible to prevent handgun sales, the only alternative was to make sure that the women buying guns knew how to use them. The paper and the police department would cosponsor a gun-training program for women. The newspaper ran a front-page story announcing that the gun-training course would take place in a city park the following Sunday.

Neal Knox, a retired journalist familiar with the story, told me that the first class of "Emily Bavar's Pistol Packin' Posse," as it was termed, was scheduled, and newspaper personnel and police made preparations for as many as four to five hundred women. To everyone's utter amazement, more than twenty-five hundred women showed up, carrying every type of firearm under the sun, some loaded and some unloaded. Knox talked to one officer who was there who said he was never so scared in his life. Apparently the cars were parked blocks away from the park, and women were walking all over the place armed to their teeth. Some had their guns holstered, others had them in their purses or pockets, and the rest had them in their hands. "It must have been some sight," laughed Knox.

Not wanting to be known for a massacre at Lake Eola Park, the police department and the newspaper decided to fall back, take cover, and regroup. They obviously weren't set up for those numbers, and they told everybody to go home. They quickly organized a three-class-per-week program, with women clipping application forms from the newspaper and the *Orlando Sentinel Star* staff arranging appointments. Five months later, they had trained more than six thousand women.

Charley Wadsworth, who administered the newspaper's portion of the program, insisted at the time that they were not trying to play upon anyone's fears, but they felt that if a woman has a pistol in the house she shouldn't be afraid of it.

Even Emily Bavar learned how to shoot, and she commented to Neal Knox, who was writing for *Gun Week,* that one of their big problems was that many women would show up every week just to practice. She also said that Chief Johnstone had told her that, although the policemen were putting in their own time for the program, it would lighten their work in the long run, thanks to the tremendous deterrent effect on crime.

As a result, the rape rate in Orlando, Florida, fell from a 1966 level of thirty-six to only four in 1967. Before the training, rape had been increasing in Orlando, as it was nationwide.

Five years later, rape was still significantly below the preprogram level, even though, during the five years after the training, rape climbed 308 percent in the surrounding Orlando metropolitan area, the Florida rate escalated 96 percent, and the national rape rate increased by 64 percent.

Another result of the Orlando training is that, while most other crimes escalated or remained steady in Orlando in 1967, violent assault and burglary decreased by 25 percent each, making Orlando the only American city of more than a hundred thousand in population in which crime declined in 1967.

Neal Knox telephoned police chief Stoney Johnstone a year later and asked him if any of the women had used a firearm to defend herself. Stoney said no, not to his knowledge. Knox wanted to know if any of his women had turned a gun on her husband or boyfriend. Stoney replied no, and added that there also hadn't been a single accidental shooting. "And believe me," Stoney said, "we looked closely at that—I had dreams of my pension disappearing."

Knox, and other experts who have analyzed the Orlando phenomenon, contend that the rape rate decreased because of the media publicity, and because the women were armed and trained. No one ever fired a gun or even pulled a gun to protect herself. What brought about the results was that the women knew how to use a gun and the newspaper was continuously telling the would-be rapists that they were trained.

Another woman who is outspoken about her gun ownership is Randi McGinn, a former violent-crimes prosecutor in the Albuquerque, New Mexico, district attorney's office. Randi has prosecuted more than two hundred criminal cases, most of them dealing with violent crimes such as murder, rape, armed robbery, child molestation, aggravated battery, and arson. More than half of the victims she saw were women who had been sexually assaulted.

Randi began legally carrying a gun before becoming a prosecutor and seeing the damaged women who came through her office. She got a gun after a series of rapes in her neighborhood. She was never fearful until the woman who lived next to her was raped, and during the next four months that woman's assailant sexually assaulted twelve other women within six blocks of her house, always in their homes.

For the first time, Randi was afraid. Her father sent her a can of Mace. Her girlfriend gave her a whistle. Neither item eased her apprehension when she came home to an empty house at night. Before opening the door, she would put the whistle between her lips and ready the Mace—all the while thinking how ridiculous she looked and wondering whether this would do any good if there was someone in the house.

"So I tried the whistle. I blew and blew one evening, and no one came. My neighbors could not hear me. I tried the Mace on a dog that snapped at me while I was jogging. He shook his head and looked madder than before. My self-defense methods were not working.

"I would never have purchased a gun of my own voli-tion," she explained. "Guns were things men used, some-thing fathers and sons shared as part of a deer-hunting manhood ritual. They had a secret code of calibers and bullet types unfathomable to women.

"Soldiers, policemen, men in uniform . . . those were the people who carried guns," she continued. "Guns were used for violence and death. I had been raised to believe that I was not capable of violence."

It was a man, a close friend, who told her to buy a gun. He could not stay at Randi's house during the rapist's rampage and was worried about her when she was alone at night. He suggested a gun. She was horrified by the idea. "He literally had to take me to a gun store and buy me a small automatic pistol," Randi said, laughing. He showed her how to use it and practiced with her many times. "Then, finally, I took a gun course."

Years have gone by since then. Now Randi has more than one gun. Wherever she goes, she carries that small automatic pistol in a jacket pocket. Randi explained, "I have a six-and-a-half-year-old daughter, and we live alone together. I feel very responsible for protecting her as well as myself. There's nobody here to protect us.

"I especially find a need to carry a gun when I'm in the car. If you're a woman driving home alone at night and someone tries to run you off the road, there's not a whole lot you can do if you don't have a gun," Randi insisted. "There aren't many circumstances when you need a gun, but when you need a gun, you need it very badly. Nothing else will do, really. I've never had to use a gun for self-defense; hopefully, I'll never have to. But if I'm in that situation, I would hate myself for having a gun but having it somewhere else."

Questioned about the possibility of killing someone, Randi replied quickly. "If I had to kill somebody, I would do it. Sure. Without a doubt. Absolutely! If I felt that somebody was threatening me or my child, I would use the gun, no question. As a lawyer, I know all of the legal consequences. Having a gun and making that kind of decision to shoot somebody in self-defense is a big responsibility. If you are wrong, certainly the law will penalize you. I think I am responsible, and I'm willing to test my judgment if it ever comes to it.

"Many, many people say that they are not entirely sure they could shoot anyone if they had a gun. Listen, if a man was in a woman's house and she knew he was going to rape her, I think most women would shoot him if it came down to that," Randi said frankly.

After counseling so many victims while she was a criminal prosecutor, Randi needed to express her views about self-defense and gun defense to other women. She wrote an article in 1984 about her experiences and why she owns a gun. Because Randi has always considered herself a liberal and a feminist, her article presented a strong feminist viewpoint in terms of self-protection and taking responsibility. She sent the article to a national woman's magazine, which turned it down; according to Randi, "The return reply clearly implied that the article was not right-thinking and that I was out of my mind."

Subsequently, *The American Rifleman,* a house publication of the National Rifle Association (NRA) with a readership of three million, accepted the article.

From the response she received from her article, Randi has found that quite a number of women all across the country carry guns. "I was floored by the number of letters I got. Nearly one hundred letters! I didn't think that any women read that magazine!" she exclaimed. "I didn't expect the tenor of the letters, which was that people are really scared. I hadn't realized how fearful people are."

Randi was further surprised about how many professional, middle-aged, matronly types of women, many of whom she knew, approached her on the street and in restaurants and told her that they, too, carried guns.

She was equally astonished to find out that people who would be called politically "liberal," who she assumed were anti-gun, are carrying guns. "These people never tell others that they have guns. They don't make it apparent at all and wouldn't come out if the NRA conducted a survey. These people would never, ever admit they owned guns.

"They are not politically vocal and do not see it as an issue whether or not they should be allowed to own and to carry guns. The reason they have guns is that they're scared and they want to protect their families," explained Randi. "I found out that they had guns because they called me and said they had liked my article."

Andrea Frank had a different reason for buying a gun. I met Andrea on Ladies' Night, when women shoot free at The Target Range, a San Fernando Valley, California, indoor gun range. Andrea sells pharmaceutical supplies and covers southern California for a major manufacturer in Chicago. She comes to the range to shoot at least twice a week.

Andrea took up a gun for self-defense after her home was broken into for the third time. On a warm September Friday night, a man entered her home through a back window. Andrea was in her den, preparing weekly sales reports and listening to her stereo with headphones. She didn't know the man was there until she saw him walking through the living room toward the den. She started screaming for help, hoping that he would be scared away, but he kept coming toward her as she backed into a small bathroom.

He grabbed her by the hair and smacked her across the face, telling her to shut up, and then punched her in the stomach, knocking her to the floor. The man saw Andrea's purse on the desk and grabbed it, demanding more money and jewelry. Andrea started to get up, but he punched her again, this time bloodying her nose. Unable to fight, Andrea began crying and begged him to stop hurting her. As she lay on the floor, the man pulled off her watch and gold chain, and then laughed at her as he kicked her in the chest. Within moments he was gone.

Andrea learned of her assailant's arrest two months later. She was subpoenaed to testify at his trial, where he was found guilty of a series of five robberies in Andrea's neighborhood. She also learned that the twenty-four-year-old man who beat her up was addicted to drugs and alcohol, had been in prison once before, and was out on parole.

It was interesting for me to find out that felons, in general, are young males from socially marginal backgrounds who were exposed to, or experimented with, drugs, guns, and crime before their sixteenth birthday. The late teens of these men were mostly spent getting into relatively serious trouble with the law; most wasted the largest portion of their twenties in prison. The average felon left school in the tenth or eleventh grade and had an erratic employment history thereafter. In the Wright/Rossi study, about 80 percent had committed at least one felony before the age of eighteen; many had committed large numbers of them, property crimes being by far the most common. About one-half the felons were or had been either alcoholics or drug addicts, or both, at some point. An additional one-quarter appear to have been rather heavy drug users, if not addicts.

According to the Bureau of Justice Statistics, of the U.S. Department of Justice, robbery ranks among the most serious and feared criminal offenses, because it involves both threatened or actual violence and loss of property to the victim. The Bureau also finds that, among commonly recorded crimes, only homicide and rape exceed robbery in violence. Over half of all robbery victims are attacked, and female robbery victims are more likely than men to be attacked and injured. Also, one in twelve robbery victims experiences serious injuries, such as rape, knife, or gunshot wounds, broken bones, or being knocked unconscious.

Since her violent encounter, Andrea keeps a gun in her house and often carries it in her car when she feels that she will be traveling to unsafe areas. She wonders whether there are any safe areas left.

Although she started shooting for self-defense, Andrea realized that she really enjoys shooting as a sport. "It can be very relaxing. The kind of work I do can be aggravating at times. When I shoot target practice, it uses up all of my frustrations, so I can start the next day feeling good," she explained.

"Women seem to excel at shooting. We seem to learn more rapidly, because we don't have any fixed ideas, and we don't have a macho attitude on how we're supposed to shoot, like men do. Men look at cop shows and Western movies and use the stars as role models. Women don't even think about guns unless someone finally hands us one, and then we look and we learn," Andrea said emphatically.

According to combat masters Mike Dalton and Mickey Fowler, who operate the renowned International Shootists, Inc. (ISI), a gun-training school in Mission Hills, California, women do just as well with guns as men do, especially in the type of shooting events where accuracy counts most.

Many women are intimidated by guns at first, looking at a gun as some mystical piece of steel that almost has a life of its own and can do some harm by itself, Mickey told me while I was taking the ISI weekend course. Many women also think that you have to be big and strong to shoot and that only men are good shooters. But Fowler insists that, once instructors get them to overcome these intimidating beliefs, women can become excellent shooters.

Ironically, women who have been the most frightened of the gun tend to end up enjoying shooting more than almost anybody else. People get into shooting for different rea-

sons, and usually a woman's motivation is self-defense.
Not too many women Dalton and Fowler train are interested in either hunting or just going out and plinking tin
cans for fun. They don't think it's feminine to shoot nor
have they had the experience of shooting. But after they've
fired a few rounds, it's easy for them to get hooked on
serious shooting.

If a woman has taken an introductory gun course and
continues to practice, within a few months she will be good
enough to join a league of competitive shooters. Many
communities have combat-shooting or action-shooting
leagues, and competition is worldwide. I have tried a number of these action-shooting courses and improved my
shooting tremendously.

Actually, competitive shooting is much more than a
sport. It is an enjoyable way to learn to use a handgun
safely and effectively under time constraints and in stress
situations, which will prepare you to save your life or your
family's life, should the need arise.

There were hundreds of other women I met who told me
why they learned how to shoot for self-defense, but one
woman stands out in my mind.

Margo Feldman is an energetic, nonstop advertising
woman whose enthusiasm at first seemed inappropriate to
the story she was about to tell, but as I got to know her I
found that she was actually heroic and offered an inspiring
message to women. For Margo, her experience was a rite
of passage, and as a result of it she developed an honest
and worthwhile feeling about herself, which she believes all
women who rely on themselves must acquire for a successful life. But I'll let her tell her story.

"The story is pretty simple," began Margo as we sat in
her office during lunchtime. "A young man came through
my closed bedroom window late one night when I was in
the bathroom showering before bed. When I opened the
shower curtain, he was standing in the bathroom doorway,
leaning against the doorjamb, holding a large knife and

grinning. I don't want to go on about how startled and instantly frightened I was. That's pretty routine: I was scared to death. I want to tell you about what happened with the gun, and what a vital role it played.

"My father died four years ago. I was the oldest of his three children, all daughters, and always sort of stood in for the son he didn't have. I liked it, though, and he was such a wonderful man that he always made me feel responsible and important—qualities I'm sure he felt were generic in men and only occasionally learned by women—and I responded always by being true to my word and clear about my preferences," said Margo, smiling, as if she knew a secret.

The night before Margo's father died, he asked her to go to his top dresser drawer to bring him a wooden box. He took a pistol from the box, checked to see that it was unloaded, and handed it to her. "It's yours. I'm going to show you how to use it right now, and don't forget what I tell you—it may someday save your life," he said. "With this gun, you may someday save your mother's or sisters' lives, or your future child."

"He showed me how the gun worked; I never even knew he had a gun. He watched me load and unload it; I was being responsible for him by following instructions and learning, although I never, ever planned to touch it again. I hated guns—sorry, Dad!" joked Margo, laughing at herself.

She took the pistol home and put it in the top drawer, as he had instructed her, loaded, as she swore she would keep it always. "I felt half stupid about the big deal Dad made of the whole thing, but, you know, the eldest daughter and all," said Margo, as she rolled her eyes toward the heavens and laughed again.

It was many months after Margo's father's death that the assailant broke into her apartment.

"So, this huge guy is standing at my bathroom door," continued Margo. "I fling open the shower curtain and there he is. And there I am, wet, more than naked, and trapped. He handed me a towel. Nice guy, huh?

"He came into the bathroom, making the big knife very obvious. He sat on the toilet-seat cover and told me to dry off. Scared? Phew, I was numb. This was bad any way you looked: I'm naked, rubbing my body all over with a towel. All I could think to do was to dry myself slowly, hoping time would reveal something—a weak spot—about this guy I'm now seeing as a rapist at the very least, and a murderer second.

"This guy—I know his name now, but I guess it isn't important—gets comfortable and, I guess, turned on by me drying myself. So he tells me to put on some perfume. I do. Then he orders me into my bedroom. He sits on the bed, flashing the knife, and tells me to put on my sexiest underwear for him.

"I still remember my instant anger about his demanding that I get sexy for him," said Margo, successfully slinging a pencil into a wastepaper basket. "But that instant of anger didn't last too long; he pointed toward my body with his knife when I was slow to move."

Going to her underwear drawer and opening it, Margo remembered the whole scene with her father. She couldn't understand at the time the significance of his stressing the top drawer, but there she was opening her top drawer, while this stranger sat eight feet away from her holding a knife. As she reached into the drawer, there was absolutely no question about what she was going to bring out. Her father's words were in her head—"With this gun, you may someday save your life—"

"I turned, with the gun in my right hand and a pair of red bikini underpants in the other. I'm laughing now. It was a scene out of some corny movie. Here I am in my birthday suit, pointing a gun and a pair of bikinis at this big, bad criminal sitting on my bed with a butcher knife in his hand waiting like a cat for a mouse. You should have seen the look on his face!" howled Margo.

The gun surprised the intruder so much that he launched himself back in the bed, dropped his knife on the floor, and banged his head on the light over the pillows, squealing like a pig. She told him that if he made a move, even scratched his head, she would shoot him with every bullet in the gun. She ordered him to put his hands on top of his head, which he did.

"It was at that moment that panic overcame me. What was I going to do with him, and how was I going to get dressed?" asked Margo, throwing her arms in the air. "I decided that getting dressed was not my priority until I called the police.

"Just then I saw the phone on the nightstand next to where this shithead was trying to disappear into the wall. I don't know where I came up with the idea—I don't even watch TV very much—but I handled this like I was on the SWAT team," laughed Margo.

She told the man to keep his right hand on top of his head and reach across his body with his left hand and pick up the phone and dial 911 for the police. He relaxed just enough to start complaining about calling the police, and Margo lifted up the gun, which was getting heavy even though she was holding it with two hands as her father had shown her.

"I reminded him again that if he moved or didn't do exactly as I told him I would empty the gun on him and probably get a medal for doing it, from—I think I said—the PTA. He got jumpy again, begged me to calm down, and lifted the phone and dialed 911 and repeated everything to the police that I told him," said Margo excitedly, feeling very proud of her maneuver.

Margo was beginning to get weary then, and a little lightheaded. Next she told the man to keep his hands on top of his head and, without moving off the wall, turn toward it and slip down until he was lying on the bed face down. He did this all very deliberately, but complained that he couldn't breathe with his face down and his hands on top of his hand; Margo reminded him that it would be a lot easier trying to breathe with his face in the pillow than trying to breathe with holes in his back. Margo felt that he looked secure in that position, so she reached around the dresser into the closet and grabbed her bathrobe. "I felt a whole lot better being dressed," said Margo, "but I was beginning to shake badly. I was pretty glad that he couldn't see me."

The police arrived twelve minutes later. They yelled to Margo through the front door, because she couldn't leave the man alone to open it. They told her to keep the man covered with the gun while they found a way into the apartment.

Moments later, two policemen popped up in the open bedroom window. One officer gave Margo the okay sign as he yelled to the man not to move. They climbed through the window, and one officer handcuffed the man while the other took the gun from Margo and put his arm around her to comfort her.

"The rest of the details don't matter," said Margo as she got up from her desk and paced the office. "There was paperwork that seemed like it would never stop, detectives, district attorneys, and court, and all that." Margo stopped pacing, looked at me steadfastly, and said, "What does matter is that I saved my life, or at the very least I saved my sanity, with a gun that I never had to shoot. And I saved the lives of who knows how many other women. And you know what else? I would have shot the creep if I had to. I would have shot him gladly—the look on his face, holding that knife and sizing me up like I was a slave girl. . . ."

Margo Feldman was very lucky. She had never shot a gun before, nor did she know anything about gun safety—all of this could have contributed to her demise. What was most important was that Margo had the ability to remain cool under extreme pressure.

World-renowned gun combat master Jeff Cooper says

that if you lose your cool under deadly attack you will probably not survive to make excuses, so don't bother to improvise any—just keep your head. Anger, as long as it is controlled anger, is no obstacle to efficiency. Self-control, Jeff Cooper says, is one thing the psychopath does not usually possess. You must use yours to his undoing.

This final personal account was most difficult to obtain and demanded hours of interviewing and every ounce of emotional energy, from Mrs. Bower and me.

Mrs. Maxwell Bower is sixty-five years old and lives with her seventy-two-year-old husband in a condominium on a respectable eighteen-hole golf-course development in Phoenix, Arizona. On an early Monday evening in January, Barbara Bower shot and killed one of a pair of intruders who broke into their home to steal their money and have some fun.

"Max saw the men first—or maybe, I should say, the men saw Max first. He was sitting in his chair, watching the end of a baseball game he had videotaped from last year's World Series. He's a nut for baseball," laughed Mrs. Bower.

She was in the kitchen, which shares a breakfast bar with the living room but can't be seen from the television chairs over near the sliding glass door opening onto the patio. She had just cut some flowers from the patio and was trimming them for a vase when she heard the television go off and knew something was wrong—her husband hadn't growled about some umpire's call or a pitcher's curve ball. So Barbara started for the living room. When she came around the corner, two men, stockings on their faces and dressed in white T-shirts, were lifting Max out of his chair, holding a gun to his neck.

"They must not have known I was in the house," recalled Mrs. Bower, "because, when I walked into the living room, one of the men flew across the room and almost yanked my arm from its socket and jerked my reading glasses right off my head, pulling me into the middle of the room."

Max Bower started to protest, but the man pointing the gun at him slapped him so hard across the face that his glasses smashed against the wall and his nose began to bleed.

"I can't say that I have feared a thing like this," said Mrs. Bower, "but, coming from a big city, you always hear about these things happening, and I guess what you always fear about these things is that the statistics about it happening to you are really that great."

Mr. Bower had bought a gun in 1975 when the Bowers lived in Saint Louis. He'd discussed it with his wife, and they'd both agreed that their neighborhood was no longer the safe, family neighborhood it had once been, so that a handgun in the house for added protection was both appropriate and prudent. He purchased a .45-caliber semi-automatic, because he was familiar with its operation and reputation from the army. After shooting it once, Mrs. Bower said she would prefer a revolver, which she would find simpler to use, but Max convinced her that she could learn to operate the .45 easily with some instruction and that the shooting efficiency of the automatic greatly outweighed the hard-shooting revolver in the horrible event they should ever need the weapon.

The Bowers learned to shoot with an instructor recommended by a police lieutenant Max knew from the municipal golf course, and the gun was put in Max's top dresser drawer, loaded. Although it was shot every summer by both of them, they were always aware that they didn't really know enough about the gun to consider using it except in a life-or-death situation. When they moved from Saint Louis to Phoenix, the gun moved along with the contents of Max's drawer, but it wasn't shot again.

"I saw the kind of trouble we were in," said Mrs. Bower, nervously rubbing her hands. "They were talking so fast, and I tried to calm things down by offering to give them whatever they wanted if they would leave us alone and not hurt us. Max's nose was bleeding down his face onto his shirt and to the carpet. I begged the one man to help stop Max's bleeding and offered to take the other man throughout the house to find what they wanted," continued Mrs. Bower, wiping back tears that she couldn't control.

The two men only wanted cash and jewelry. They took the forty dollars Max had in his pocket, both their wedding rings, and Mrs. Bower's diamond studs. The man holding Max at gunpoint mashed the heel of his hand into Max's bleeding nose, breaking it and squirting blood all over both men. They weren't happy with forty dollars, and told Mrs. Bower that they would kill Max if she didn't come up with one thousand dollars.

"I don't know who keeps that kind of money around; for us, one thousand dollars earns interest in the bank. I was so frightened that I panicked and told them I would get it. I don't know what I was thinking of when I blurted that out, but something had to happen," sighed Mrs. Bower. "It was a nightmare."

The one man grabbed her arm again, shoving her toward the other room, and told her to "get it." Mrs. Bower led him into the bedroom, where the only thing she could think to do was empty her purse on the bed. She knew there couldn't possibly be twenty dollars in her wallet. As he was looking through the contents of her purse, holding her with one hand, she was mentally searching the whole room, trying to think where more money might be forgotten or saved. Just as her inventory took her to the drawer with the gun, the man found eighteen dollars and change in her wallet. Angry and swearing, he flung her on the bed and left the bedroom, laughing derisively.

Mrs. Bower said she sprang off the bed to the gun drawer before the heel of her assailant had left the door frame. She picked up the .45, released the safety, and walked out her bedroom door. The one gunman saw her in the hallway pointing the gun toward him. Her size and appearance added no additional menace to the pointed .45, so the gunman jumped for his gun, lying on the bar in front of him. His hand reached it just as the bullet ripped through his chest. He was dead before he hit the floor, and his partner bolted through the patio door.

"The most amazing thing—and it's easy now for me to say 'the most amazing thing,' because at the time everything was so amazing—but the amazing thing was that I don't remember hearing the gun fire," recalled Mrs. Bower. "Max always insisted, when we went for our annual practice session, that we fire the gun at an indoor range. Now, I don't know if you have ever fired a .45-caliber gun inside, but even with ear protection, the noise and percussion is quite impressive. And on that night I never heard the gun go off."

The details of what happened next are routine: the police, the paramedics, the coroner, and the investigation. Max fully recovered from the surgery necessary to repair his broken nose and cheekbone; the hallway and living room were recarpeted and painted; the whole family came from back east to visit; and the Bowers are once again taking two long walks a day, playing golf, reacting to baseball games, and feeling very close and strong and happy to be alive.

"What I did had nothing to do with courage or shooting or murder; what I did had to be done. It was necessary, there was no other choice. I just thank God and I thank Max for that gun. Without it we would have spent the rest of our retirement that night, or have been injured beyond repair and lived with pain and fear and tragedy," said Mrs. Bower, smiling for the first time.

And, yes, the other man was caught within an hour of Mrs. Bower's call to the police. He was stopped for a speeding ticket and was detained because of the blood splattered all over his chest and face, and his behavior, which was reported by the traffic officers as being erratic and frightened. Barbara Bower has no fear that he will ever want to see the inside of her house again.

After talking with these women, as well as many others, I realized that there is a quiet but definite trend among women to shoulder the responsibility for their personal safety. They feel that they have been made fools of by the experts who advise the use of "personal weapons" for protection against vicious assault and are buying guns in astounding numbers.

Many women are open about their gun ownership, and more than willing to discuss with anyone their reasons for having a gun and their methods of using it should the time come. Yet many women gun owners consider the subject intimate and personal, and refuse to talk about it or be associated with any trend or gun culture. But the evidence is inescapable: the threat of assault against women continues at an alarming rate; law enforcement is virtually incapable of preventing such assault; and women are arming themselves in self-defense.

2

Futile Defense

GUN DEFENSE FOR women is not promoted by the media or encouraged by many law-enforcement agencies, for reasons even they are not clear about. Rather, they recommend a potpourri of measures, from hat pins to karate to Mace, from reasoning to nonresistance.

In the early 1980s, classes in using Mace (tear gas) were popular in most large metropolitan areas from coast to coast. I organized a class with the hope that I would find a means of self-protection, as did most of the thirty women in the course. Our instructor, an off-duty policeman, began the two-hour session by telling us that Mace cannot kill or permanently injure anyone. Ironically, we all sighed in relief, because we didn't want to hurt our assailant! We learned that, if Mace is used properly and sprayed in an assailant's face at close range, it can be expected to stop an attacker temporarily, long enough for the potential victim to run away.

It was only years later that I learned the truth about the efficacy of Mace. Dennis Ray Martin, president of the sixty-eight-thousand-member American Federation of Police, told me that "Mace canisters are so small that the amount of gas they spray cannot possibly slow down a mugger even if you spray him directly in the face at short range. If you are too far away, and we're talking inches here, he may easily grab your arm and turn the canister against you. And what the public doesn't know is that the Mace formulas available to them have been diluted to such an extent that most people can take several direct streams to the face with virtually no effects. In fact, drunks and narcotized individuals are almost immune to the chemical. I wouldn't advise a woman to be dependent on Mace for protection."

Bobby pins, keys, hat pins, nail files, and eyeglass temples are other things that have been endorsed as personal defense weapons for women over the years by the so-called experts. They have suggested that such "personal weapons" be used as an element of surprise to puncture the attacker's eyeballs.

Using a key or a nail file as a weapon sounds good in theory, only because they are sharp, but these "weapons" are inadequate in most situations and have little effective stopping power, because of the unlikelihood and repulsiveness of actually poking out an eye. They can only be used at close range, and can be taken or knocked away because of a woman's inferior hand and arm strength, not to mention the powerful adrenaline reaction, which immediately disables motor function in the arms and legs.

Some of these experts have even suggested using a stun gun, which they say will stop an attacker. In fact, a stun gun will only work if the victim manages approximately three seconds of constant application into a major muscle group or nerve center. According to nationally recognized gun-defense trainer and martial-arts and weapons trainer Lieutenant Massad Ayoob, a Concord, New Hampshire, police officer, the public needs to understand that you must be physically close to the assailant—belly to belly—so that you can wrap your arm around him and dig the small electrodes into him and hold the position for three seconds. During that time, a man trained in violence is going to do a great many unpleasant things to you. And Ayoob suggests that if you can do that for three seconds you're probably strong enough to subdue your assailant without the stun gun. Ayoob also reports that a number of people are relatively immune to the effects of a stun gun, including a large number of outlaws who have their own stun guns and play with them and "zap" themselves until they have built up a tolerance. Anyone who's done a lot of electrical work and has developed a tolerance to electric shock will not be affected the same way by a stun gun. Also, anyone wearing a leather or heavy wool jacket, as well as very obese people, or people with a high pain tolerance, are not affected by a stun gun. These are all enough reasons not to rely on the stun gun to deter an assault. Just as with a can of Mace, luck plays a large part in its effectiveness.

Well, if not a stun gun, what about using a taser? This is a very bulky instrument that reaches out to eighteen feet and is known to be wildly inaccurate. It throws a barb that must actually penetrate the body. Another button is then pushed, to distribute an electrical charge. If, however, the barb catches on heavy clothing, it won't work, and there are numerous stories of suspects who were tasered by police and simply ripped out the barbs and continued to attack. It certainly would not be a good self-defense tool for a woman; anyway, since it is a projectile device, it is sold and controlled as if it were a firearm.

Another weapon that is occasionally recommended for self-defense is a knife, and at one time I resorted to carrying one. When I lived in Washington, D.C., I was absolutely petrified to walk alone at night from the car to the house. I lived near the Capitol, a neighborhood never considered to be safe, just chic. On the nights when I walked alone from my house to the car, I would openly carry a steak knife for protection. A friend I told about my tactic laughed and said, "I didn't know you were a street fighter! You better have won some knife fights, or you're going to be in deep trouble if you're attacked."

Then I was told that using a knife requires speed and

skill and that unless you are well trained a knife will be taken away from you in a matter of moments by an assailant. Basically a knife is an assassination weapon: lethal but without stopping power. To stop someone by stabbing, you would need to stab twenty to thirty times. As mentioned earlier, knife-armed resisters are six times more likely to be injured than gun-armed resisters, and about twice as likely to suffer injury as victims who do nothing.

Nonresistance is another form of self-defense that is also advocated in instances of rape, and many times a woman will find it the best strategy for certain circumstances. Nevertheless, it has been found that women who do not resist are more likely to suffer from severe psychological consequences than women who make attempts to resist, and just as likely to be hurt.

A case in point is Philadelphian Sandra Frankel. Late one Saturday afternoon, Sandra purchased a birthday gift for her husband and walked quickly to her car in the shopping mall's subterranean parking lot, hoping to get home before her husband got back from golf. For years, Sandra told me, every time she parked her car there, she thought about how empty the lot always was, even though it was well lit and full of cars.

"It was always so hard to find a parking space, yet there never seemed to be a soul around, except for the occasional parking-lot employee who would drive around in a little motorized cart, usually more concerned with citing cars that were parked improperly than with patrolling the area," Sandra nervously recalled.

She never felt quite safe, and always walked rapidly to and from the escalators. Sandra even deliberated that day about not locking her car door, something that she always did. She thought about what might happen to her if someone accosted her and she needed to get into the car immediately. As it was, Sandra had a hard time fumbling with her keys and unlocking the door under normal circumstances, and she knew that in a crisis situation it would be even more difficult.

When Sandra got to the car that Saturday, a man came up behind her and tightly grabbed her right arm, commanding her to open the door.

"I absolutely froze. He told me again to open the door, and I did. He shoved me into the passenger seat while he got into the driver's seat. He snatched a clump of hair on top of my head and wanted the keys to the car. He yanked at my hair so hard that I thought all of it would come out, and I screamed. He told me that if I shut up he wouldn't hurt me, and I believed him. I was paralyzed. I did everything he told me to do."

Holding her neck, the man drove to a secluded area in a nearby park. He threatened repeatedly that if she didn't comply he would hurt her, maybe kill her. She never cried. She barely made a sound. Sandra let him rape her.

"I don't know why I did what I did. I don't know why I didn't do what I might have. It was so much like television that I couldn't believe it was happening to me. Pictures ran through my head of a woman screaming and kicking, and poking out the guy's eyes. I just couldn't do anything, because I didn't know what to do," Sandra explained softly.

"I am a very passive person, and in my entire life I never fought with anyone, nor have I ever had big yelling, screaming arguments. I guess that my mother raised me to be that way, or maybe I was born that way," Sandra said, giving a slight smile, almost asking for forgiveness.

"In retrospect, I think there was time for me to do something when we were in the park, and when he told me to get in the back seat I knew that I had some choices. I knew that I could have tried to hurt him and get out of the car, or I had opportunities when I could have tried kicking him. There were certainly other moments in which I could have reached out and done some damage to his face. But I wasn't confident that I could stop him, and, if you can imagine this, I was also scared that I might hurt him,"

Sandra told me. "I was too afraid that I would escalate the situation that at the time wasn't that threatening to me. What was threatening to me, now that I think back, was thinking I would be killed, so I chose to do nothing."

Six months after the rape, Sandra would not leave the house alone, and she still won't go alone into underground parking lots. For more than two years, she had recurring nightmares and would awake screaming. During the day, she would have uncontrollable crying episodes that would leave her exhausted. She revealed to me that it was almost a miracle that her husband didn't leave her because of her despondency and sense of isolation from people.

It has been more than five years since Sandra was raped, and although she finally underwent therapy and learned some self-defense techniques for women at the YWCA, she still feels guilty and angry at herself for not even attempting to resist her assailant.

Sandra has gone one step further: she is learning to shoot a gun. When she began telling me of her gun training, she surprised me with a newfound confidence that hadn't been present in her accounting of the rape. She described to me how well she was doing in target practice and how fast she could load her gun. Her enthusiasm was similar to other women's excitement when they are learning how to shoot.

The big question, of course, is, could she use that gun? "I'd like to tell you that I could. I think I could. I just know that I will never, ever be a victim again if I can do anything to change it," Sandra insisted.

Traditional self-defense techniques—karate, judo, and ju-jitsu—are still the current rage to make women think they are powerful and can defend themselves. It is true that self-defense methods can make you physically stronger and more confident, but commercially learned confidence can get you killed in hand-to-hand combat. It takes a tremendous amount of rigorous training and physical conditioning for many years to become effective at fighting someone even your own size, let alone someone bigger than you. Without training, practice, and correct follow-through, if you kick a man in the groin, poke him in the eye, or break his finger, you have not necessarily incapacitated him. He could get angrier, and you might turn a would-be burglar or rapist into a killer.

Even if you're an expert in karate, judo, or some other martial art, you still are not prepared for street fighting. In most practice situations or even in tournaments, you will never hit anyone, except by accident. Also, some people are inured to pain. I was told that boxers often win matches with karate masters, because boxers have so much experience with pain.

Dr. Elyse Singer, a neurologist at UCLA, has taken a number of self-defense courses since her early college days in Buffalo, New York, and in fact, was able to fend off an attacker by using self-defense techniques.

"It was in the basement of a health clinic. I was going for some supplies when I was attacked. I was very shocked and froze for a few minutes. But instinctively I responded by side-kicking into his abdomen—a technique that I practiced the most in class. In retrospect, I think that there were a number of other moves that would have been better, but I wasn't accustomed to target the groin—an area definitely out of bounds, for obvious reasons—but certainly I had the opportunity and would have been more effective if I had either kneed him or kicked him lower."

As it was, she didn't disable him. The man kept attacking her after she initially repelled him. Elyse couldn't remember what had happened next, except that he hit her quite hard a number of times, knocking her to the floor. She did remember seeing him coming toward her, about to jump on her.

"What I did was something that I had watched people do in class but never practiced myself," Elyse recalled. "I picked up my knees up to my chest and I kicked both feet into his stomach as hard as I could. He flew over my left shoulder, just like you see in the cowboy movies, and fell on the concrete floor," Elyse gleefully said. "That's what really discouraged him. He wasn't severely hurt, but I think he was amazed. He had expected me to give in immediately, but I was able to keep him off long enough that he must have begun to realize that people were going to be looking for me.

"He looked real scared at that point, and I began to get angry. Up to then, I had been dizzy and felt nauseous. I started raving and threatening him, and that produced a real change in his attitude. I couldn't believe it. This big, bad guy, afraid and backing away from little me," laughed Elyse.

"I think that I was just incredibly lucky that I came up with that cowboy move at the last minute, because I never learned how to defend myself if I was knocked onto my back. I just lucked out," admitted Elyse. "The training gave me the psychological edge to deal with the situation, but had he actually pinned me, I don't think I would have known what to do. My training had been classical fighting from an upright position. My instructors never taught us how to fight from the floor. They always assumed that you would be attacked 'John Wayne-style.' "

Elyse advocates that all women take a self-defense course, but she quickly points out that there are limitations in traditional martial-arts training that are not addressed. One drawback is a tendency to make martial arts into a sport in this country, rather than a form of self-defense, so that a great deal of class time is spent learning techniques that are very spectacular and flashy and may earn points in tournaments but are not effective in immobilizing an attacker on the street or after being taken down. "Some of the very high kicks, for example, often lack power and accuracy, and can put you off balance. While they may look very good in class, they are not a good first choice in a real fight," Elyse points out.

What displeases Elyse the most is the lack of contact

fighting. "Partly as an attempt to popularize the martial arts and partly as a response to the liability crisis, most schools teach purely noncontact fighting," said Elyse. "You develop a tendency to pull your punches, and in times of crisis you may not be able to hit with full strength."

I met Elyse at a four-week self-defense training called Model Mugging Women's Self-Defense Course, which was begun in northern California and has been studied at Harvard, Stanford, Radcliffe, and Wellesley. Model Mugging was founded in 1971 by karate, judo, and kendo black belt Matthew Thomas, following the assault and rape of a female karate student and successful state-tournament competitor who was unable to defend herself in real-life combat.

Matt studied three thousand assaults against women to find out how men attacked women. He found it very different from the way men attack men. What women need, Matt concluded, is not to spend four or five years in an art, but to learn a stopgap measure to take advantage of surprise by using only a few time-honored, disabling techniques that will terminate any attack from any-size man.

Model Mugging is truly an extraordinary method of self-defense. Unlike other self-defense courses, Matt has developed a twenty-hour, four-week course that teaches women aggressive fighting skills that emphasize using the strength of the legs from a prone position—the position where all rapes take place. Women actually fight many times with a "mugger" who is a highly trained martial artist dressed from head to foot in fifty pounds of protective equipment. During these practice sessions, the mugger attacks each woman in the class and continues assaulting her until she delivers one or more blows with enough power to convince the padded model mugger that the blows would render an unprotected assailant unconscious.

Model Mugging instructors, who are all women selected and personally trained by Thomas, have graduated more than six thousand women since 1971. Of the graduates, thirty-two have been violently assaulted. All but two of these successfully disabled their attackers, and the two who didn't faced men with knives and deliberately chose not to resist.

The training assault scenarios are all different and can be quite frightening. The model mugger will threaten his victim and use the most vile verbal abuse. Situations include being attacked at a bus stop, an underground parking lot, or an automated bank teller, where conversation begins simply, then escalates to threatening behavior and attack; also bedroom scenes, where a woman asleep in bed is surprised by a rapist, and various other high-risk encounters.

During my four-week course, I was attacked forty times by the model mugger in a variety of scenarios. This was the first time that I had ever battled with an attacking man. Each fight was difficult and at the same time exhilarating. We were all surprised to be told how quickly our fights had gone. It took from three to ten blows to score a KO, and the average time was eight seconds. One time, while I was waiting my turn and watching another woman being attacked, my adrenaline got so high that I became dizzy and had to sit down for a few minutes. When it was my turn, I had regained my composure and was able to knock out the mugger with three ax-kicks to the head. I felt triumphant!

Matthew Thomas explained to me that women have always been perceived as weak and as victims, not having the capacity to fight back, but that women need to believe in themselves and to know that they have the capacity to defend themselves. He tells the women in his classes that his instructors cannot teach self-defense in only twenty hours. What they can do, however, is provide a path for his students to release the power that has been within them all the time.

Model Mugging is only step one. Even Matt confesses

that Model Mugging has limitations that are overcome by having a firearm. In an attack, he explained to me, the victim needs distance and time; if nothing else works, Model Mugging affords the time and space to use a gun. Why depend on a primitive system, Matt insists, when you can use a highly developed one? "We are toolmakers; that's what sets us above brute strength. Firearms are our most efficient tool for defending life and freedom."

Women can use two types of strategies in response to fear. They can use restrictive, passive behavior, which limits or restricts their life style—such as refusing evening engagements—or they can learn risk-management techniques that involve engaging in defensive tactics in the presence of danger. A U.S. Department of Justice report defines risk-management behavior as a way to minimize or manage the risk of victimization in the face of danger by learning self-defense or carrying a weapon.

Unfortunately, the majority of women still do not take self-defense seriously, even though studies show that fear of crime is twice as high for women as for men. One study conducted by Northwestern University's Center for Urban Affairs reported that 48 percent of the women, compared with 25 percent of men respondents, thought of "their own safety all or most of the time" or "fairly often." The study also pointed out that women worry more than men do that someone might try to harm them while they are engaged in a variety of day-to-day activities.

It was once thought that women were more frightened because they are smaller and less powerful than their potential assailants, but Professor Paul J. Lavrakas of Northwestern University, the nation's leading authority on fear of crime, says that someone's height has hardly anything to do with fear of crime; even tall women (over five feet six inches) are more fearful than short men (under five feet four inches). His studies indicate that gender, for whatever reason, is the most important independent factor.

Women are fighting and winning rights equal to those

that men have always enjoyed, yet they do not have the same liberties. Many feminists contend that the impact of potential victimization on women is linked to perpetuating women's lower status in society. Women think twice about taking, or decline to take, jobs that may be better-paying because the workplace may be located in an unsafe area. Women select housing first for safety, then for comfort and fashion. They skip many evening affairs, classes, or meetings for fear of coming home alone late at night.

We know that women are at a distinct disadvantage in a world that is dominated by men—perhaps simply for the most obvious reasons. As young girls, they don't learn how to box or wrestle, nor do they play with toy guns. They are not taught to defend themselves either in playground tussles or through military training. On a more insidious level, socialization processes that connect femininity to various styles of weakness and helplessness may paralyze many women, teaching them the fear that restricts their ability to defend themselves. And if women lack assertiveness and self-confidence about their physical competence, they most certainly will be easier prey for attackers.

Often women are literally intimidated out of the possibility of behaving aggressively in a self-defense situation. New Yorker Deborah Stein confided that if she were ever attacked she would not fight back, because, as we have heard from other women, she would be afraid of hurting her assailant. Questioned whether she would feel that way if an assailant were trying to kill her, Deborah still maintains that she couldn't fight back, because she is a nonviolent person. Instructors who teach women's self-defense courses such as Model Mugging observe many physically strong women who at first are so frightened of violence and of fighting that they cower and cry uncontrollably, unable to defend themselves in a simulated mugging situation. Sometimes it takes weeks or even months before these women begin to realize that they are physically and mentally capable of successfully defending themselves against an aggressor.

Moreover, a great many women also dislike and fear guns and consider it normal female behavior to react in that manner. These emotions may be a consequence of a myth that perpetuates the idea that guns belong to men as if they were some sort of cultural prerogative. Some women, as well as some men, endorse the Freudian theory that the gun is a symbol of a phallus—the Priapic Theory, although I'm sure they're thinking of rifles and shotguns rather than small handguns—or they perceive guns as an extension of a man's masculinity, giving him perhaps an undeserved power.

Jane Clarenbach, a spokesperson for the Handgun Information Center, reflected the attitudes of a number of women with whom I have spoken when she told me that she is a very nonviolent person and that the most violent thing she has ever done was to smack someone across the face, which upset her and was remorsefully remembered for many years.

Clarenbach carefully and persuasively continued to explain that she also wouldn't want the changes that would be required in her life to prepare herself for that one possibility of being assaulted. She compared carrying a gun with taking out life insurance before getting on a flight.

"If it does happen that I'm attacked, and if I survive, I might change my mind," Clarenbach told me during an interview in her Washington, D.C., office. "I don't feel a whole lot different about being on a plane. But once you've been in a plane crash or in an emergency landing, then maybe it's a little different. But I don't choose to take on the other responsibilities that I feel are involved with a handgun in order to prepare myself for that one possibility."

Jane Clarenbach's attitude is not uncommon. However, for a brief time during America's frontier days, many women had the means and the skills necessary to defend themselves and their homes from animal predators, Indians, soldiers, drifters, and drunken cowboys. And in the big American cities of the mid-1800s, and later in the Gold Rush towns of California and Nevada, it was not uncommon that women were armed, concealing Derringers under hats and in boots, corsets, garter belts, bodices, muffs, and purses. Annie Oakley became an American folk heroine throughout the land and in Europe with her extraordinary demonstration of shooting skills, earning more than a hundred thousand dollars and shooting more than one million shells.

Even though there are many women who refuse to take the time and precautions to ensure their own safety, others are actively defending our security as members of the police forces of every city in the Western world.

Being called on to use a weapon for self-defense is perhaps as remote a possibility as Jane Clarenbach implies with her analogy of the plane crash and the flight insurance, but being prepared for the statistical long shot of being a victim of violent crime is really no more extraordinarily prudent than wearing seat belts in a car or having a fire extinguisher in the kitchen. And the time it takes to learn how to use and maintain those pieces of emergency equipment should be evaluated only in terms of the severity of the threat they could eliminate, not by comparing the efforts in time and trouble with other, less critical occupations.

Having a gun for self-defense brings with it the responsibility of knowing how to use and maintain it. Without that knowledge, the firearm defeats your purpose and should not be relied upon to furnish protection. If you don't have the time or will to make time for instruction in the use of a self-defense gun, and if you cannot assume the responsibility of maintaining your skills with regular practice, it is my opinion that you should not buy a gun.

If, for whatever reason, you think it is time for you to do your share to end the victim status of women, and if you can bear to undertake the attendant responsibilities, you should know that finding a gun in the hand of a potential victim is one of the most feared and avoided incidents a felon can imagine—feared and avoided even more than the police.

3

Rape and Consequences

RAPE CAUSES PSYCHOLOGICAL damage so serious it can't be measured; some victims are so grievously injured physically and psychologically that their lives are beyond repair.

The following vivid descriptions of rape trauma come from the court cases and the literature on rape: Perhaps the most succinct expression of the effect of rape upon its victims is that rape approaches a death experience. . . . At best, the rape victim will suffer the ultimate violation of self. . . . Rape victims uniformly report their feelings during rape as horror and terror induced by fear of being killed, maimed or mutilated, in addition to fears of pregnancy and venereal disease. . . . Even those victims who recover from or escape serious physical injury suffer psychological damage that continues long after the attack. . . . The psychological consequences of rape are sufficiently definite and well-documented to have their own name, Rape Trauma Syndrome.

Melody Sparks was raped when she was nineteen, and her life was mostly ruined for the next two years, never to be the same again.

Melody was the pretty flower of the Sparks family. She lived at home in Rehoboth Beach, Delaware, with her parents and brother, Michael, who was just one year older. Melody was a mature, caring, and gifted child—a source of happiness to her family, teachers, and friends—who graduated in the top 10 percent of her class with awards in leadership and community involvement. Brother Michael was proud of his little sister—"Loony Tune," he called her when he wasn't standing too close—who cheered him to victory at football games and cried with him when he lost his black Labrador under the wheels of a truck.

Melody's parents couldn't afford a college education for her, so she enrolled in evening courses at the local community college and during the day was a valued employee who controlled the inventory and kept the books at the same construction company where her brother worked as a carpenter. She was determined to save enough money for tuition, and wanted to major in journalism and become a newspaper writer.

Life was always going well for Melody Sparks, and her dreams were being fulfilled; she even sold a short story to a popular magazine. And as if life wasn't good enough, Melody fell in love with a young man she met at a church function, and plans were being made with great excitement to marry after her fiancé finished another year of college. She was to join him as his wife during his senior year at the university—she had already been accepted as a freshman.

It would all change in ten short minutes on one Friday afternoon in September.

Melody was at her desk finishing up the payroll checks that would be handed out to the crews within the next hour. A young construction foreman whom Melody hardly knew poked his head into her office and asked her to come down the hall to his workspace for a moment when she had a chance. She agreed, knowing that it was his last day with the company, thinking that he wanted some paperwork to take with him to his new job in Boston. After completing the page of checks she was working on, she walked into his office. He was waiting. He locked the door behind her.

"As he shut the door, he had a very strange smirk on his

face, and I moved away from him. I felt something was very wrong and wanted to leave. He kept looking at me, saying nothing. I got extremely nervous. So nervous, in fact, that I picked up the phone to call the security guard, but the phone was dead. As I put the phone down, he laughed at me," Melody said.

"He had pulled the wire out of the phone jack, and then I noticed that his job board had been propped up against the window. He laughed again and told me what he was going to do to me."

The man grabbed her and forced her to the floor. She tried to fight back, but knew from all the years of wrestling with her brother, Michael, that it was useless. Before she could scream, he made it painfully clear what he would do to her if she made any noise. He took the telephone cord and bound her arms behind her. She begged him to stop. She prayed for her brother to come for his check and look for her.

"I never was touched by a man before. You see, I was a virgin," she said with some embarrassment. "He was very vicious and he very forcibly entered me. He had a hard time, but he did it, and it hurt so much," Melody said, starting to cry. "When he realized that I was a virgin, he got even more excited. He called me all sorts of names and told me that it was exactly what I needed.

"When he was done, he untied the cord and told me not to tell anyone. He grabbed my hair as I was trying to get up from the floor, drew me up to his face and looked at me with a stare I will never forget, and told me that no one would believe me if I said that he raped me, because all the guys thought I was a whore anyway. He used the most awful words. He said that, if I told, everybody would do it to me."

While Melody tried to put herself together, her assailant picked up his check from her desk and left the building. She was bleeding and almost delirious. She didn't know what to do. She went back to work writing payroll checks.

Melody handed them all out and smiled, wishing everyone a pleasant weekend. She left with her brother. When they got home, she waited until he got out of the car so that she could wipe the blood off her seat.

"That night I took five baths. I was so scared that I couldn't stop shivering. I didn't want my mother to see me, and I couldn't tell her. We are a very religious family; what happened to me just couldn't be talked about," Melody explained. "Sitting in the bathtub, I began to feel fortunate: my fiancé was away at school, nobody had to know.

"Something possessed me from that time on. I quit my job the next week and took another one, at a fast-food place. I lived in hell for the next three months. I couldn't talk. I couldn't eat. I couldn't think. I had a horrible fear that I was pregnant, because I hadn't gotten my period. I was getting crazier every day. I stopped going to school, and I wasn't writing anymore. Nor was I able to talk to my fiancé when he called. It was all falling to pieces."

Then, one morning at work, Melody began crying uncontrollably. The manager had to call Melody's mother to pick her up. She didn't stop crying when she got home, and finally was able to tell her mother that she had been raped. Melody was taken to a doctor, who tested her and told her that she was not pregnant, yet that didn't seem to ease her condition. He said she was suffering from a nervous breakdown and needed immediate psychiatric care. Her parents balked at the idea since their religion prohibited psychiatric treatment, but the physician told them that this was the only approach that could help her. Melody's parents tried to talk to her, telling her that everything would be all right, and tried to convince her to put the experience behind her. But a few days later, they realized how troubled she had become and took her to a psychiatric hospital recommended by the doctor. When Melody was allowed to come home—three months later—

she continued to see a therapist twice a week for another six months. She was feeling better, but never feeling good.

Melody told me her story four years after the incident. We talked on the telephone; she refused to see me. Her voice was weak and toneless. She wasn't angry. She wasn't vengeful. Melody was beaten. She had moved away and eventually married another man; her first fiancé couldn't deal with the ramifications of what had happened to her and simply stopped seeing her. She wants to write again, but finds only one story to tell.

"The man who raped me took a lot from me. He took my life," Melody says with a kind of reflective sadness.

Creating joylessness, a need to look to the past for answers, rape pierces the soul. It crosses every economic and social barrier, has no respect for love or innocence, and makes victims of everyone.

Because every rape has different actors, experts can neither draw conclusions nor make predictions about causes and effects. What is known about rape is too little to illuminate any methods of escape. In the United States, the FBI estimates, a rape is reported every six minutes.

What we do know is that 87,340 rapes are *reported* to the police every year, and rape crisis centers assert that three to ten times more rapes are committed than reported, because the victims are so fearful of repercussions, including reprisal, destroyed reputations, police probing, and ultimately the humiliation of courtroom confrontation. Based on a study funded by the National Institute of Mental Health, Dr. Diana Russell estimates that 1.5 to 2 million women are victims of rape annually.

Although many people still consider that rape is sex, the police, the courts, and the psychiatric community all view rape as a crime in which sex is used as a weapon.

Helen Benedict, in her excellent book, *Recovery*, reports, "A torturer who puts his victim in a position of helplessness, makes clear to his victim that he is utterly at the torturer's mercy, breaks his will by humiliating and degrading him, and finally inflicts pain on him, usually to the most tender parts of the body. A rapist duplicates these acts."

Numerous clinical reports show that rapists frequently hold cavalier attitudes about rape and believe in rape myths, such as "Women ask for it." Probably the single most used cry of rapist to victim is: "You bitch . . . slut . . . you know you want it. You all want it," and afterward, "There now, you really enjoyed it, didn't you?" Studies of the attitudes and beliefs of convicted rapists suggest that, despite living proof to the contrary, essentially most believe that their actions did not constitute rape and were justified by the circumstances.

A survey conducted at California's Atascadero State Hospital shows that 50 percent of rapists raped their victims to achieve dominance, humiliation, and/or revenge. Twenty-seven percent reported becoming excited when their victims resisted their attacks, 34 percent admitted that overcoming their victims' resistance made them feel powerful, dominant, and good, and 35 percent beat their victims into submission.

One of the few other facts we know about rape is that 65 percent of all rapes and rape attempts occur at night, with the largest proportion striking between 6:00 P.M. and midnight. The Bureau of Justice Statistics shows that 44 percent of the completed rapes occur in the woman's home, while nearly half the rest happen on the sidewalks, or in a park, field, playground, parking lot, or parking garage.

The most terrifying form of rape, an assault by a total stranger, is the most commonly reported rape, according to the Bureau of Justice Statistics, which finds additionally that a woman is twice as likely to be attacked by a stranger as by someone she knows. The rape crisis centers and private or university researchers find that rapists usually live or work in the neighborhoods they prey upon and know where the victims live in 65 percent of the cases.

The chances of a rapist's getting caught and convicted

are one in six hundred, and the average among them has assaulted seventeen women before he is convicted.

The FBI profile of the typical convicted rapist reveals that he is somewhat more likely to be white than black, typically under twenty-one years old, and is probably drunk or high on drugs. He is usually unarmed, and beats or chokes his victims before, during, or after attack.

The Bureau of Justice Statistics reports that weapons are used in only 25 percent of the reported rapes and rape attempts. Of that number, knives were used in about 12 percent, whereas guns were displayed in 10 percent of all reported rapes and rape attempts.

The myth that a rapist will see a woman he is sexually attracted to, suddenly be overcome with an uncontrollable sexual urge, and attack has been dispelled in studies by Dr. Menachim Amir, who reports that the majority of rapes are premeditated but with no specific victim singled out for the assault.

Another type of rape is the "gang rape," in which a victim is arbitrarily selected by a group of boys or men who want to prove their masculinity to one another. Not only do "street kids" engage in this brutal activity, but so do so-called normal college students, who often rape for ritual reasons as part of a fraternity initiation. Twenty-five percent of the rapes in Amir's study were group rapes, of which 97 percent were planned, although no particular woman was targeted in advance.

What we know for sure is that rape comes usually by surprise and at night. A victim may or may not know her rapist, but he is likely to know her and her patterns. Thirty-six percent of all rape victims are injured, 6 percent seriously, and emotional trauma of some degree results in every case of rape, similar to the post-traumatic stress syndrome of witnesses to an atrocity or living victims of a plane crash.

The most prominent symptoms of Rape Trauma Syndrome are fear and anxiety about safety, which can continue for many years, if not for a lifetime. A victim's sense of safety is totally shattered, and often she doesn't feel safe anywhere. Once a woman has been raped, many things that she previously took for granted, including everyday activities, become colored by anxiety.

A high number of victims are afraid to return to their homes if they've been raped there, and even women who are raped on the street often are fearful of living in their own houses, thinking the assailant is going to find them again. Circumstances such as being alone, or in a crowded place, or in a room where a woman's back is against an entry cannot be tolerated by some victims. The heightened anxiety of being on guard and worried makes many victims suffer terrible fatigue, because they are tense all of the time.

Other rape trauma symptoms include feelings of guilt and self-blame, which are usually unrelated to the realities of the rape incident. Sometimes women blame themselves for not successfully fighting off the attacker, or for not locking their windows when it was eighty degrees outside.

Self-blame or guilt, according to Gail Abarbanel, founder and director of the Rape Treatment Center, Santa Monica, California, may seem irrational, but those feelings fulfill a need to find a reason, to explain what happened. After all, Abarbanel stresses, rape is so arbitrary. Self-blame is almost easier to tolerate than the reality that rape is a random event. It is a very common, interesting dynamic, and some people don't understand the part it plays in the recovery process. If a victim can explain something and pin it on a reason, then she may feel that she can prevent it from happening again.

Another symptom in the trauma that may follow rape is a feeling of shame. This, of course, has more to do with the cultural stigma that is attached to rape, a residual, no doubt, from lingering Puritan attitudes about sex. Many victims feel as if they are ruined women and have concerns about being held in less esteem, as less valued, seen as damaged goods. This is especially prevalent among Latino and devoutly religious victims.

Women may also have flashbacks during the day. These recurrent, intrusive thoughts about the rape will overwhelm victims, almost incapacitate their thinking for hours, days, or weeks at a time. Crime victimization surveys find that sexual assault victims are three times as likely to attempt suicide, and four times as likely to receive psychological treatment.

If those early feelings of fear, guilt, anger, and even hatred are suppressed, they will eventually affect the woman's love life, her home life, her work, or her health and fitness. The rape experience doesn't fade away or heal with time.

According to the Boise, Idaho, YMCA's Women's Crisis Center, 80 percent of their calls are from women who were raped or assaulted one to ten years ago and who then suppressed their horror, never telling anyone of their episodes. Professionals who deal with assault victims on a daily basis discover that they suffer from low self-esteem. In studies of women who experience posttraumatic syndrome, those who suffer the most are women who feel that they were attacked because of their character, and they think that if they had been better persons they would not have been assaulted, says Danielle Molles-Evans, a founding member of the Cleveland Women's Counselling Center, and currently the president of the Personal Empowerment Center, the umbrella organization for Model Mugging.

Evans insists that, if these women are not treated, low self-esteem can manifest itself in many areas of their lives. "It is not uncommon," Evans explains, "to find assault victims who are compulsive overeaters, almost purposely making themselves unattractive, and subconsciously hiding their sexuality they somehow feel contributed to their rape. Others hide in alcohol or drugs. Many develop phobias or sleeping disorders. And, interestingly enough, almost all are unaware of their destructive behavior."

Other reactions that may endure for months or even years include nightmares, physical ills, depression, the development of twitches, and even taking absurd risks such as walking alone on dark, deserted streets or going to unsavory bars to prove renewed strength. One woman who spoke to Evans said she experienced panic attacks and blackouts in which she couldn't remember if she had fed her children or changed their diapers.

Donna Henderson is a victim who buried her rape experience for sixteen years before confiding in anyone. When I spoke to her, she had just completed a year of therapy and a defensive-tactics course. A reticent woman who hid behind large tinted glasses and layered clothing, Donna at first wanted only to discuss the theories she had learned concerning rape. My probing for her experience and her feelings made her nervous and even more theoretical. Finally, she accepted my desire to know her story and how her experience affected her life.

In 1973 Donna's life was altered. At the age of thirteen, she was returning with a church youth group from a day at a Charleston, South Carolina, beach. The trip was chaperoned by the special-activities director and elder of the church, who drove the van. Donna was the last to be dropped off, and before the elder reached her house, he pulled over into a secluded meadow and ordered her to go to the rear of the van. Confused by his demand, Donna hesitated, knowing that something was wrong, but then he yelled at her and she fled to the back.

Wrapped in a wet beach towel and a skimpy bikini bottom, Donna cowered in the seat as she watched the man unzip his pants and lunge toward her. Immobilized by fear, she stifled her screams as he tore off her towel, pulled off her bikini, and raped her. Afterward, he shook her and threatened that if she informed her parents they wouldn't believe her, and the church authorities certainly wouldn't believe her, because she and her family weren't parishioners of the church.

Donna never told her parents about the rape. She was afraid that her father might go after the man, which would certainly mean trouble for everyone. She told me that she wasn't afraid for herself, but for her father.

"So I took on the burden and felt it was my fault that it had happened," Donna told me sadly with an impatient sweep of her hands. "It changed my life. I was shy before, but after the rape I became extremely shy and introverted. I became a homebody. I didn't date like most girls. I never went to any dances. I decided that other things were more important, but later in my therapy I learned that it was fear. I was afraid of men. As a result of being raped, I never trusted men again and never had any boyfriends. It was okay when I was with a group of people, but I shied away from getting into a conversation with a man. I still find that difficult even today. It's only been in the last year that I've really been able to relax a little and enjoy the friendship of a man," explained Donna as she fidgeted with a piece of her hair.

"For a long time, I couldn't remember a lot of what happened to me—I blocked it so totally out of my mind. Now, as an adult, I am angry. I separated myself so much from the rape all these years, and all I can say is that during therapy I had to go back as an adult to take care of that bruised and injured child in me. I had to go back as an adult and fight this man. I was helpless then, and so frightened, and so overpowered, not only by the authority that this man represented in my life, but also his physical strength. Besides, I never had any association with any kind of sexual encounter." Later she added, "I do remember being practically totally paralyzed."

When Donna told me how many years she had kept her rape a secret I was quite surprised. She explained, "Part of the reason that I didn't say anything is because of the shame of it. Another part of it is that internal blaming of myself, thinking that it was my fault. It's not something that I want to talk about," she quickly reminded me. "It's something very shameful, and you take it and it kind of grows into some kind of malignancy, to the point where it is so ugly that you stuff it so far down you never allow it to surface." Donna sighed as she slid lower in her chair. She paused for a moment, then straightened up.

"Now I know differently. It's so important not to push it down. It's so important for women not to feel that it was their fault," Donna said with renewed vigor.

Would her life have been different? "Yes," she said. "I would have been more outgoing. I would have taken advantage of a lot of different situations that I refused to participate in because I was afraid. Now, after therapy and taking a defensive-tactics course, I no longer will allow fear to dominate me, but I have a lot of lost time to make up," Donna said, smiling for the first time since we had begun talking about her ordeal.

Months after this conversation, Donna called to tell me she had quit her computer programming job and had enrolled in a university woman's studies program to further her education and make possible a new career.

The psychological consequences of rape are not just limited to the victim. In a way, the victim's family is raped as well. According to psychotherapist Albert Potash of the Los Angeles Rape Resource Center, a rape victim will bring her husband or boyfriend with her during counseling, because men just can't deal with all of the woman's emotions. Potash counsels husbands and significant others to help them know that their life will not be the same for months or even years. Regrettably, Potash asserts, people in primary relationships with the victims don't understand rape. They feel their own failure, and often a typical kind of reaction is to withdraw from it and say, "You were upset, now we need to go on." It's the same kind of response as to grieving over the death or loss of a loved one. There isn't a great deal of understanding of the rape experience in our culture.

Often husbands will want to help, but rape victims are

unable to talk about the incident or how they feel. Linda Stern, who was raped in her Staten Island home while her husband was away on a business trip, recalls that, after the police had gathered information for their reports on her rape, her husband patiently and lovingly asked to be told the story. "I said, 'No, I can't!' What I was saying to him, and I didn't explain it accurately, was, I can't discuss it now because I'm too upset, I'll tell you when I can, and I want to tell you everything. He never asked me again, and I never said anything to him, because I was so lost in myself that I forgot about his feelings," admitted Linda, who was divorced sixteen months after the rape.

It was only years later that she heard what he had been feeling. They met for dinner in Manhattan, and he told her that one of the things that he assumed when he married her was the responsibility for protecting her. He felt that he was a failure because Linda had been so severely hurt and he wasn't there to help her. He blamed himself for the rape and felt guilty that he hadn't taken better home-safety precautions, especially since he was away so often. He apologized to her for his wrongdoing. Linda tried to explain to him that it wasn't his fault, but she realized that it was too late in their communication to change his feelings.

In many cases, a husband or boyfriend is truly incapable of coping with his loved one's emotions and experience. Michael Leon is one such man, who struggled more with his own feelings about his girlfriend's rape than he realized, making the situation more difficult for her and ultimately impossible for both of them. Psychologists say this is not an unusual reaction. Michael was, at first, angry with Melissa because she was late and hadn't called him, but when she walked into their New York City apartment looking as if she had been hit by a car, he turned that anger toward her assailant.

"I wasn't the least bit concerned about Melissa when I saw her. I was concerned that some son of a bitch violated someone that belonged to me. All I wanted to do or could think about was finding the guy and killing him. Melissa actually had to calm me down, take care of me, me. And all the while it was she who needed to be taken care of. I'm pretty disgusted with myself about that now," worried Michael. "She was such a strong woman."

After Michael recovered from his rage, he helped Melissa clean up and treated her bruises and cuts. She didn't want to go to the police, because she felt, as so many victims do, that it wouldn't do any good. But Michael wanted to go. "I wanted this guy to get caught and pay for what he did to us," Michael said, his eyes still showing his anger. "Am I making any sense? It was an unbelievable shock, seeing my future wife so beat up and sexually violated."

They went to the police the following day to report the rape, and Michael realized that it was a futile exercise. That night, they went to Melissa's favorite Italian restaurant, where they talked about the rape. "I brought it up. I wanted to know what she was thinking now, after what happened, but I guess really I wanted to know what she was thinking about when it happened," explained Michael. "She said she couldn't remember what she thought about when it happened. She said she was so frightened, all she was doing was hoping it would be over and she would be alive—like a bad dream just before you wake up.

"I think, now, that I was more than a little disappointed that she wasn't thinking that I would somehow miraculously appear to save her," he said simply and honestly. "I was hurt that this guy was on top of her, having sex with her, like I do, and she didn't even think of me. I know it is wrong of me to think like that, but, damn it, I loved her, and she was being used by someone else," Michael said with intensity.

That night, he was apprehensive about sleeping with her and admitted that he didn't know how she wanted him to behave. Their communication seemed to be getting worse and worse, but finally, many weeks later, they were able to enjoy sex again.

"I wanted it to be exciting for Melissa, to snap her out of it. And for me it was sort of exciting knowing that the last time she had sex was when she was raped," he said, nervously laughing and looking away. "The therapist told me that thought was common. Somehow it was like having sex with a virgin or a child. It was good for me. I broke through some of my problems about the whole thing."

A few days later, Melissa decided to go to her parents' home in Ravenna, Ohio, for the rest of the summer. She surprised Michael with the idea, telling him that her two sisters were planning to visit at the same time and it would be a rare chance for them all to be together. While on this trip, Melissa wrote to Michael telling him that she wouldn't be returning to live with him and she didn't want to talk to him about it—that was just the way it was. Michael didn't interfere. "After all," he said, "she'd been through a horrible experience."

Rape can ruin people's personal lives and their relationships. The economic ramifications of rape can often be as serious as the psychological consequences. A rape victim's business career or job can be profoundly affected by the experience. If the rape occurred in the office building where a woman is employed or while she was traveling to and from work, she may quit her job because she suffers flashbacks every time she is back in the area, fearful of being raped again.

In Helen Benedict's book *Recovery,* one of the victims, identified as Claire, explains, "People need to know that they may not be as good at their work as before for a long, long time. And the money thing is hard, too. You take cabs because you're afraid of public transport, you pay more for a secure place to live, moving costs you. The rape was a huge setback for me financially, and I still can't save anything because I need to live in someplace safe, and that costs all I earn in rent. . . ."

The preceding stories about the experience of rape are only a fraction of those that I was told by rape victims. I found that most of these victims weren't ready for any assault. It was only after they were mugged, robbed, or raped that most of these women took a self-defense course or learned how to shoot a gun. Almost all of them told their instructors that if they were assaulted again, they wanted to be better prepared to make choices and defend themselves. They wanted to have a fighting chance.

Demanding the right to survive is the issue; the possibility of killing in defense of that right is the ultimate consequence.

The Second Amendment to the Constitution of the United States specifically permits stable, law-abiding citizens to own guns for their own defense and for the defense of the community. Somewhat different from other rights of individuals defined and guaranteed by other amendments to the Constitution—free speech, assembly, religion, and so on—the right to own and bear arms brings with it the implicit right to kill. It is a huge burden to stand with a firearm in front of something, intent on surviving, prepared to kill for food or in self-defense. The burden is so monumental that most of us choose to avoid it altogether and let professionals do the killing and protecting for us.

Perhaps the politics of the amendment should be looked at first; the issue of rights of the accused and rights of the victim stem from constitutional safeguards protecting against wrongful prosecution. But many people feel that the rights of the accused have now overshadowed rights afforded to victims. Technicalities of arrest and indictment and prosecution, plus the shortage of judges, have turned many guilty felons loose to commit more crimes—more than those who are found guilty in a court of law and are sent to prison. In fact, FBI Crime Reports indicate that only 1 percent of all those arrested ever serve jail time, and they serve only 25 percent of their sentences because of poorly funded, overcrowded prison systems.

4

The Politics of Self-Defense

ALTHOUGH HARD TO believe, the D.C. Supreme Court *(Warren* vs. *District of Columbia)* has upheld the decision that police are not responsible for the safety and defense of the individual citizen. The police and other law-enforcement agencies are responsible for the safety and protection of the general population in the districts they serve. That means that, if your life is threatened by a trespasser, an intruder in your home, and you summon the police, there is no legal requirement for the police or sheriff to respond to your call.

At midnight on April 22, 1987, in Cincinnati, Ohio, Margaret Franklin was at home alone reading in bed when she heard a window break in the kitchen. Immediately recalling advice given to her by an acquaintance who worked in crime prevention with the local police department, she quietly got out of bed and locked her bedroom door, went directly to the telephone on her nightstand, and called 911 for the police. When the police answered, she took a deep breath and, as calmly as she could, explained that an intruder had broken into her house and that she could hear him in the other room. She identified herself and the location of her house and said that she was in the bedroom with the door locked.

All she could do was wait and pray that the police

would arrive before the intruder discovered her locked
bedroom door. Overwhelmed with fear, and trying to buy
as much time as she could, Margaret went into the bathroom adjoining her bedroom and locked that door, too.
She waited. First the door to her bedroom was smashed in,
and she heard the intruder rummaging around through the
dresser drawers and the closet.

Margaret began to reason that the intruder probably
didn't think anyone was in the house, given the way he was
noisily searching all the rooms. The thought that he might
not know she was home and that he had broken a window
to gain entry and had just now broken her locked bedroom
door frightened Margaret even more—he was bound to
break through the locked bathroom door, just as he had
broken through the locked bedroom door. He was looking
for valuables, she concluded, and a locked door just adver-
tised something of value.

Later, during the police report, Margaret estimated that
the burglar had been in the house for fifteen or twenty
minutes before he found her hiding in the bathroom. He
was in the house for another fifteen minutes raping Margaret. She thinks that his brutal handling of her was the
result of his being surprised to find her hiding behind the
shower curtain.

The police never arrived until they came with the ambu-
lance to take Margaret to the hospital. Questioning her in
the hospital, they apologized for not responding to her first
call; somehow it had gotten misplaced.

Margaret's crime-prevention police friend came to visit
when Margaret was healed enough to get around. Privately he told her that the reason the police hadn't responded that night was that she hadn't sounded alarmed
enough when she made her report over the telephone.
"You have to scream and yell to get them to take you
seriously," he said.

This is not just an isolated instance of random police
error. The fact is that the police cannot protect individuals,

notwithstanding the legal fact that they are not even required to. There is just too much crime and not enough police to cover it all, and crime is increasing every day, especially violent crime.

Our capacity to prevent crime is wholly inadequate, and deterrence to crime virtually does not exist. So where do we turn? If we look at the statistics, we must recognize the imminence of the threat of violence. Are we just to hope against all odds that we will not be victims? Are we expected just to be careful when it comes to rape, and again ignore the statistics that almost half of all rapes happen in the victims' own bed? Do we just have faith that drugs will soon disappear and the primary motivation for robbery and burglary will dry up? What do we do if we are not willing gamblers?

A former police chief of the Los Angeles Police Department, Ed Davis, said, "Crime is so far out of hand, we can't protect the average citizen. He must protect himself."

So it comes down to this: we must take responsibility for our own safety. That means at the outset that we must get involved in our communities to make sure that our law enforcement is the best our communities can afford. It means that we must organize or support neighborhood citizens' groups that have a clear-cut plan of communication throughout the neighborhood we live in, so that we know of all criminal incidents that take place and hear about any suspicious activity on the streets around our houses.

Being responsible for our own safety means that we equip our homes with intrusion and fire-detection devices. We learn that we don't walk in the middle of a city park at night; we don't drive late at night through dark, dangerous areas; we don't park in underground garages away from pedestrian activity; we walk briskly from bus stops; we don't pick up hitchhikers or get out of our car on the highway or on a lonely street to exchange information with someone who has just suspiciously rammed us with his car. We learn that we take the responsibility not to run out of gas, or let an unscheduled electric-meter reader into the house or open the door to anyone we do not know or expect. We learn to think about our safety all the time, never get trapped, and never depend on anyone to help.

Many say that the best deterrence to personal attack is the gun. The police depend on the gun to deter crime, armies use the gun to resist invasion, and criminals rely on the gun to stay in business.

But a dispute rages. There are those who would have the government confiscate all firearms, especially handguns, under the heartfelt conviction that the systematic elimination of these instruments of death would reduce the violence that accompanies crime, and at the same time reduce accidents and gun-related suicides. They call themselves gun-control advocates. Their intentions are honorable, and their influence often is targeted directly at legislators who continue to introduce federal and state laws that work toward disarming the American public. Their goals cannot be achieved without a fierce struggle.

On the other side of the debate is the pro-gun position. Attorney Don B. Kates advances it with a vigorous assertion that just fourteen words in the Second Amendment to the U.S. Constitution guarantee every citizen the right to own guns: ". . . the right of the people to keep and bear arms, shall not be infringed." The pro-gun banner gets carried further by attorneys like Mark Benenson and David I. Caplan of New York City and Stephen P. Halbrook of Washington, D.C., criminologists James D. Wright and Peter H. Rossi of the University of Massachusetts, Professor Gary Kleck of Florida State University, David J. Bordua at the University of Illinois, and others who argue the interpretation of those fourteen words and defend their positions with exhaustive research into the crime statistics compiled by the FBI, the U.S. Department of Justice, and public and private studies of the role the firearm takes in the balance between crime and crime prevention.

The pro-gun cause, flush with defensible data, is helped to a very large extent by the NRA, headed by Warren Cassidy; The Citizens Committee for the Right to Keep and Bear Arms, guided by John M. Snyder from Washington; Gun Owners of America, with lobbyist Larry Pratt at the helm; The Firearms Coalition, piloted by Neal Knox, former NRA head of legislative affairs; and the Second Amendment Foundation, in the hands of Alan Gottlieb. The anti-gun banner is carried by Pete Shields and Handgun Control, Inc., and Michael Beard's National Coalition to Ban Handguns. This public issue revolves around the constitutional guarantee to bear arms. The private debate takes place in the 115 million households across the country whose occupants own two hundred million firearms.

The debate is a hot one and each side truly despises the other. The anti-gunners accuse the pro-gunners of supporting a position that was never guaranteed by the Constitution except with regard to the individual state's having the ability to muster a militia to defend its franchise from the domination of the federal government. Moreover, the gun-control advocates add, that misinterpretation costs the country eleven thousand gun-related suicides each year, more than twelve hundred accidental deaths, twenty-five murders each day, and the death by gun of one child under the age of fifteen every twenty-four hours.

Neither position can be dismissed lightly. Here is the background of the two sides, and their arguments. Be sure about which side you lean toward, because if you follow the path of one side and really believe in the truth of the other, you may have a problem; the subject here, after all, is killing.

Gun control was not a national issue in this country before the assassination of President John F. Kennedy, and really didn't begin to attract active proponents until the 1968 murders of Senator Robert F. Kennedy and Dr. Martin Luther King, Jr. I was one of the Kennedy presidential campaign staffers in Washington, D.C., who immediately upon his death began work on organizing the first pro-control group, called the National Committee for Handgun Control, which, along with other lobbying groups, was instrumental in pressuring President Lyndon Johnson and Congress to pass into law a highly controversial bill that is known as the Gun Control Act of 1968.

The passing of this act was the first attempt at federal gun control and the first occasion since its inception in 1871 for the NRA to take a highly visible, aggressive, anti-control posture that endures to this day. With a membership of close to three million, five full-time lobbyists with a budget in excess of six million dollars, an extensive network of state and local gun clubs, and three hunting-and-shooting magazines, the NRA is a powerful grass-roots organization that one can easily say represents the gun owners of America.

Just as impressive is the NRA's intransigent position with regard to all gun-control issues. The NRA's stated political goal is to work for the defeat of all present and future firearms restrictions on the federal, state, and local levels. Along with the Second Amendment Foundation, which campaigns for gun owners' constitutional rights, the NRA feels it is the watchdog of personal liberty in this country—liberty that can only be guaranteed by the freedom to own and bear arms for sport, defense against crime, and protection from a government that may attempt to dominate, enslave, or otherwise usurp the freedoms of its citizens.

The NRA and the Second Amendment Foundation feel strongly that they carry the banner of a noble cause, patterned after the cause the Founding Fathers championed in writing the Bill of Rights. The anti-gun camp sees the NRA as intractable, right-wing, old-fashioned, and a dangerous threat to domestic tranquillity.

The pro-control side of the issue is divided into two separate but mutually sympathetic voices. The most radical is the National Coalition to Ban Handguns which works for the complete elimination of handguns. It contends that the handgun causes far more damage to the innocent than possible value as a deterrent or an effective weapon against crime. The National Coalition is underfunded to such a degree that it cannot get its message to the public. In effect, the Coalition actually serves as a whipping boy for the NRA.

Without some uncompromising effort at completely banning the sale and ownership of handguns, such as the National Coalition, the NRA would not be able to keep sounding its horn about freedom and constitutional rights. The NRA spends more than fifty million dollars in gun-related projects. I don't know what the budget of the Coalition is, but whatever it is, it might as well be contributed to the NRA, considering the opportunity it presents to the NRA to answer back.

A more moderate anti-gun expression comes from Pete Shields and Handgun Control, Inc., which raised $3.9 million in the first three quarters of 1988 and has a membership of one million. Pete lost his college-aged son in 1974 at the hands of the infamous "Zebra Killer" in San Francisco. Nick Shields was shot three times in the back, at point-blank range, by a lone assailant. His was one of many senseless deaths in a series of killings by the Zebra Killer that plagued the city that year.

The shooting death of his son prompted Pete to campaign for handgun control. His involvement was predictably strenuous and not without conflict. Within a year, Pete had taken a leave of absence from his job to lobby Congress for a gun-control law; after another six months, he formally resigned his job to become the executive director of Handgun Control, Inc.

Pete Shields is a fighter, not a fanatic. He has positioned Handgun Control, Inc. in what he calls a "centrist" position. "This is the most difficult position, because it satisfies the ideals of neither side," Shields says in his book, *Guns Don't Die—People Do.* "Yet, if we continue to allow the debate to proceed along purely idealistic lines, i.e. extreme lines, I don't believe we will ever achieve effective handgun control nationally. What's more, I think that's why the pistol lobby encourages this all-or-nothing kind of debate. They agree with me that such debates only serve to polarize the issue and end up turning off and even alienating the public. Consequently they achieve exactly what the pistol lobby wants—nothing."

By a "centrist" position, Shields means that his group is not anti-gun. In his book, he advocates control rather than ban, and rallies his supporters behind the slogan ". . . working to keep handguns out of the wrong hands." The NRA retorts that any control of handguns would only keep self-defense guns out of the hands of law-abiding citizens, not the criminals who get their guns without regard for any of the twenty thousand gun laws and controls already existing. The NRA returns an echo of "Control criminals, not guns."

This gun-control debate stirs up deep-rooted emotion from just about everybody. We all have an opinion about capital punishment, euthanasia, abortion, violence, terrorism, child abuse, and killing, don't we? And, without having been continually exposed to the arguments of both sides, we really only hold the opinion that made the last impression on us.

The Second Amendment's constitutional guarantee to keep and bear arms is certainly one of the most hotly debated topics in the gun-control theater. The pro-gun scholars, such as Halbrook and Caplan, devote most of their research to the analysis of the Second Amendment to the Constitution and how it affects gun possession, proposed or existing restrictive gun laws, law-enforcement treatment of gun owners, and the court's administration of gun-law violations.

The debate over the Second Amendment, as well as the

other amendments, has been raging since the day after the Constitution was signed in 1787. The framers of the Constitution were not all satisfied with the document as it was negotiated, insisting that it be amended to specify rights afforded to the individual. The founders were primarily concerned that the newly formed federal government not have legal access to usurp the individual freedoms of the population and the states within which they resided.

After the ratification of the Constitution, founder James Monroe wrote that the "right to keep and bear arms is a basic human right," which he would propose to have added to the amendments to the Constitution. Similarly, the principal exponent of the Constitution, James Madison, voiced his opinion about how the just-created federal government would differ from the enslaved European countries, which he described as "afraid to trust the people with arms." Americans would never fear their government, because of "the advantage of being armed, which Americans possess over the people of almost every other nation. . . ."

Samuel Adams recommended to the Massachusetts Convention the ratification of the Constitution conditional upon an appended guarantee of personal rights, stating that "the Constitution be never construed . . . to prevent the people of the United States who are peaceable citizens, from keeping their own arms."

George Mason and Richard Henry Lee are together credited with negotiating the compromise that allowed the ratification of the Constitution subject to the signing of the Bill of Rights. Lee wrote, "To preserve liberty, it is essential that the whole body of the people always possess arms and be taught alike, especially when young, how to use them." Again, fearing the domination of the new federal government, Noah Webster wrote, "Before a standing army can rule, the people must be disarmed; as they are in almost every kingdom in Europe."

The historical precedent for the constitutional right of

the people to keep and bear arms is abundant. However, Pete Shields, speaking for the anti-gun movement, decries the pro-gun philosophy erected on the foundation of only the popular fourteen words of the Second Amendment.

"To understand the supposed constitutional argument," Shields points out in his book, "it is essential that the reader be familiar with the full and complete wording of the Second Amendment to the Constitution of the United States. It reads: 'A well-regulated Militia, being necessary to the security of a free State, the right of the people to keep and bear Arms, shall not be infringed.' " Shields continues: "It would be interesting to take a poll of Americans and see how many have forgotten, or never knew, the Amendment's initial twelve words. Certainly, the pro-pistol lobby has not seen fit to clarify that point. The 'Militia' of the Amendment is what we all know today as the National Guard."

Countering Pete Shields' assertion, Don B. Kates explains that the militia was not a military unit but a system under which every household had to have a gun (as a deterrent to both crime and foreign invasion) and men of military age had to appear regularly for militia drill bearing their own guns. And as Congress was enacting the Bill of Rights, both Federalist and anti-Federalist commentaries on it appeared that hailed what would become the Second Amendment as a guarantee that individuals could never be deprived of "their own arms," "their private arms."

This subjectivity of the amendments in the Bill of Rights mitigates the strict interpretation of each and every passage and paragraph of the Constitution. In fact, constitutional scholars insist that the Constitution and its amendments must be read as one complete document, so as to produce a total and unified effect. Moreover, it seems logical that the Bill of Rights was intended to amend the main body of the Constitution to reflect a concept of natural rights and define limits on the government's power to sanction or regulate the affairs of citizens.

The basis of the Second Amendment argument is without regard to the types of weapons the constitutional guarantee safeguards. The courts have generally interpreted that only weapons that could have naturally evolved from the weapons used at the time of the writing of the Constitution qualify under the meaning of the amendment. It is therefore unreasonable to expect protection under the amendment to extend to weapons such as machine-type guns, flamethrowers, artillery, and atomic weapons, which would commonly be thought of as "dangerous or unusual," whose display would cause enormous fear and distrust in one's neighbors.

The no-interference concept notwithstanding, reasonable gun controls are no more troublesome or less sensible than, for instance, regulating the First Amendment guarantee of speech to disallow the yelling of "Fire!" in a crowded assembly of people if there is no immediate danger of fire. So it is from this evolving position that we accept, even expect, the law to ban guns to convicted felons, lunatics, children, and other individuals who are proved to be irresponsible or a threat to the peace and freedom of law-abiding citizens. In fact, as Kates points out, gun registration and licensing cannot be considered contrary to the intent of the Second Amendment, whose framers conceived of and practiced periodic inspections of all able-bodied men to assure that they had appropriate arms and ammunition.

United States vs. *Miller,* a 1939 case, is the Supreme Court's first and last extended analysis of the Second Amendment; it emerged from a challenge to an early federal gun law, the National Firearms Act of 1934. This law encompassed several provisions against sawed-off shotguns and submachine guns, including a prohibition against the interstate shipment of a sawed-off shotgun, which Miller and his associate were charged of violating.

The court said: "In the absence of any evidence tending to show that possession or use of any 'shotgun having a barrel of less than eighteen inches in length' at this time has some reasonable relationship to the preservation or efficiency of a well regulated militia, we cannot say that the Second Amendment guarantees the right to keep and bear such an instrument. Certainly it is not within judicial notice that this weapon is any part of the ordinary military equipment or that its use could contribute to the common defense."

The Supreme Court holding is apparently so ambiguous that it is interpreted differently by the proponents of the individual-rights position and the states'-rights advocates, and a discussion on this issue could go on for many pages.

Since the Miller case, a number of lower federal courts have ruled against challenges to federal gun-control laws. When Morton Grove, Illinois, banned the civilian possession of handguns, the Supreme Court refused to comment.

It seems, then, that the intent of the Second Amendment was to guarantee individual citizens the right to own ordinary weapons to defend themselves against personal threat and against the tyranny of government. But this is the twentieth century, argue the gun-control advocates. Our government is established and has had a long enough time to show that it isn't about to tyrannize the populace. Yet is that really true? Just take, for example, early gun-control laws and how they were administered by law enforcement and adjudicated by the courts. The tyranny-of-government theory might not be so farfetched.

Gun-control laws started in the West before the 1870s, but occurred more frequently and with more force in the South and the East from the 1870s to 1934, because of the massive immigration of Europeans into the urban areas. Jobs were often rare for people with poor English-language skills and only an agricultural background, and the times were filled with repeated economic slumps, panics, and depressions.

"Under these circumstances," writes Don Kates in his fine book *Restricting Handguns: The Liberal Skeptics Speak Out,* "it is scarcely surprising that some of the new immigrants followed their adopted country's fine old tradition of violent crime. In fact, like all ghettoized minorities, their depredations were largely confined to their own people and their own neighborhoods."

As early as 1903, New York City began canceling pistol permits in the Italian and Jewish sections of the city. This was followed by the 1905 state law that made it illegal for any alien to be found with a gun of any kind in any public place. Foreigners were often considered anarchists and radicals, not to be trusted with firearms. They were believed to be the organizers of the labor unions, which at the time were thought to be ruining the American standard with their collective demands for better working conditions and decent pay. Feeling helpless, preyed upon, and threatened by the perceived agitation of the foreign element, authorities throughout the Eastern states began restricting gun ownership in order to control the influence these new troublemakers had in the highly organized Eastern society.

In 1911 New York City passed the first of its sweeping gun-control laws. The Sullivan Law, as it is known, outlaws the ownership of firearms in the city without a police permit, which to this day is expensive and difficult to obtain. Other states followed the lead of New York City wherever dissidents surfaced.

The Southern states had their own form of conservative fears that led to gun-control laws. At first these laws made it illegal to own a handgun of less than a certain size and caliber, effectively preventing the poor black from owning the more expensive "Army"- or "Navy"-model handgun, which was available to the white Klan members returning from the army in the 1870s. These so-called Saturday Night Special laws with stiff jail sentences were enacted throughout the South by white-supremacist legislators acting on behalf of their land-rich constituency to quiet the restless blacks and the poor white tenant farmers aroused by examples of labor victories in the Northeast.

Kates points out that the Arkansas, Michigan, Missouri, and North Carolina laws were expressive of one of the lowest periods of race relations in modern American history. A younger generation of blacks—led by soldiers returning from World War I familiar with guns and willing to fight for the equal treatment they had received in other lands—had to be painfully reintroduced to the forces of social control. Once again, in the 1910s and 1920s, the Klan became a major force in the South. Once again the public authorities stood by while murders, beatings, and lynchings were openly perpetrated. Once again the handgun legislation of Alabama, Arkansas, Mississippi, Missouri, Tennessee, and Texas deprived the victims of the means of self-defense, cloaking the specially deputized Klansmen in the safety of their monopoly of arms.

What we may be able to deduce from this brief history of the framing of the Second Amendment and the beginning of gun-control laws in this country is that perhaps keeping an eye on our government isn't such a bad idea. It is hard to believe, in this era of high-profile politics and global power plays and democracy versus communism, that the government in America might benefit if the population in this country were categorized, numbered, and also disarmed. But certainly, at least in theory, it is far easier to govern a body that is homogeneous, obedient, and dependent than an assembly of individuals who refuse domination and have the strength to resist.

In the words of the late Senator Hubert Humphrey: "The right of citizens to bear arms is just one more guarantee against arbitrary government, one more safeguard against a tyranny which now appears remote in America, but which historically has proved to be always possible."

5

Gun-Control Laws

GUN LAWS CAN be local, state, or federal. State and local laws make up the bulk of the existing laws and vary to such extreme proportions that it is illegal to own a handgun in Washington, D.C., and against the law *not* to own a gun in Kennesaw, Georgia.

Federal law dominates local statutes, and at present bans the sale of extreme firearms, such as machine guns, and restricts gun ownership to permanent U.S. citizens with no criminal indictments, previous felony convictions, history of mental illness, drug addiction, allegiance to a foreign power, interest in overthrowing the U.S. government, or dishonorable discharge from the armed services. Federal law also prohibits the sale of handguns through the mail and across state lines, and further requires all new guns to be sold through federally licensed dealers.

Notwithstanding the anxiety ever present since the Founding Fathers identified government as a threat to the people and firmly proscribed in the Bill of Rights any interference by government with the natural rights of citizens, the primary objective of gun control, we must believe, is to keep innocent people from being maimed or killed by criminals or madmen with an instrument so expressly designed for killing. An equally important aim of gun control is to reduce gun-related suicides and accidents.

For the most part, the handgun has been the focus of gun-control activity—this, we are told, because of its concealability and high usage in crime and gun-related homicide. The handgun was designed for killing humans and is the weapon of choice in more than 80 percent of crimes and homicides involving firearms.

Everyone wants to take handguns out of the hands of criminals and psychopaths, yet researchers point out that the twenty thousand gun-control laws enacted over the past century have done little to achieve the goal. Why?

Pete Shields, speaking for the pro-control advocates through Handgun Control, Inc., asserts that present federal, state, and local gun control is not succeeding in taking the handguns out of the hands of criminals because, without a strong nationwide standard of control, criminals will get their guns from states that have little or no control and distribute them wherever there is a market.

The anti-control campaigners, using Professor Gary Kleck's research (645,000 defensive handgun uses annually versus 580,000 criminal handgun attempts), respond by pointing out that criminal use of guns involves fewer than 1 percent of the sixty million handguns in circulation, and restricting the sale or ownership of firearms would serve only to handicap the law-abiding citizen who feels a need to own a gun for self-defense. And more restrictive laws, they add, will do nothing but make black-market guns more expensive to the criminal, who will commit more crime to afford them.

NATIONAL REGISTRATION OF HANDGUNS

The gun-control supporters have suggested many gun-control measures to limit the number of handguns owned and used by criminals. One of those recommendations is to register all gun-ownership transfers with a federal agency. The Gun Control Act of 1968 requires that all new handguns be sold through a system of federal firearms dealers, and the FBI claims that as a result of that system they can trace more than 90 percent of all new-gun sales in the country. But used-gun sales are subject only to state and local laws, and, given the difficulty of controlling the transfer of used guns, most states don't even try.

So the next logical step in identifying where all the handguns are is to register or license the owners themselves and make the owners responsible for registering with the appropriate authority the guns they own. This licensing would also include a national system of issuing and enforcing permits to carry a concealed handgun. Currently, concealed-weapons permits are issued or denied by state or local authorities usually at their sole discretion, which of course suggests a great deal of opportunity for them to reward or punish individuals within their jurisdiction. A national law controlling the issuance of carry permits could standardize acceptable reasons for issuing those permits.

According to Pete Shields, licensing is nothing more than the law-abiding citizen's standing up to his accountability. And registration, Shields asserts in his book, is nothing more than that same law-abiding citizen's standing up to his accountability for a deadly commodity he has chosen to own; it's the law-abiding citizen saying: "I'm a responsible citizen. Check me out. And when you find I'm right, put the number of this gun down after my name, so that if it's ever misused, you know who to come and get." Shields insists that that is responsible citizenship.

Shields would like a federal law passed that would license all the gun owners and require them to register their guns. The first question that the anti-control voice demands to have answered is, Who enforces the law, and how does the enforcement authority—let's assume it is the police—find the criminals, who would obviously be unlicensed and have unregistered guns? And, further, they ask, how would a licensing-and-registration law be enforced on the owners of the sixty million handguns in circulation now? Would present owners voluntarily comply with a licensing-and-registration law? Numerous polls and surveys among current gun owners have indicated that 75 to 92 percent think registration is the first step toward confiscation and would not voluntarily comply.

So, if even a minority of current handgun owners would resist, how would they be punished when they were found? Our law-enforcement and judicial systems are already overburdened with dangerous criminals, say the gun owners. We don't have the resources, they insist. And how would licensing law-abiding citizens and registering their guns affect the use of handguns in crime? And perhaps one more question should be asked relative to licensing and registration: How much would it cost, and where would the money come from?

The biggest question about passing a national law requiring the licensing of handgun owners has to be whether such a monumental undertaking would result in fewer handguns in the hands of criminals, and therefore less violent crime, resulting in fewer victim deaths and serious injuries.

The anti-control voice insists that licensing and gun registration are just the first step—the investigative step used to compile lists of gun owners—toward a total ban and confiscation of handguns. They cite Washington, D.C.'s experience of more criminal shootings after legislating one of the country's toughest gun laws as an example of that kind of escalation, but for now let's assume that licensing and registration are just as Pete Shields says, nothing more than the law-abiding citizen's standing up to his accountability.

It seems that the logical way to assess whether licensing and registration will have any effect on keeping handguns out of the hands of criminals is to look at the states and cities that already have existing handgun restrictions that are as tough as or tougher than national registration would be. Having already been warned by the pro-control lobby that local laws are impotent because of the likelihood of criminals' going into adjacent states and other cities that have more lenient laws to obtain their weapons, then returning to commit their crimes, we should still find that some trend should be apparent in gun-tough jurisdictions.

It can be concluded from the continuing reports of the FBI and the Department of Justice that the areas of the country with the highest homicide rates have the strictest gun controls. It is estimated that 20 percent of American homicides are concentrated in four cities that have some of the most restrictive gun-control laws, with only 6 percent of the population—New York, Washington, D.C., Chicago, and Detroit.

The Bartley-Fox Law took effect in Massachusetts in 1975, legislating a mandatory one-year jail sentence for persons carrying handguns without a license or owning other firearms—including BB guns—without a firearms-owner identification card. When the Bartley-Fox initiative became law, Massachusetts was the nineteenth most violent state in the nation, and Boston was the fifth most violent city with over five hundred thousand in population. By 1983 Massachusetts had moved to the eleventh most violent state, and Boston captured the number-one distinction. And between 1974 and 1983, gun-related assault rose 20 percent in Massachusetts while it rose only 6 percent nationwide.

Hawaii, Michigan, Missouri, New Jersey, New York, North Carolina, and Puerto Rico all have laws that prohibit their residents from purchasing or possessing a handgun without a discretionary police permit. All these gun-control laws have endured for thirty to seventy years in each jurisdiction, and were amplified and enlarged by the federal Gun Control Act of 1968, prohibiting the importing of handguns from across state lines. There has been ample time for these laws to reflect a change in the crime statistics of each region.

Six independent criminological studies have compared the homicide and violent-crime rates in these states and Puerto Rico with those of states with more lenient handgun control. The results of all the studies reveal that the jurisdictions restricting optional handgun possession have homicide and violent-crime rates as high as or higher than states with no special emphasis on handgun ownership.

New York City has some of the toughest gun-control laws in the nation, and it probably should, if gun-control laws can be counted on to chip away at gun crime. It is, after all, the largest city in the nation, and can thus be expected to have the most crimes of all kinds. In fact, New York City has more homicides than the total number in twenty-four states with a total population of 40 million.

The gun-control laws in the state of New York are known as the Sullivan Law, and were legislated in 1911. In New York City, the Sullivan Law has been supplemented a number of times during the years, making the laws tougher. It is now unlawful to own a firearm of any kind, kept in your home or your place of business, without a police permit.

A target-practice handgun license does not grant the holder the right to keep a loaded handgun in his home or place of business, but he can transport it in a locked container to and from a licensed shooting range. An on-premises license permits the holder to possess a handgun in his home or place of business—loaded, we assume—but he can obtain only two authorizations a year to transport it, unloaded in a locked container, which, of course, doesn't allow for any target practice. Each additional handgun must be registered and listed on the owner's license.

An additional license and registration is required in New York City for rifles and shotguns, and no firearm can be carried concealed unless a separate carry permit is granted; in this city of more than eight million people, there are only six thousand carry permits—in fact, there are only thirty-one thousand permits in all categories, including private detectives and armed guards. At least one of these gun licenses is needed to buy a gun, to buy ammunition, or to shoot at a target range. Now, that's gun control! Yet the police estimate that there are two million unlicensed handguns in New York City—one for every four men, women, and children within the city.

In 1980 Mayor Koch pushed through legislation calling for a mandatory penalty for anyone carrying a handgun without a proper permit. The mayor said that nice guys who owned guns weren't nice guys, and an assistant district attorney said that he could "sympathize with and understand people's wish to have guns for their protection, but when you're living in a civilized world you have to subjugate that for the greater good."

In the past twenty years, the national homicide and handgun-homicide rates rose approximately 40 percent. The homicide rate in New York City rose 150 percent, and the handgun-homicide rate increased 350 percent. Handgun use in robbery in New York City over that period rose from 20 percent to 30 percent.

Nationally, 13 percent of criminal homicides are robbery-related; in New York City the figure is 25 percent, and among Caucasian homicide victims the figure is in excess of 50 percent. New York City, with 3 percent of the population, accounts for 17 percent of the gun-related robberies committed in the whole country, and close to 10 percent of the reported robbery-related murders. New York City is without a doubt not a typical American city. Given the city's unique problems among those of all the cities in the United States, it is no small achievement that New York City runs as well as it does.

However, it seems obvious just from these examples that the licensing and registration of guns do no more than to disarm the law-abiding resident, who, many think, could be better prepared to assist the police in fighting crime by policing his own domain.

Colin Greenwood, former superintendent of the West

Yorkshire Metropolitan Police, Great Britain, and a leading authority on gun control, argues that, although at first glance it may seem odd or even perverse to suggest that statutory control on the private ownership of firearms is irrelevant to the problem of armed crime, that is precisely what the evidence shows. According to Greenwood, armed crime and violent crime generally are products of social, economic, and cultural factors unrelated to the availability of a particular type of weapon. The number of firearms required to satisfy the crime market is minute, and these are supplied no matter what controls are instituted. Greenwood feels that controls have had serious effects on legitimate users of firearms, and claims that there is no case, either in the history of Great Britain or in other countries, in which controls can be shown to have restricted the flow of weapons to criminals or in any way reduced armed crime.

If licensing and registration affect only the gun owner who never uses his gun in criminal activity, and do not come close to controlling the criminal's access to weapons, there is no need to bring up the mountainous problems of enforcement, punishment, and cost. Perhaps the only control that will work is an outright ban of handguns.

BANNING ALL HANDGUNS

Again, Pete Shields freely admits that he guided Handgun Control, Inc. into a middle-of-the-road position, working for handgun control rather than a handgun ban, so that he wouldn't have to lock horns in what he calls "purely idealistic lines" that would not achieve effective handgun control nationally. Advocating control instead of a ban, Shield says in his book, "is the most difficult position, because it satisfies the ideals of neither side."

So, instead of soft-soaping this issue, let's come right to the point: the only way to keep the handguns out of the hands of the criminal is to ban the manufacture, sale, and possession of handguns. However, Shields freely admits that "The polls have consistently shown that the people do not want an absolute ban on handguns. A total ban is perceived as taking away their self-defense, and until their fear of the criminal, the crazed, the drug-addicted, the violence-prone psychotic is reduced, they will never agree to such a law."

If Handgun Control, Inc. really wants a handgun ban in the future, but is pushing for more moderate controls like licensing and registration, perhaps they believe that, after the lawmakers see how expensive registration laws are for all their ineffectiveness, the anti-gun forces will have a better shot at asking for more restrictive reforms.

In the 1960s Washington, D.C., adopted a gun-registration ordinance, assuring gun owners that registration would only record ownership of firearms within the District, and would not, as the pro-gun group asserted, lead to confiscation.

But in the mid-1970s there was a vigorous attempt by the U.S. Congress to ban the possession of all handguns in the District. Met with equally vigorous resistance, the District of Columbia enacted substitute legislation that forbade the new registration of handguns, and then demanded a ban on the manufacture, importation, and transfer of handguns, full registration of rifles and shotguns, a prohibition on the sale or possession of ammunition except for firearms lawfully registered to an individual, and a prohibition on guns being usable for self-defense in the home—not exactly what was promised in 1965 with a simple registration ordinance.

In 1976, the year before the law took effect, Washington, D.C., was the seventh most violent city with over five hundred thousand in population in the nation. Six years later it had moved into first place as its violent-crime rate increased 48 percent. Before the gun law took effect, guns were used in about 40 percent of the city's violent crimes.

Six years later guns were involved in almost half of the city's violent crimes, prompting then police chief Maurice Turner to remark in a speech, "What has the gun-control law done to keep criminals from getting guns? Absolutely nothing . . . City residents ought to have the opportunity to have a handgun." And it sounds as if Chief Turner had a point: justifiable homicides of felons by civilians in the District were effectively reduced by about two-thirds under the gun-control law.

Again we see that even the most severe form of gun control—prohibition—does nothing to control the handgun in the hands of the criminals. It controls law-abiding residents of Washington, D.C., but allows crime to escalate. The slogan of the old-time pro-gunners echoes off of some of these statistics: "Guns don't kill, people kill." We need to find a way to control the criminals, not the guns.

Here are some more attempts at controlling crime through banning guns and their implications:

The most recent battleground is the state of Maryland, where in May 1988 the governor signed a law establishing a commission that will decide which handguns are legitimate for sport, law enforcement, and self-protection and prohibit the manufacture and sale of all others. The measure is aimed at banning the cheap, lightweight handguns known as Saturday Night Specials. Critics of the law contend that serious criminals do not carry Saturday Night Specials but prefer to carry, and actually do carry, relatively large, well-made guns. And according to the Congress on Racial Equality (CORE), Saturday Night Specials are purchased for self-defense by poor people, especially poor black women. CORE maintains that the law would deprive these people of their only means of self-protection. Groups opposing gun control collected signatures to put the new law to a November referendum. It was defeated by a 58 to 42 percent vote. Both supporters and opponents say the 1988 November referendum is crucial, because of the state's proximity to Washington, D.C., and the effect the outcome could have on gun-control efforts in Congress. Not surprisingly, state gun dealers report a dramatic rise in handgun sales.

Morton Grove, Illinois, banned the private possession of handguns in 1981. The town is small and relatively crime-free. There have been no homicides since 1979. Since the ban, burglary has increased 12 percent. This, it may be argued, could simply represent only one or two more burglaries. But the real impact of the Morton Grove ban comes out of a survey by Northwestern University following the ban, indicating that, from the twenty-four hundred households possessing handguns, fewer than twenty guns were turned in or confiscated. The only result of the law to date has been to criminalize the private possession of handguns by up to 20 percent of the households, representing at least 10 percent of the population of Morton Grove, Illinois.

Evanston, Illinois, became the second jurisdiction in the country to ban the private possession of handguns. The ban took effect in 1982. The number of homicides rose from four to seven in 1984, and robbery increased.

Oak Park, Illinois, adopted a handgun ban in 1984. None of the town's estimated twenty-five hundred handguns were surrendered.

Many scholars emphasize that the critical question is whether, and how, a handgun ban would affect the one in fifty-four hundred handgun owners who commits murder.

If guns are used for criminal purposes approximately 535,000 times a year, and used for protection against criminals by 645,000 law-abiding Americans annually, clearly guns are used for protection more often than for crime. And according to Dr. James D. Wright, who did the Wright/Rossi study for the National Institute of Justice, for an American family picked at random, the probability of being victimized by crime in any given year is on the order of 10 percent and over five years would therefore be on the order of 50 percent, all else being equal. To put these odds in a comparative framework, Wright stresses the probability for the same family of being victimized by a natural disaster (flood, tornado, hurricane, or earthquake) in the same year would be on the order of 1 to 2 percent, or some five to ten times less risk. And as far as he knows, Wright observes, nobody has seriously argued that, because the risk from natural hazards is so small, no protective measures need be taken against them.

Don Kates adds that it is difficult to call defensive gun ownership an irrational overreaction if it is deemed reasonable to pay twenty times as much to ensure against a danger less than one-tenth as likely. Indeed, Kates asserts, the gun owner could reasonably consider his weapon a better instrument in that it may actually avert the harm while insurance only recoups its costs.

Moving in the opposite direction, the town of Kennesaw, Georgia, not far from Atlanta, passed a law in 1981 that required every household to have a working firearm and suitable ammunition. Between 1981 and 1982 there was a 74-percent drop in violent crime and burglaries, and further decreases in 1983 and 1984.

Dr. Paul H. Blackman, research coordinator for the NRA's Institute for Legislative Action, concludes that, since there has been no noticeable increase in the number of households in Kennesaw with firearms—just as there had been no decrease in Morton Grove or Evanston—the crime drop may be attributed more to chance and to publicity than to the law itself. Potential criminals were reminded, as they were in Orlando, Florida, that Kennesaw residents had guns and that protection was acceptable behavior against criminal aggression.

In Highland Park, Michigan, police offered a highly publicized gun-defense training program for retail merchants. Armed robberies decreased from eighty during the four months prior to the firearms training to zero in the four months after the training.

In Detroit, an association of grocery-store owners instituted a firearms-training course for its members. The program received extensive publicity, first through denunciations of it by the chief of police, and afterward when seven robbers were shot by grocers. Grocery robberies in Detroit decreased by 90 percent.

In New Orleans, an association of pharmacists was publicly acclaimed by police and federal narcotics agents after a gun-training program for member pharmacists resulted in pharmacy robberies' dropping from three per week to three in six months.

And, of course, in Orlando, rape fell 88 percent the year following a well-publicized gun-defense course attended by more than six thousand of the city's female residents.

So who is winning in the war against crime? It seems that the criminals always win, even when guns are controlled, and crime marches on with bigger steps every year.

BANNING COP-KILLER BULLETS

In light of the dramatic failure of strict gun-control laws enacted in various cities and states throughout the country, the pro-control advocates—motivated, it appears, by a recruitment drive to enlist the support of police—are beginning to stress other areas, notably the sale of machine guns and what Handgun Control, Inc. is calling cop-killer bullets.

Pro-control organizations have continued to insist that, since fully automatic weapons are designed only for use in war, their outright ban would make the streets safer from the lunatic fringe that would turn a machine gun loose on a crowd in the commission of a crime.

Under pressure from Handgun Control, Inc., the most recently enacted federal law, the McClure-Volkmer Firearms Owners' Protection Act of 1986, included, among other things, a prohibition of the sale of fully automatic weapons and the sale or possession of carbine, armor-piercing handgun bullets (cop-killer bullets).

Pro-gun groups do not understand this argument. Fully automatic weapons have been carefully restricted and registered in this country, and there has never been an incident in which a *lawfully* owned machine gun has been used in a crime. Again, the pro-gun voice cries, another example of registration leading to restriction leading to confiscation.

The issue of what Handgun Control, Inc., is calling cop-killer bullets is another appeal to emotion rather than fact, according to the pro-gun group.

Cop-killer bullets have never once killed a cop; in fact, they were developed *for* police use and in the handgun calibers have generally been available only to the police, for a decade or more.

These are regular cartridges with very hard, carbine bullets that can penetrate car doors and bulletproof body armor. They are not effective man-stoppers, however, and even the police don't use them in their handguns, preferring the more lethal hollow-point bullet, which expands in size when it strikes its target. The assertion made by Handgun Control, Inc. in full-page newspaper advertisements throughout the country that these are cop-killer bullets is seen by the pro-gun forces as misleading, as well as another attempt by the government to erode the freedoms of the people. The NRA still defends the sale of carbine ammunition—all but unavailable for handguns—on the grounds that more than 80 percent of the rifle hunting cartridges (carbine cartridges) would be prohibited if such a ban were made law.

NATIONAL WAITING PERIOD

And, finally, the most important control being campaigned for in Washington, D.C., was the standardizing of a mandatory national waiting period and background check for prospective buyers of handguns. On September 15, 1988 the House of Representatives turned down the "Brady Bill," which would have imposed a national seven-day waiting period, by a 228 to 182 vote. The "Brady Bill" had been attached, as an amendment, to the Omnibus Drug Abuse Act, but the House substituted the McCollum amendment, which could establish an "instant" check system for felons.

At present there are sixteen states requiring waiting periods and background checks (plus scores of cities and counties that have their own laws), and six additional states that do background checks along with licensing. Typically, between 1 and 3 percent of the applicants wishing to buy handguns are disapproved. Again, the anti-control groups insist that the overwhelming majority of handgun buyers who purchase guns through licensed dealers are law-abiding, and that waiting periods and background checks only serve as *de facto* registration on the way to confiscation.

However, on the other side of the coin is the concern for spur-of-the-moment crimes of passion and suicide that may be avoided if people have to wait a week or two before taking delivery on handguns. There is just no way of knowing if the waiting period deters these overemotional shootings, or in fact if another weapon or means would be employed. The anti-control group points out that crimes of passion and suicide attempts almost always occur at night, when gun stores are closed anyway.

The waiting-period advocates only specify a handgun waiting period. We do know that long guns are far more lethal than handguns. If the pro-control people really want to stop the killing, I wonder why they don't have a waiting period for all guns. Given their philosophy, that certainly seems reasonable. It seems to boil down to politics; the waiting-period advocates simply don't want to anger or lose some of the support of the millions of hunters in the United States.

Handguns represent one-third of the total number of guns owned in this country, and probably 90 percent of the guns kept loaded at any one time. Yet handguns are involved in only 10 percent of the accidental firearm fatalities. It is easy to conclude that the number of accidental firearm fatalities would multiply enormously if even a small number of those who think it necessary to keep a loaded gun in the house for self-defense substituted long guns (shotguns and rifles) for their handguns.

The handgun is a relatively inferior weapon whose victims have approximately a 90-percent survival rate, comparable to the rate of survival from wounds inflicted by knives and ice picks. In contrast, rifles and shotguns are so much more powerful and accurate that a wound inflicted by one of them is on the order of four times more lethal.

In the "Task Force Report on Firearms" to the National Violence Commission, Franklin Zimring, the leading academic opponent of handguns, asserted that a national system of restrictive handgun licensing "would not appear to risk a massive shift to the use of long guns in crime." The day after the "Task Force Report" was released, Professor Zimring was asked by Senator Thomas Dodd in Senate hearings on firearms legislation to define "massive," to which Zimring responded, "My guess would be that no more than a third of handgun violent assaults in the city would be supplanted with long gun crime." Assuming Zimring's estimate is correct, criminologist Dr. Gary Kleck calculates that firearms homicide would only double. If, however, Kleck is correct in estimating that long guns would be substituted in 50 to 75 percent of all present handgun assaults, homicide would triple or quadruple.

The pro-gun dialogue adds to Kleck's assessment by observing that a handgun is far easier to hide, or lock away from inquisitive children, than a long gun.

OTHER ARGUMENTS SURROUNDING THE GUN CONTROL ISSUE

ACCIDENTAL DEATH AND SERIOUS INJURY

According to the National Safety Council (NSC), there are an average of 1,800 accidental gun-related fatalities per year. Since 1979 (when the figures first became available) the NSC can identify only 247 of these deaths as having involved handguns, which places accidental handgun deaths about twenty-seventh on the list of accidental fatalities, behind:

Motor-vehicle accidents	47,900
Falls	11,000
Drowning	5,600
Fires, burns	4,800
Poison by solids and liquids	4,000
Suffocation, ingestion	3,600
Posion by gases and vapors	1,200

Data from the NSC 1986 *Accident Facts* concerning accidental firearm fatalities of children under the age of fifteen point out 270 total firearm-related deaths. If handguns were involved in 25 percent of those, as claimed by the NSC, then there were 68 accidental handgun deaths of children under fifteen years of age.

However, Professor Kleck, who is considered to be pro-gun by anti-gun proponents, considers the NSC figures too low. He has gone behind the published figures to ferret out the ages of gun-accident victims from the mortality-detail files of the National Center for Health Statistics. His figures include an estimate of what proportion handgun accidents make up in the unidentifiable gun deaths: he calculates that one-third involved handguns, because that is the ratio of handgun to long gun in those cases that are identifiable. Based on that, he has calculated the following annual child-death totals from handgun accidents: for children under five, fewer than 24; for children under fifteen, 115 handgun accidents. Thereafter the total goes way up: if you count anyone under twenty as a "child," the accident total is 230.

As a consumer product, firearms (both long guns and handguns) are involved in 26,000 accidents requiring emergency-room treatment annually, with only one-third requiring hospitalization, usually for less than overnight, according to the Consumer Product Safety Commission. Accidents among the sport-related consumer goods ranking ahead of guns are:

PRODUCT	INJURIES
Bicycles	574,000
Basketball	458,000
Football	433,000
Baseball	432,000
Skating	183,000
Soccer	93,000
Volleyball	78,000
Fishing	65,000
Wrestling	64,000
Exercise Equipment	58,000
Gymnastics	53,000
Playground Equipment	53,000
Skiing	43,000
Squash/Racquetball	35,000
Tennis	29,000

Anti-control spokespeople summarize these comparative statistics by remarking that doubtless we could react to such figures by prohibiting bicycle ownership, requiring the destruction of all swimming pools, and making it a crime for anyone to enter voluntarily water that is more than one foot deep. Most people would, however, consider widespread publicly sponsored training in water, bicycle, vehicular, and gun safety a more appropriate policy approach.

The retort of the gun-control advocates is that, for example, bicycle accidents cause few serious injuries, but anti-control people say that the statistics show that most gun accidents are not considered serious, either. The gun-control side also claims that all the comparative sports activities have a redeeming functional purpose and only incidentally result in death and injury, whereas firearms are unnecessary to anything but killing and injuring.

Firearms Suicide

Suicide is not well understood, even though there are many, many scholars devoting the abundant resources of most universities, research hospitals, and government agencies to finding a common cause or discovering a hint of cure. Taking one's life is the final decision of personal responsibility, and is always preceded by deep, seemingly incurable depression. We all wish suicide wouldn't be necessary for those who choose it, and yet some of us have recognized it as an available alternative if life ever should become too dark with pain or grief.

There are approximately twenty-six thousand suicides in this country each year; roughly half are from firearms, and half of those from handguns. It is inarguable that if there were no guns there would be thirteen thousand people who would not have voluntarily concluded their lives with a firearm. But it seems to be the conclusion of most suicidologists that the people committing those thirteen thousand suicides by self-inflicted gunshot wounds would find another means to take their lives, especially since nearly 40 percent of all suicides from every means have attempted the act at least once prior to its successful completion.

Additionally, Dr. John Brinkley, resident psychiatrist at Seattle's Harbor View Hospital, points out that the data on suicide depict a very specific, small subpopulation, mostly made up of depressives and alcoholics, who do not represent the population at large.

In the book *Firearms and Violence in American Life,* pro-control authors George Newton and Franklin Zimring, summarizing their research for the 1968 Eisenhower Commission to Restrict Handguns, wrote that cultural factors appear to affect the suicide rates far more than the availability and use of firearms. Thus, they conclude, suicide rates would not seem to be readily affected by making firearms less available.

Their conclusion was based primarily upon data from the 1967 United Nations *Demographic Yearbook* that placed the United States ninth in suicide among sixteen nations, almost all of which had more restrictive firearms laws and considerably fewer firearms per capita. The Eisenhower Commission estimated there were twenty-seven million handguns in the United States in 1967. By 1975 the estimated handgun ownership grew to forty-one million, yet the United Nations' 1975 *Demographic Yearbook*'s comparative ranking of national suicide rates drops the United States down to fifteenth place.

Finally, psychiatrist Bruce Danto, former director of Detroit's Suicide Prevention Center, who continually reviews domestic and foreign suicide studies for any thread of evidence that may help define a treatment to stop suicide, insists that data show that people will find a way to commit suicide regardless of the availability of firearms.

I will not pursue this argument. I am certain that, even though the experts say that the suicidal individual will find a way to reach his or her goal, at least a few suicides would be postponed or avoided altogether if a gun hadn't been so immediately available. There is no defense to that, and it would be facetious of me to suggest that there would be fewer suicides if bridges were not so high and doctors didn't prescribe so many sleeping pills and automobiles couldn't go so fast.

UTILITY OF HANDGUNS IN HOME DEFENSE

The usefulness of civilian firearms in reducing crime is one of the main issues of the gun-control debate.

Anti-gun proponents argue that having a loaded gun is a relatively ineffective defense in the home. Their position relies mainly on local and fragmentary statistics found in Newton and Zimring's twenty-year-old book, *Firearms and Violence in American Life*. The authors say that burglary is the most common type of home intrusion, causing the greatest property loss, but rarely injures or threatens the victim's life, since burglars usually enter when no one is home to shoot them. Rather, they say, a burglar is more likely to steal a home-defense gun than to be driven off by it.

They contend, further, that few burglars and robbers are killed by their victims. To corroborate their anti-defense stand, Newton and Zimring cite mid-1960s statistics from the Detroit Metropolitan Area Police Department whereby, out of eighteen thousand burglaries occurring in 1967, only one burglar was killed by the intended victim. Also, police reports from January 1964 through September 1968 documented only seven Detroit householders shooting and killing burglars.

For robbery, Newton and Zimring reiterate, guns are of limited utility in self-defense, since a robber is usually able to surprise and overwhelm his victim. Again, they cite Detroit, where the police reported only three cases in five years in which the householder killed a robber.

Criminals do steal many guns. They aren't concerned with our handgun-control laws. If they don't steal guns, they can get them on the black market. No comparisons have been made between gun thefts and gun self-defense, and no exact figures on residential gun theft are known.

Estimates of the percentage of stolen guns among crime guns vary. Studies on police-confiscated weapons claim 20 percent of stolen guns among crime guns. The Wright/Rossi study for the National Institute of Justice, which involved a sample of two thousand prisoners, finds that 30 percent of handguns recently owned by these criminals were stolen. Of that percentage, 29 percent were reported to have been stolen from houses, apartments, and automobiles of strangers, while 31 percent were stolen from friends or family (another 30 percent were stolen from various gray- and black-market sources, and about one-tenth were stolen directly from retail outlets). Because of the high percentage of stolen guns, pro-gun advocates strongly state that law-abiding citizens owning guns for self-defense must safely secure their guns when they are out of the house, so that if a burglar breaks into a residence he will not be able to steal the gun. Further, they say that if a gun is kept in the car, it should not be left unattended in the car.

Those opposed to the Newton/Zimring conclusions come prepared with new national evidence. Although 87.3 percent of burglaries occur when there is no victim at home, the injury figures for burglary, as presented by the National Crime Survey (NCS) data through 1984, contradict the Newton/Zimring assumptions. Included in the NCS ten-year sample were 2.8 million burglaries that occurred when a victim was home, and in over 30 percent of these the burglars used violence, including 623,000 aggravated assaults and more than 281,000 rapes. And these figures don't count the number of victims actually killed by violence-prone burglars, because NCS data come from surveys of survivors. The critics go even further by citing Zimring's own 1986 research showing the potential deadliness of occupied-premises burglaries. His newest study finds six times more victim deaths in such burglaries in Chicago than in street muggings.

Yet those confronting Newton and Zimring, like Professor Gary Kleck, admit that in many burglary incidents the offender has the initiative by taking the victim by surprise, with situations often developing too quickly for victims to get to their guns. However, they challenge the Newton/Zimring opinion that few burglars and robbers are killed by their victims. Kleck, using 1980 FBI statistics and more detailed 1980 studies from Detroit and Dade County, Florida, estimates that on a national basis armed citizens *legally* killed in self-defense approximately 1,525 intruders. Kleck and others also strongly argue that the outcome in most defensive gun uses is not that criminals die but that they are wounded, apprehended, or scared off without being injured. As mentioned earlier, Kleck has another study, based exclusively on surveys done by anti-gun groups, that concludes that guns are used in defending against 645,000 crimes per year, with only one-third of the guns actually being fired. According to Kleck, the frequency of defensive gun use approximates the total number of U.S. arrests for violent crime and burglary by the estimated six hundred thousand police officers across the country. He says that being threatened or shot at by a gun-wielding victim is about as probable as being arrested, and substantially more probable than being convicted or incarcerated.

The anti-gun proponents continue to be challenged and frustrated by new statistics, and embarrassed by people within their ranks. Until 2:00 A.M. of June 15, 1988, nationally syndicated columnist Carl Rowan was a vocal supporter of handgun control, even to the point of advocating, in print, an automatic jail term for anyone using an unregistered pistol. He also called for a complete and universal federal ban on the sale, manufacture, importation, and possession of handguns.

That early June morning, Rowan pulled out an unregistered .22-caliber gun in self-defense and shot a young man who had scaled his Washington, D.C., fence.

The next day, in his *Washington Post* column entitled

"At Least They're Not Publishing My Obituary," Rowan wrote, "A lot that is theoretical, ideological is being written by people who have not been threatened, have not had a stranger at their bedroom window at 2 A.M. and have not been confronted by a doped-up intruder just outside their door. Let my political enemies crow. But let them know that as long as authorities leave this society awash in drugs and guns, I will protect my family."

Naturally, the opposition were ecstatic; Rowan had made their day, and the NRA sent him an honorary membership. But even if Rowan proved to be a momentary embarrassment to the well-organized anti-gun movement, this movement still holds its ground against the usefulness of gun defense.

DOMESTIC VIOLENCE AND SELF-DEFENSE

A major argument of the pro-control forces is that citizens aren't safer when they have handguns. Shields maintains in his book that the "facts show clearly that a handgun kept for self-defense is far more dangerous to its owner and his family than it is to the criminal. There are far more accidents and acts of passion with one's handgun than there are either criminal murders or prevention of criminal attacks."

The 1987 FBI "Uniform Crime Report" shows that there were 19,257 homicides in 1986. Of these, 3,236 were domestic homicides and 8,554 were acquaintance homicides. These perpetrators, however, are not exactly what we think of as ordinary law-abiding citizens. Most of the acquaintance homicides are not committed by neighbors shooting one another in a neighborhood argument. These people are drug dealers killing customers, gangs killing members of other gangs, Mafiosi killing rival Mafiosi, and loan sharks killing nonpaying clients.

Shields seems to stress the idea that shootings involving family members are spontaneous crimes of passion involving nonviolent people, but his perception does not coincide with existing reports. A study conducted by the Kansas City Police Department finds that in 85 percent of the domestic homicide incidents, the police were called to the address at least once in the preceding two years; in half of the incidents, police were called five times or more in the preceding two years.

In a 1977 study at the Women's Correctional Center in Chicago, all the women who had killed abusive mates reported that they had called for police assistance at least five times before they murdered their mates. A large number claimed the violence became more, rather than less, severe after their attempts at gaining assistance.

Professor Murray Straus, a leading authority on spousal and intrafamily homicide, affirms that family murders are rarely isolated outbursts of previously nonviolent people but tend to be preceded by a long history of assaults engaged in by people who are known to the police and to others as violence-prone. Professors Wright and Rossi, in *Under The Gun,* say they have also found that often domestic homicide is not an isolated occurrence or outbreak but, rather, the culminating event in a pattern of interpersonal abuse, hatred, and violence that stretches back into the histories of the parties involved.

Occupationally, these people are generally of low socioeconomic status; nearly a third of the males and a fourth of the female victims are unemployed, and there is evidence of alcohol abuse by either the victim or the offender. A vast majority of these domestic homicide cases involve a history of wife or child abuse. Since the police often treat such incidents as family disputes, few result in a felony arrest until a death occurs. And the 1980 National Crime Survey found that spousal victimizations were not reported to the police 43 percent of the time, and not all of those reported resulted in an arrest.

Intrafamily "murders" are often committed in self-defense. Only recently has information come to light about children who are killers. Approximately three hundred children each year murder one or both of their parents; fathers are most often the victims. An October 1987 *Time* magazine reported that more and more children are arguing that they acted in self-defense, admitting readily to the crime but pointing to years of abuse that left them fearful for their lives. According to Los Angeles attorney Paul Mones, over 90 percent of children who commit parricide have suffered physical, sexual, and mental abuse.

Women don't usually kill; they perpetrate fewer than 15 percent of the homicides in the United States. When they do kill, it is often in their own defense. A government commission on violence estimates that homicides committed by women are seven times more likely to be in self-defense than homicides committed by men. Further, women charged in the death of a male companion usually have no criminal record. A 1987 study of Detroit homicides finds that, although more women actually killed their spouses or lovers than men did, twice as many husbands were tried. Seventy-five percent of the wives had no charges filed against them, because it was determined that they had shot in self-defense.

Battered women who kill in self-defense are now receiving support from some feminists. At a June 1987 news conference in New York City, the Committee on Domestic Violence and Incarcerated Women announced their determination that it is "reasonable and necessary" for battered women to kill their abusive husbands in some cases. "Options for battered women are few," stressed the group, composed of social, legal, and church organizations. "Domestic violence can lead women to believe with justification, that their survival depends on protecting themselves." The group also questions the appropriateness of the state's jailing such women.

A few months later, a group of women who are members of the rape intervention program at Saint Luke's–Roosevelt Hospital Center in New York City wrote a letter

to *The New York Times* in reference to the acquittal of
Karen Straw, tried for the stabbing death of the husband,
who had abused her. The group asserted that, although
this case should never have come to trial, it did serve to
publicize the inadequate system that fails to safeguard the
woman who does everything within the law to protect herself. In their Saint Luke's program they have seen women
who have been slapped, choked, kicked, punched,
scratched, bitten, and hit with objects. They've been
pushed down stairs, thrown against walls, knocked off
chairs, and dragged out of bed. They've had knives, ice
picks, bats, belts, and guns shoved in their faces. They've
endured cigarette burns on arms, lacerations on scalps, and
knife wounds on breasts. They have suffered bruises and
broken limbs. At one time or another they've lost blood,
hair, their dignity, and a sense of hope. "We can only wish
that the acquittal of Karen Straw is the beginning of a new
sensitivity by the criminal justice system. Battered women
do not need to be further victimized by the very system to
which they turn for help," is the political point of these
women's message.

Unfortunately, Pete Shields and many other anti-gun
proponents never address the issues of intrafamilial self-
defense shootings, and simply lump them together with
criminal murder. His only comment on self-defense in
Guns Don't Die—People Do is that, "As police officers have
said for years, the best defense against injury is to put up
no defense—give them what they want, or run." Needless
to say, some battered women have put up no defense, and
they have died; some who defended themselves are free,
others are in jail, and the vast majority are trapped, with
nowhere to run, in "lives of quiet desperation."

Anti-gun proponents also contend that stricter gun-control laws would cut down on the number of domestic
homicides every year. This is difficult to prove, but, again,
statistics contradict their argument. The domestic homicide rate has actually decreased from 2.4 per hundred

thousand in the mid-1970s down to 1.3 per hundred thousand in the 1980s, while the number of firearms grew at the rate of an estimated five million a year, with more and more women owning guns, principally handguns.

How can this be explained? One theory suggests that the decrease in the domestic homicide rate has been caused by men's realization that many women have guns for protection, so that they have not attempted to physically abuse or kill these women, and the women, in turn, have not had to use their guns. This phenomenon may be similar to what occurred in Orlando, Florida, when the rape rate was drastically reduced because of the publicity surrounding the thousands of women who took gun-safety courses.

So where do the pro-control and anti-control arguments lead? It seems to me that they lead nowhere, for each side is putting forth a different argument. To ensure orderly coexistence in our increasingly small world, we have understood the need for and accepted a great variety of laws and controls. Life in major metropolitan areas—which house 90 percent of the population—would be bedlam without traffic signals, health and sanitation laws, reckless-endangerment statutes, and decency requirements. Even in rural areas, where sheer numbers of people don't pose environmental problems, laws control hunting, fishing, and trespassing.

You might say that all laws in some way restrict someone's freedom. Yet we recognize the need for demonstrating the skills necessary to drive a car or fly a plane or perform open-heart surgery. So why is it so unacceptable to have enforceable laws that require gun owners to demonstrate their abilities—both emotional and physical—to operate such deadly weapons? And why do some people so ardently want to prohibit gun ownership, even in light of convincing evidence that handguns deter and terminate so much violent crime?

It seems to me, now that I have put myself in the middle of this battle, that the real argument of the anti-control camp traces back to a fear that the government will eventually disarm and subjugate its citizens. This fear of the Founding Fathers continues to the present day. And the real argument of the pro-control group focuses simply on killing. They are campaigning to stop the killing, and who in their right mind wouldn't agree?

6

Ethics of Using Lethal Defense

THERE IS NO question that guns kill. We could go on for volumes debating the benefits versus detriments of firearms, and in fact millions of pages of rhetoric have already been and continue to be written and argued. And what is it all for? Guns kill, just as fires burn. But it is equally true that guns preserve life, as fires warm homes. Indeed, it is more true. Criminals do not pick victims who are stronger than they.

Without guns, the violence-prone criminal will find another way to terrorize, but the defender of innocent life, the designated victim, cannot possibly offer a more adequate or effective resistance.

No one ever suggests that in the United States the police should be prohibited from carrying guns. Yet the citizens whom the police are employed to protect somehow aren't considered responsible enough to exercise the same judgment, when it comes to life-threatening incidents, as an employee who most certainly has less at stake. In fact, armed citizens use guns to prevent more crimes and shoot more criminals each year than do the police. And even if that were not the case, any attempt to disarm the owners of the estimated two hundred million guns in this country would result in nothing short of a civil war. So the point is moot. Enough.

The real issue has to do with the use of lethal force, not with the means. Without question, a rapidly growing number of American women are arming themselves. Whether this trend is in reaction to the escalating incidence of rape, criminal assault, and domestic violence, or is a predictable attitude of assertiveness that has developed out of the seasoning of the women's movement, the real issue is not the polemics of guns versus no guns; rather, for some women it is the choice of being victor or victim.

The amount of serious crime reported to police increases each year. The FBI's crime index level for the first six months of 1988 was up 1 percent in the Midwest, 7 percent in the Northeast, 6 percent in the South, and in the West, a 4 percent increase. Commenting on the crime data, Alfred Blumstein, dean of the School of Urban and Public Affairs at Carnegie Mellon University in Pittsburgh, said in 1987 that we may well be seeing the start, five years early, of an increase in crime that many members of the academic community anticipated would begin in the 1990s. Researchers have predicted that crime levels will increase as children of the baby-boom generation reach the most crime-prone age group, the late teens and early twenties.

Special Agent Roy Hazelwood of the FBI Behavioral Science Unit doesn't hesitate to say that the crimes he sees today are more vicious than those the FBI saw just ten years ago. The FBI, according to Hazelwood, is seeing more brutality in assaults themselves, with the caseloads of serial murders and serial rapes obviously increasing.

So the situation is this: the police cannot completely defend us from predator crime; the courts cannot keep the predators off the streets or otherwise occupied in noncriminal activities; and the gun is the most effective deterrent to crime available.

Handgun laws vary from state to state, concerning for the most part restrictions on carrying a handgun loaded and concealed. In no state is it a crime to defend oneself, and though local laws may differ somewhat in interpretation of what kinds of threats justify what kinds of responses, nowhere is it considered unreasonable to use lethal force by any means available to stop a threat that may endanger your life or the lives of innocent people, or that may result in grave bodily harm.

In common law, which for the most part was handed down from English law, the equal-force doctrine requires the innocent party to respond to attack with little or no more force than that which he perceives is being directed against him. However, with victim crimes becoming directed more toward women and the elderly, the law is recognizing the great degrees of difference that may exist between the potential physical force of victims and the physical force of attackers.

Massad Ayoob, police lieutenant and author, explains that this disparity of force between the unarmed combatants is measured in one of two ways. It exists if the victim is attacked by one who is physically much stronger or younger than he, or by two or more attackers of equal or similar size.

Almost without exception, Ayoob counsels, reasonable force is the concept upon which the court disposition of a self-defense shooting will ultimately rest. The judgment of a reasonable man is the measure used in the American system of justice. Some call it a vague yardstick, others a flexible one; it is certainly the most practical determinant, given the great variety of circumstances under which it becomes the criterion for legal judgment.

Massad Ayoob, in addition to being a police officer in Concord, New Hampshire, is one of the world's leading experts on the use of lethal force in self-defense by citizens. He teaches a five-day course at various locations throughout the world, in what he calls "threat management." I was fortunate to have taken Massad's course in Las Vegas, Nevada, and learned, in addition to gun handling, the justifiable use of deadly force. Much of what follows is from that course, as well as Massad's excellent book, *In the*

Gravest Extreme, and most of it is taught by every reputable firearms instructor and all police academies.

The accepted definition of the justifiable use of deadly force is an immediate and otherwise unavoidable danger of death or grave bodily harm to the innocent. There must clearly be no hope of escaping an attack safely, and according to Massad, the attacker must fulfill three conditions to justify a lethal defense on the victim's part:

1. ABILITY—   The attacker must have the power to kill or cause crippling injury, or be advantaged with a disparity of force or a disparity of skill, such as a prizefighter or black-belt karateist (which the victim must know of beforehand).

2. OPPORTUNITY—The attacker must be capable of employing bodily harm immediately. He must be within range.

3. JEOPARDY—   The perpetrator must be acting in such a manner that a reasonably prudent person would assume he intended to attack.

Under what is termed "the doctrine of the reasonable man," the three elements must be present for lethal defense to be legally justified. It sounds like a lot to think about, especially when an attack is in progress and adrenaline is pumping and fear is so strong you can smell it. However, as you become more comfortable with handling a gun in a combat situation, which will be discussed later, assessing the danger of any circumstance will come more naturally and quickly. If you take on the responsibility of preparing to defend yourself and your family with a gun, you take on the additional responsibility of knowing beyond the shadow of a doubt that, if you ever think of using that weapon, there must exist no hope of escaping an assault safely.

It would be a shame to shoot or kill someone with obvious criminal intent and then go to prison for attempted murder or manslaughter because some district attorney could prove that you acted a second before your assailant had the ability, opportunity, or intention to cause you grave bodily harm. Again, the more familiar you get with your gun, the later you can wait before you are forced to use it.

These three important conditions can actually be distilled further, especially in the case of female victims. If an assailant is taller or heftier than his female victim, it is safe to assume that there exists a disparity of force. Even if a man's size is not that much greater than a woman's, there is usually a disparity of strength. He has the power to kill her or cause crippling injury even if he is unarmed, as has been grotesquely illustrated to the courts on countless occasions of rape.

With respect to the third condition, jeopardy: If a stranger breaks into your house, you may assume that he is acting in such a manner as to jeopardize your safety. If however, a burglar breaks into and enters an empty house, you would not be justified in coming in after him and shooting him unless he turned on you with the intent and ability to cause grave bodily harm.

And when does a potential assailant display the opportunity of employing his attack? If he has a gun in his hand or in a holster on his waistband, he has the opportunity. A handgun can be fired in one-quarter of a second, and it can be drawn from a holster and fired in less than one second by a skilled gunfighter. Since I have learned to draw and accurately fire a gun from a holster in 1.25 seconds, I know that a handgun, rifle, or shotgun at any distance gives an assailant the opportunity to inflict death or grave bodily harm.

How about a knife? Again, I learned from Massad Ayoob what has become known throughout the self-defense industry as the Tueller Drill. To our amazement, everyone in our class demonstrated that any person, no matter his age or physical condition, can cover twenty-one feet from a standing start and plunge a knife into a target in an average of 1.5 seconds—just a little slower than I can draw and fire a handgun. I wouldn't have believed it if I hadn't done it myself. Twenty-one feet is about two car lengths.

So, if a man is twenty-one feet from you with a knife upraised and is acting as if he is intending to stab you, he certainly has the ability (the knife), the intention (jeopardy), and, as you will know after you try the Tueller Drill yourself, the opportunity to inflict grave damage to you or any other innocent person around you. You may assume that you are in immediate, unavoidable danger of death or grave bodily harm and use as much force of whatever kind as is within your means to defend yourself.

Now, what if this situation is the same, except that, instead of a knife, the growling, threatening man is holding a baseball bat? Are you justified in using lethal force to defend yourself? He again has the ability, given the bat, and is acting in such a manner that a reasonably prudent person would assume that he intended to attack. But unless he is closing the twenty-one-foot distance and has that bat poised to strike, he does not have the opportunity, and you would not be justified in using a greater force to stop him. I know that this sounds a little silly, but if you were to shoot and kill a maniacal, three-time-convicted rapist who was shouting that he was going to beat you to a pulp, and a witness could testify that he wasn't moving toward you, you could be found guilty of manslaughter.

You are embarking on very delicate ground when you use deadly force in self-defense. Those very same criminal rights that turn career criminals loose on the streets demand that a shooting, no matter how justified, be investigated down to the last question of ability, opportunity, and jeopardy. Some say, though, that they would rather be tried by twelve than carried by six.

It must also be noted that lethal force is never legal just to protect property. You can shoot a robber only if he is threatening you in order to get your property. That is what robbery means: theft by threat or use of force. But a sneak thief is taking only property. If you see him enter your car, you cannot shoot to stop him from driving off. Nor can you shoot a shoplifter or a burglar whom you discover leaving with your TV.

Massad Ayoob advises that there is still another tricky legal doctrine waiting to trap you if you *chase* a thief. Your quarry could not claim self-defense if he had hurt you in the initial struggle, since he was in the wrong, and self-defense is a privilege reserved for the innocent. But if he made an obvious attempt to desist and escape and you pursued him, remember that you will not necessarily be continuing the initial confrontation but, in the eyes of the law, opening a new one—opening a confrontation in which the criminal will be blameless since you, not he, are now the aggressor. He is trying to avoid the combat, and you are now carrying the fight to him. Therefore, he now possesses the privilege of self-defense. He can now, in short, turn around and kill you, and get away with it.

In fact, the law and good common sense require a victim to exercise some degree of retreat, withdrawal, and avoidance of a conflict before lethal force is an acceptable alternative to risking one's life and safety. Just how far you are expected to retreat is the subject of continually changing laws. These so-called back-to-the-wall laws are steadily giving way to more reasonable interpretations of imminent danger.

The acquittal (but convicted of illegally carrying a gun) by a New York jury of Bernhard Goetz—the man who shot in self-defense at four thugs on a New York subway—is an important case that clearly indicates that the public's perception of what constitutes self-defense is changing in favor of the victim. A *Newsday* poll published on June 28, 1987, showed that, by an overwhelming 71 percent, New Yorkers did approve of Goetz's actions, including 83 percent of the city's non-Hispanic whites, 78 percent of local Hispanics, and 45 percent of blacks.

Even Mayor Koch, an outspoken anti-gun advocate, stressed on the June 21, 1987, edition of "This Week With David Brinkley" that, although he did not encourage people to go about armed, they had a right to self-defense. He said that the jury had deliberated at length and that their decision had to be accepted.

Philosophically, Koch contended that those who do use a firearm in self-defense might have to prove before a jury, as Goetz did, that their response was a "reasonable" one with respect to the laws regulating the use of deadly force.

Finally, there is one more condition or state of mind that must be fully understood. Past incidents may not be the cause for a present use of lethal force. We have all heard tragic stories about people asking for and being denied police protection from individuals who made repeated threats upon their lives, later to have those threats fulfilled. As mentioned previously, the police have no prescribed duty to protect any one individual citizen. However, the subject of someone's harassment, or the victim of previous assaults, cannot assume that previous threats or even beatings are grounds enough to use deadly force unless the aggressor displays all the conditions of immediate, unavoidable attack. The law makes a distinction between bare fear and reasonable fear, or reasonable apprehension. Bare fear can sometimes be the misinterpretation of past episodes as cause for present defense, and is generally considered paranoia.

Still, courts are beginning to make exceptions. Another landmark decision ended the *Georgia* vs. *Norman* case, in which a Georgia jury in 1987 acquitted Doris Jean Norman of Atlanta of murder. Norman had stabbed and killed her boyfriend, Luke Johnson. Her defense was that long-term verbal abuse, which included threats to beat and kill her, often in front of witnesses, had triggered "battered woman's syndrome," the psychological term used to describe the actions of women who endure repeated physical abuse by their husbands or lovers and then one day retaliate by killing them. According to Margaret Nichols, an Atlanta psychologist who testified in behalf of Norman at her trial, what Norman did was what a responsible person would have done, given the circumstances.

Finally, Massad Ayoob stresses that one cornerstone of a legitimate claim of self-defense is the innocence of the claimant. He must be entirely without fault. If he has begun the conflict or quarrel, or if he has kept it going or escalated it when he had the power to abort it before it becomes a killing situation, he shares a degree of culpability. The self-defense plea, in this case, will not be allowed.

All of which brings the discussion around to the most critical issue of all, pulling the trigger. It would be nice not to have to deal with this issue. Nobody in his right mind wants to shoot another person.

Dr. Ashley Montagu of Princeton University and author of *The Nature of Human Aggression* writes in *The New York Times,* "As a scientist who has made a lifelong study of the nature of human nature, and especially of the alleged innate aggressiveness of humankind, I find, as many of my colleagues have, that there exists no evidence whatever to support the notion of a 'human propensity to injure and kill.' "

However, a segment of the population defies Montagu's analysis, and no matter what our social institutions do to eliminate or rehabilitate that element, they fail. And as the FBI and others point out, the sociopathic element are growing in size and escalating their violent activities.

Dr. Murray J. Friedman, also writing in *The New York Times,* states, "There is substantial evidence that violent behavior is related to both social conditions and early life experiences. Poverty, discrimination, poor education, substance abuse, broken families or parental neglect have all been found to be associated with subsequent violent adolescent and/or adult behavior. . . . It is reasonable to believe that reducing these conditions will also reduce violent behavior in the future, perhaps in 10 to 20 years. However, large-scale social solutions will not solve the immediate problem of violent behavior among many of today's adolescent or young adults. Once violent or antisocial behavior become a part of the personality, it does not follow that eliminating antecedent social causes will change already internalized patterns of behavior. . . . Unfortunately, changing existing behavior is much more complicated because the effects of early experiences are not easily reversible. . . . To date, neither psychotherapeutic nor criminal sanctions—nor any other techniques—have been very successful in eliminating violent behavior among large numbers of perpetrators. . . . Being safe from violent attacks ought to be a crucial civil right in civilized society."

This has been a lengthy discussion, in which thoughts, motives, and commitment must be analyzed before one moves on to assume the responsibility of choosing a gun as a possible defense against violent crimes.

One of the axioms of gun safety has always been: Do not aim a gun at anything you are not willing to destroy. To pick up a gun and aim it at someone in self-defense must be a decision that comes after you see there is no escape from an immediate and certain attack that will result in death or grave bodily harm. And once that gun is pointed, you must be able to drop the hammer without hesitation. If you do not feel that you are capable of shooting a person to prevent your own death or crippling injury, DO NOT BUY A GUN.

And how are we to know if we would be able to pick up a gun and shoot it at someone? Unfortunately, there isn't any test or any formula to arrive at that answer, but by learning how to use a gun and conscientiously practicing with targets, you will be forced into an answer at your own pace.

As a former campus Vietnam War peace demonstrator and an early staff member of the first national gun-control organization, I have always championed the causes of peace and nonviolent behavior. But as a mother of two sons, I have always recognized in me a deeper, almost animal-like rage capable of causing me to do anything within my power, even kill, to protect my children. Every mother knows this undercurrent; we would die for our children, and most of us would kill to protect them. In a way, a person must know this warrior spirit is there, and can be called upon in a life-or-death crisis, even to think it would be possible to shoot someone in self-defense. If you recognize this kind of instinct in yourself, then I would say you should continue with your plans to learn self-defense skills with a gun.

If, on the other hand, you have never been in touch with a feeling like that, and believe completely that you could not possibly fight back in a life-threatening crisis, do not buy a gun, whatever you do.

Pointing a gun at someone who intends to hurt you and not being able to pull the trigger can get you killed. Even though statistics indicate that in more than 75 percent of the cases guns were displayed in self-defense situations they were successful in deterring the assault without being fired, each time you point your gun at anything you must be prepared and able to pull the trigger.

More will be said later about the tactics of gun defense, but it is interesting to note here that, after I had attended the courses of all the major gun-defense instructors during the research phase of this book, my shooting skills improved and exceeded my wildest expectations of my ability. Also, my confidence about when to shoot and when not to, and whether in fact I could shoot, grew to a comfortable level. This is interesting because, if my experience is typical, and the instructors all say it is, then it can be expected that a quality course of instruction in gun defense will not only eliminate the fear of guns that everyone who is unfamiliar with guns has, but as a result will develop judgment and certainty about if and when to bring a gun into use.

Again, the privilege of killing in self-defense derives from "the universal judgment that there is no social interest in preserving the lives of the aggressors at the cost of those of their victims," as one of the great twentieth-century legal analysts, Herbert Wechsler, said. And we can conclude from the reasonable-or-prudent-man test that it is the privilege of the innocent to use lethal force to interrupt or prevent any attack that is perceived to threaten death or grave bodily harm.

But is it reasonable or prudent to perceive rape as an assault threatening death or crippling injury? It is obvious that death is an unlikely result of forcible sexual intercourse in itself, with one very notable and new exception that will be discussed momentarily. And the concept of grave bodily harm resulting specifically from nonconsenting forcible sexual intercourse—accompanying threats of physical harm notwithstanding—is reasonably limited to relatively minor pain, psychological trauma, and pregnancy. None of this justifies the use of lethal force to repel it. But in fact the law does recognize the right to repel rape with deadly force.

Our legal scholar Don Kates observes that many sexual attacks begin with an explicit threat of death or great bodily harm, or the display of a weapon capable of producing those effects. Moreover, Kates observes, the superior physical strength and combat skills of most men over most women enables even the unarmed rapist to carry out his expressed intent to kill or grievously injure his victim if she does not comply. In such cases, the threat of death or great bodily harm clearly justifies the privilege of defending with deadly force.

It is common knowledge that many rapists kill or seriously injure their victims incidentally to raping them. There is continuing dispute among criminologists and psychologists about the profile of rapists. Some contend that rapists are essentially normal men, indistinguishable from the general population except in their belief that they can get away with rape. Other experts insist that rapists are severely disturbed individuals. Both groups admit, however, that the motivation for rape is likely to be antagonism toward the individual victim or toward all women, rather than a desire for sexual satisfaction.

Seventy-five percent of the convicted rapists at California's Atascadero State Hospital had weapons with them during the rapes for which they were found guilty. And a study of Philadelphia rapes reported that 20 percent of the victims had been beaten brutally before, during, or after rape, and more than 85 percent of the victims in reported rapes were subjected to some sort of violence, consisting of roughness, beating, or choking.

So, Kates concludes, whether or not rape alone constitutes great bodily harm, the risk of other grievous injury is substantial. Consequently, it is not unreasonable for a woman to believe from the outset that a rape attack may result in her death or serious injury.

And this reasonable expectation of death or grave injury as a result of rape is not limited to rape by strangers. Many studies reveal that rapes committed by former husbands or boyfriends, business associates, or social acquaintances are frequently more brutal.

If the law allows the use of lethal force against rape because of the physical threats of the rapists, irrespective of the rape itself, there now exists a new issue that not only justifies the use of deadly force to prevent rape but almost demands it. The issue is AIDS.

Seventy-five percent of career criminals are admitted drug users, and a sizable proportion of them have a history of intravenous drug use. Add to them the rapists who statistically commit seventeen rapes each before being caught and convicted, and the ones who prey upon prostitutes and the ones who are bisexual, and you find the odds substantial that at least one of every two active rapists could be a carrier of AIDS.

This line of investigation has yet to be pursued, to my knowledge, but it is of particular interest to note that, in a study of Michigan prisoners, sex offenders were found to be afflicted with some kind of venereal disease more than twenty times as much as the general prison population. Although this is not AIDS, such widespread venereal disease among known sex offenders suggests that the sexually communicated disease of AIDS will in some proportion follow, in this population at least, which experts estimate to be responsible for between 25 and 40 percent of all rapes.

So, instead of debating whether a rapist's manipulation of his victim for compliance is more potentially damaging than forcible intercourse and the attending risks of pregnancy, emotional disorders, etc., I would like to suggest that rape now presents a very clear and present danger of causing a disease for which there is no known or foreseeable cure, resulting in certain death.

The prospect of contracting AIDS as the result of rape forces women to prevent the occurrence by any means available. The only deterrent that has been found to be universally respected by every aggressor is the gun.

7

Professional Advice

PROFESSIONAL ADVICE COMES clothed in many different garments. Most police departments are not the best source of objective advice on whether or not to buy or carry a gun, and there is a very good reason for that. The police are mandated to protect and serve the community in the area of law enforcement and crime prevention. You might say that they have a territorial imperative when it comes to dealing with criminal activity, and, not unlike any other highly trained professional, they do not welcome encroachment from outsiders. So the official police position on citizens' having guns for self-defense is usually disapproval. Perhaps they don't want the competition, or they don't want poorly trained people adding to the perils of their profession, and they are understandably apprehensive about any situation that would present more danger to their lives, which are at risk the moment they leave their houses every day. Answering a call in which a gun has been reported complicates an officer's options, no matter who is holding the gun.

Yet, when the officers themselves are questioned about owning a gun for self-defense, another viewpoint comes into focus. Officer Evan Marshall of the Detroit Police Department sums it up rather well: "Let me say that I carry a gun all the time, and I don't carry that gun all the time just because I have a badge. I carry a gun all the time because I am aware of what kind of a world we live in."

A number of law-enforcement associations are publicly in favor of private gun ownership. The nation's largest professional police association, The American Federation of Police, states: "There are many Americans who fear for their lives. They know that often they will have to protect themselves, their own families and their own property. Should these people be disarmed? There are enough laws. No, we don't need to disarm our loyal citizens, our friends and our neighbors. We just need judges with the guts to make the use of a gun in a crime a risk that few will undertake in the future."

The National Police Officers Association of America declares: "We feel that an American citizen of voting age and of good character should have the right to purchase without restriction a handgun, pistol, revolver, rifle, shotgun, or a like item without interference by a governmental body. . . . For every criminal that uses a gun to rob and kill, we have ten times that number of armed citizens who are able to assist the police in capturing these potential killers *because they are armed.*"

A group that represents police officers' wives, the Chicago Police Wives Association, says: "Although the people proposing these anti-handgun bills appear to be well-meaning, and their bills appear to be well-meaning, these bills would apply only to honest citizens who register their handguns. It would seem that a better solution would be to enforce the present gun laws."

A national study commissioned by Boston police chief Robert diGrazia seeking opinions from the chiefs of the fifty state police agencies and all the county sheriffs revealed that 42 of these officials opposed a ban on private handguns; 40 approved of the private possession of handguns in the home or business; and 25 were in favor of citizens' carrying handguns. Yet the total does not equal the sum of the parts.

Dr. Martin Reiser, director of Behavioral Science Services of the Los Angeles Police Department, contends that police departments are conservative traditionalists, reflecting the conservative point of view until that view is perceived to change in society. "Laws are made after the fact, after something happens. Laws, and police opinion, get changed and get amended when enough people want them amended," explains Reiser. "My own point of view is that people are becoming more proactive, saying, 'Hey, wait a minute, I have to protect myself, and I am not going to sit here and be victimized or raped or assaulted by some idiot and just fill out some police report and hope that he's among the fifteen or twenty percent that get caught.' Police administrative viewpoints are beginning more and more to move in the direction of acknowledging and asserting that policing is a responsibility of the total society and not just the police-force part of society."

What seems to be at issue with the police, whether or not the departments are in favor of private arms, is the quality and amount of training private individuals need to be safe and competent with using a firearm. The subject of training has come up with every professional I talked to, and it is certainly one of the important components of this whole subject of taking the responsibility of defending yourself.

It is believed that the typical private firearm is fired no more than once or twice a year. Only fifty bullets are fired from each privately owned gun, including hunting and sporting guns. And that is not anywhere near enough training, according to police administrators, whose officers have in excess of eighty hours of instruction and fire thousands of rounds each year. Moreover, practicing only once or twice a year is hopelessly inadequate compared with the case of the typical gun-toting criminal, whom criminologists Wright and Rossi find to practice once a month or more and to shoot their guns at someone 75 percent of the time they have threatened to do so.

With respect to the positions defended by the pro-gun and anti-gun activists, there seems to be emerging from the two camps a common ground regarding the issue of training. Along with the police agencies, many thinkers on both sides are beginning to advocate some kind of required training and competency testing as a prerequisite for buying a gun, or, more precisely, for carrying a gun concealed. Pete Shields of Handgun Control, Inc. likens this kind of training and testing to the requirement each state makes on the driver of a motor vehicle.

Combat instructor Massad Ayoob concurs. "Contrary to public belief, there is a form of firearms control law that a few members of the 'gun lobby' actively support: legislation requiring competency tests before the issuance of permits to carry concealed, loaded weapons. The very application for the carry permit indicates that the applicant believes that there is a chance, however remote, that he will someday have to use that gun in a tense situation in public. It is only fair, therefore, to require him to prove that he is capable of using his gun with precision under pressure (in this case, the stress of knowing that a poor score would cost him his pistol permit). I feel there should also be a written examination to determine his grasp of the laws that govern self-defense and deadly force."

As Don Kates pointed out in the discussion on the Second Amendment, the constitutional guarantee to own and bear arms was qualified in the Bill of Rights to include periodic inspection and training for those residents of the community who were looked upon as active members of the state militia. So some kind of demonstration of basic safety procedures and competency should not upset the traditional pro-gun advocate, and would probably further deter criminals from risking confrontations with intended victims, as seems to have been the case in Orlando, Florida.

The NRA has a hunter-safety course that teaches basic skills in the use of a rifle, and is required in many communities before a hunting license is issued. The state of Florida, in an attempt to standardize the hundreds of county gun laws, has embarked upon a statewide system that will issue a permit to carry a concealed weapon to anyone who qualifies under the federal requirements—prohibited are mental patients, felons, etc.—and who can verify spending a certain number of hours in handgun training. It will be interesting to see how this will affect the crime rate in Dade County, which has the highest in the country.

So, if the police would rest easier knowing that the law-abiding gun owners in their community were knowledgeable in the use of their weapons and had some training in the tactics of gun defense, why don't they provide the instruction? The police are, after all, fully equipped.

Some police agencies do offer handgun training to their communities, but most do not. When I questioned the chiefs of some of the departments that do not assist their residents, the best explanation of the reasons they managed had something to do with the liability the community would face should they advocate gun defense and be sued by a resident who accidentally shot someone. I have heard that rationale a number of times, and it is still not clear to me how a community agency could be held liable for anything just by providing safety classes to the public. How would gun-safety classes expose a community to more liability than, say, community swimming pools and playground equipment, which injure and kill more people each year than are accidentally injured or killed by all firearms combined?

It must be just as Dr. Reiser of the Los Angeles Police Department said: the police follow public policy, they do not make it. It is up to the residents of a community to pressure their officials to make changes—changes, in this case, that would unify the community and their law-enforcement representatives to fight effectively the crime that is rapidly consuming their freedoms.

Another view to be considered is a moral one. Some

people find it repugnant—on moral or religious grounds—to use a gun in self-defense. Reverend R. J. Mahoney, a Catholic priest and former chairman of the sociology department at Rockhurst College in Kansas City, Missouri, in "The Morality of Home Defense," addresses the issue by saying that shooting in self-defense is moral under certain conditions. He cites Saint Thomas Aquinas, who, according to Reverend Mahoney, "argued some seven centuries ago that homicide could be justifiable in self-defense. Saint Thomas argued that since 'it is much more lawful to defend one's life than one's house,' that therefore, 'neither is a man guilty of murder if he kill another in defense of his own life.' "

Mahoney identifies three conditions that must be met before the full legitimacy of self-defense can be established: (1) The defender (or his neighbor) must be the object of an unjust aggressive action. (2) The defender must use only the force necessary to prevent the threatened harm to self or neighbor. "If the warning and the sight of the defender's gun causes the attacker to surrender or flee," says Reverend Mahoney, "the purpose of defense is accomplished, and additional violence would not be morally permissible." (3) The defender's primary intent must be to stop the aggression, rather than to kill or injure. However, he strongly points out that a defender with a gun can shoot to kill.

Reverend Mahoney explains it this way: "To stop a determined aggressor . . . by using a gun, the defender must aim at some part of the body of sufficient vulnerability to stop the attack. The only way in which a handgun may stop a determined aggressor with any reasonable hope of success is to 'shoot-to-kill' in the sense of aiming for a vital spot—this would seem morally acceptable in these special circumstances, particularly since the primary purpose is to stop the attacker through striking a vital spot, which indeed can be effective without causing death. This should make clear, as a side consideration, that one may never use self defense as a pretext for killing someone we hate, feel revengeful toward, etc."

Reverend Mahoney believes that for many women neither Mace nor karate offers any meaningful protection. "On the old frontier, the six-gun was the 'equalizer.' On the urban frontier—in a period of social flux, with great turmoil and strain and uncertainty and change—sadly enough, the six-gun may still 'equalize.' Little else," sums up Reverend Mahoney, "can put a 105 pound woman on a par with a 260 pound rapist, or a septuagenarian widow on even terms with a 20 year old thug."

The next group of professionals I consulted, and perhaps the most qualified to advise on guns as a deterrent to crime, were the career criminals themselves. I spoke to a number of convicted felons at the California State Penitentiary at San Quentin. The prisoners I interviewed were selected because each had been convicted for, among other crimes, sexual assault. The men I talked to had not murdered any of their victims, but each had sufficiently defiled his victim to serve time in one of the country's most hardcore prisons. They were escorted to the reception area in handcuffs. One of the prisoners was in a maximum-security area, and I was permitted to talk to him only over a telephone while we looked at each other through a soundproof, bulletproof glass window about the size of an oven door. They all complained of the indignity of being strip-searched every day before leaving their cells and after returning from meals or exercise. I was unsympathetic.

When Dennis Raymond and I sat down to talk, he was as nervous as a cat. The ordeal of coming down to talk to me caused great anxiety in Dennis. It took us almost half an hour to develop Dennis' concentration to the point where he could answer questions and follow the line of thinking. Surprisingly, Dennis is in favor of women having handguns.

"If women had guns, and criminals knew that women had guns, there would be a lot fewer incidents. Hey, a gun pointed at someone is a very big intimidation. And if the gun holder, even if she is a woman, is shouting orders, there isn't anyone except the crazies who won't stop," Dennis spoke with authority.

Dennis Raymond advises a woman to use foul language when she confronts an assailant. "These guys are all used to hearing bad talk. We've been talking bad all our lives. We don't know any other way to talk," Dennis said with animation, as if I were deaf. "So, if they don't hear bad talk, they don't understand. And you got to yell it. We have been yelled at all our lives, too—cops, mothers, jail guards, and tough guys all yell. You got to yell if you are pointing a gun at someone. He'll listen."

Dennis is also very sure of another thing. "The only way for women to change what's happening to them is for the media to help promote it. A few reported cases of women shooting bad guys, followed up with some more media reporting that more and more women are owning guns and are prepared to shoot, is the only way for the criminals to notice."

From where Dennis comes, violence is a way of life. He thinks, however, that if more women had guns there just might be less violence in the long run. "Since violent crime is on the rise, women are being pushed into a corner. If women didn't have guns they would eventually be forced, maybe, to commit more deadly things to get back at their attackers. At least with a gun they have a very good chance to frighten an attacker away without having to sneak up on him with a kitchen knife and kill him."

Dennis tells a story of a girl he knows who was gang-raped. She didn't tell anyone. Every day after the incident she had to continue to walk past her violators on the way to school. Every time she passed them they jeered at her, "Coming back for more, baby? You really liked it, didn't you, baby?" Dennis told me that after a while the girl began playing up to the boys, teasing them sexually. At first, he said, the guys didn't trust her new interest in them and avoided her. It didn't take long for them to respond; she wouldn't let up. One night she engaged them all in another group episode and killed three of them with a knife she had taken from her mother's kitchen drawer.

"You gotta believe that this whole thing wouldn't have happened in the first place, and these punks wouldn't be dead now, if this little lady pointed a little gun at one of these guys' zippers and told him what she was going to blow off if any one of them came within five feet of her," Dennis said.

Another prisoner, Alvin Sanders, has spent most of his life behind bars. He gets out long enough to be put right back in. At San Quentin, Alvin Sanders is a senior citizen at the age of thirty-two. A small man wearing a blue knit sailor's cap pulled down over his eyebrows, Alvin looked at me through five inches of glass with small, angry, suspicious eyes. I don't know why he agreed to an interview with me. He was certain that our conversation was being tape-recorded by the guards. Alvin spoke through closed lips in a hushed tone, as if he didn't want what he had to say to get back to his fellow inmates.

Alvin had a lot of very interesting things to say about the roots of crime. He believes that criminals are made in the prisons, not on the streets. He traced for me the steps in the making of a career criminal, starting with the welfare mother too broke or too preoccupied to give the kids what they need, forcing them into the streets with the other kids in the same predicament to steal what they want any way they can. After a while they get caught, and after they get caught enough times they spend some time in juvenile detention, where they sharpen their street skills. They learn drugs early, even at the age of twelve or thirteen, and steal to keep up with as much as a thousand-dollar-a-day interest in them. Alvin said that drugs are the driving force behind criminal activity, and a lot of criminals are not afraid to land back in prison, trying to keep current, because in prison, Alvin told me, drugs are easier to get than on the street.

Alvin Sanders knows a lot about crime. He has spent years committing crimes, and has spent more years thinking about crime in prison. He thinks that women get raped because the rapist just needs to control a situation, control he never had while being brought up by his single mother, whom he grew to hate because she couldn't provide the things he needed. He insists that, if a woman in a rape situation did not struggle or offer any resistance, she would not get hurt. Yet he admits to the instability of the criminal.

"Criminals do not want to find people home when they burgle a house. But if they do find someone home, they panic, because they are afraid to begin with. And if that person is a woman, there is a strong possibility that she will get sexually abused, just because the criminal doesn't know what else to do to control the fear and excitement," Alvin Sanders whispered as his eyes darted around at every moving shadow.

The monstrous issue of AIDS not only threatens rape victims, but in a perverse way it presents a threat to the rapist, too. Alvin knows this much: "And now, with AIDS, rape will happen more to younger girls and the children instead of the whores and the older women. I'm sorry, but that's the way it's going to be after a while."

Alvin Sanders does not want women to own guns, which is understandable. "Are you kidding me?" Alvin said, wide-eyed, when we finally got around to talking about women with guns. "I don't think that is a good idea at all. Hell, before you know it, they going to be shooting up everybody that just winks at them. It's a real bad idea. I'm not for it."

Alvin does not want to get shot when he gets out of prison. He feels deeply that the woman he "claimed" and then received a ten-year sentence in San Quentin for raping was asking for his sexual attention. She was a nurse coming home from a night shift at the hospital. Alvin thinks that she shouldn't have been showing so much bare chest in her white nurse's uniform. He taught her a lesson.

Before we finished talking, Alvin detailed a four-point plan for women to be safe from criminal assault. It was actually comical that this career punk had a plan, a four-point plan. Here's the advice Alvin has given to his wife, so that she and their two children may be safe until he gets home to take care of them properly.

1. If you use a gun (Alvin gave his wife a gun just before he left for San Quentin), use it to scare, to intimidate your assailant. Fire a warning shot to impress the criminal that you have a gun and are willing to use it. "Word will get out real fast that your house shoots," Alvin counseled.

2. Get a dog. Even a small dog barks enough to make a criminal leave, Alvin says. The last thing a criminal wants is trouble, he says. He doesn't want to get hurt or caught, "and he can pass your house if a dog is barking and maybe letting you know someone is around, giving you time to call the police or get a gun."

3. Keep the lights on, especially outside, where a criminal might think that he will be seen. Inside, keep the television or the radio playing. "It works every time," Alvin emphatically said.

4. Finally, the way a woman carries herself will dictate whether she will be assaulted. "Like a pack of wolves, rapists will pick out the weakest, not the strongest," Alvin concluded.

Alvin's advice is sound, according to most authorities. There is a difference of opinion about firing a warning shot, but prevention is certainly the best defense against crime. We must be alert all the time to our exposure to crime and minimize our chances of being victimized.

Vincent Sullivan is also a resident at San Quentin. He is younger than the other convicts I talked with, a little less worldly in the manly art of victimizing, but he has one very valuable insight to pass along.

Vincent thinks it is okay for women to have guns. He said that rape and assault would happen even so, but that the criminals would do more research before they selected a victim, and pick out victims who they believed were not armed. "When a guy goes out to rob a store," Vincent explained, "he avoids the store that has a security guard and robs the store with no protection. It works the same with homes and people."

Another group from which to take advice are the professional gunmen, the firearms instructors, the men who refine the techniques and teach the police how to defend themselves. One of those men is Massad Ayoob, whom I have quoted before. On the subject of professional advice, Massad can be counted on to give us carefully deliberated and tested opinions.

For Ayoob, a gun is nothing more than a special-purpose item of emergency equipment, to be used only in the face of immediate and unavoidable danger of death or grave bodily harm to oneself or another innocent person. "If you want to reinforce your self-image, join a karate club or take up weightlifting. Both these things would be a lot better for your health," contends Ayoob.

He further explains that, if a case comes to court, the judge and jury will be looking at background evidence from long before a person went for his or her pistol, and the whole ordeal won't end for months or years, if ever. Ayoob stresses that, when a person doesn't know the law and uses a firearm outside the parameters of the law, he or she has endangered our rights to keep firearms for self-defense.

Among all the self-defense experts, Massad Ayoob occupies a very special niche. In addition to instructing police and private citizens in the use of the gun in combat, he is called upon extensively as an expert witness in court cases to establish forensic possibilities in shooting cases. He teaches and writes, and contributes greatly to the field of forensics. If you ever have the opportunity to take his course, don't miss it.

Ayoob feels that the possession of a gun is the ultimate degree in personal, physical power, giving a woman an edge that improves her chances in more ways than one. He says, "An unarmed woman threatened with physical assault responds largely from fear. A danger she is ill-prepared to cope with has two results: it clouds her thinking with fear, even panic, and it provokes her to extremes to ensure her own survival. One who is armed is not above fear, but experiences it to a lesser degree. The knowledge that she is prepared to cope with and survive the worst, relieves her mind of the heaviest fear," says Ayoob, "and lets her turn her full mental powers toward a non-violent escape from the situation."

Mickey Fowler is generally considered to be one of the world's top handgunners. He has won as many world titles and prestigious national championships as anyone alive. He and the equally celebrated Mike Dalton run an excellent shooting school, International Shootists, Inc. (ISI), near Los Angeles in Mission Hills, California. Dalton and Fowler run a weekend course in basic shooting, or "modern pistolcraft," as they call it. I attended the course, and it provides an outstanding twenty hours of fundamental training.

Mickey Fowler is a quiet, unpretentious, and gentle man. He represents the highest level of gunmanship, and has many valuable thoughts about women and self-defense.

"Some people like to look at the world through rose colored glasses and say 'what a wonderful place this world would be if there were no guns.' Where their illogical idealism fails is that in the reality of today's society, the person who is the biggest and strongest brute will still have you at his mercy. The handgun eliminates that problem because it serves as the great equalizer. It makes up for what strength you lack physically," Fowler says in his and Dalton's fine book, *Handguns and Self-Defense: Life Without Fear.*

Fowler talked with me after I had finished taking his course at ISI. He wanted to give this additional piece of advice to readers: "Once you explain to somebody that a gun is only a piece of machinery, and it is for you to control and learn the right procedures, it is like any other machine. You can work on a table saw as a cabinetmaker does and have your fingers cut off if you don't use it properly. The guys that still have their fingers are the guys that learn how to use it right and have formed good habits and proper techniques. There's no mystery to handling a gun properly. Methods have been developed by people like Mike and myself who have shot hundreds and hundreds of thousands of rounds of ammunition. We've drawn our guns from our holsters very quickly and never even come close to shooting ourselves, or hurting anybody with a gun. It's a matter of proper techniques, and once you have learned those techniques, you can handle this machine."

Carol Ruth Silver, a pro-gun advocate and member of the Board of Supervisors for the city and county of San Francisco, amplifies Fowler's advice by insisting that a gun "is a piece of machinery, like my Cuisinart or my drill. It's dangerous if used improperly. It is not a toy and is not to be treated as such. As far as I'm concerned," Carol Silver says, "it's a necessary piece of household equipment."

Jeff Cooper is the father of modern combat gun handling. There isn't a handgun instructor in the world who hasn't been influenced by his techniques; the Cooper method has produced the standard.

Jeff Cooper's school is in Paulden, Arizona, and is called The American Pistol Institute. Gunsite Ranch, as he calls it, might possibly be the finest training facility in the world, hundreds of acres of specialized shooting ranges and simulators, a staff of twenty-six range instructors, and a reputation that has spread throughout the world for training the best weapons specialists in all the U.S. armed forces and in the police agencies of most major American cities. I attended the API course, as I did most of the prominent pistolcraft courses in the country in preparation for the gun-defense chapter in this book. In my class of thirty, there were four women. Mr. Cooper says that women's enrollment is steadily growing.

"As society moves more and more off the land and onto the pavement, we find more and more people who never, ever get the notion that they might look after themselves," said Cooper, as we comfortably sat in his office overlooking miles of arid fields. "They feel that they are going to be looked out for in this big organization that we call government. From the time you start going to school, you're told where to go to the bathroom, you're told where to eat, you're told what to learn, you're told where to start and stop and what games to play. It never occurs to you that you might have an idea of your own, because you are overcivilized. And I would say that the majority of people are overcivilized."

I asked Jeff Cooper for his thoughts about women's using lethal force against rape.

"That's so new," he said, "but you know, it's a goddamn corruption of the human race to bring that subject up like that. You see," he continued, "I am a product of a nineteenth-century pioneer environment. I grew up in a large city where all my parents, grandparents, and uncles were from the turn-of-the-century period, and they had a different attitude. And the notion of whether or not rape was a capital offense never even came up. Because, in the first place, you didn't talk about it, and if anybody even suggested that someone might lay a hand on a woman out of sexual aggression, there was no question about what you did with him. You didn't even bring him in—you killed him on the spot.

"And so," he said, gesticulating, "the notion that rape

isn't much of a deal, that attitude is a sick attitude that has grown up in the atmosphere of the Vietnamese War. I don't know that there is any connection, but it wasn't until the Vietnamese War that anybody ever accepted the idea that a rapist had a right to be treated as a victim, too.

"You do not do that," Jeff Cooper said as he smashed his large fist into his palm. "If violent crime is to be curbed, it is only the intended victim who can do it. The felon does not fear the police, and he fears neither judge nor jury. Therefore what he must be taught to fear is his victim."

John Farnam is another of the country's top combat-shooting instructors, teaching shooting skills mainly to police academies across the nation. John is a jovial man whose unique style of instruction causes his students to become exceptionally comfortable and self-confident about shooting a handgun. I studied with John for fifty hours in Aspen, Colorado, at Executive Security International, the foremost school for instruction in executive security, and came away from his course with a real sense that the handgun is nothing more or less than a tool. "I recommend that some women own guns," John told me. "The question would have to apply to each individual woman. There are some women who might benefit immensely from having a gun around, and there are some women who would not. It all depends on the level of emotional stability. And it also depends on the willingness of the woman to acquire the necessary training, and her own ability to make that crucial decision to shoot if it ever needs to be made, and, of course, all those criteria also apply to men.

"Some women clearly shouldn't have guns," Farnam continued, "just as some men who are hotheads or irresponsible shouldn't. However, for most women, certainly the majority, a handgun is the only personal defense instrument that makes any sense at all, one that has any possibility of getting her out of a very difficult situation when she is the victim of a personal attack by someone much larger than herself."

Finally, Dr. Ann Turkel, assistant clinical professor of psychiatry at Columbia University College of Physicians and Surgeons, addresses one last consideration. "I think it has a lot to do with women's liberation. Women are more independent. More women are looking to defend themselves," she observes in an interview in a New York City community newspaper, *The West Side Spirit.* "The men didn't become wimps because they learned how to diaper babies. I don't think women have to sacrifice their femininity if they learn how to shoot a gun."

Well-known handgun-control advocate and researcher Franklin E. Zimring comments on the changing status of women and their role in public opinion about handguns. "Female ownership of self-defense handguns has historically been low," Zimring says in *American Violence and Public Policy,* "but female vulnerability to violent crime has been one of the most persuasive reasons offered as justification for household guns. . . . The American woman of the 1980s and 1990s will thus be the first and most important leading indicator of the social status of self-defense handguns in the more distant future.

"If female ownership of self-defense handguns increases dramatically, the climate of opinion for drastic restriction of handguns can't happen. Women are physically more vulnerable to crime than men, and this special vulnerability, other liberations aside, will be an important part of our culture for generations. Women, predominantly, are targets of sexual violence.

"Further, female attitudes toward household burglary, far and away the most frequent form of home victimization, seem to diverge sharply from male attitudes. Many men tend to shrug off burglary as a loss of property; women experience it as a gross invasion of personal privacy that produces high levels of fear and insult," says

Zimring. "If single women demand guns for self-defense purposes, federal firearms control will, at maximum, require screening, waiting periods, and some registration. The 50-million-handgun society of the future may be fore-ordained."

8

Kids and Safety

IF YOU'VE DECIDED that you want a handgun in the house but are apprehensive because of your children or grandchildren, you are certainly justified in your concern. There is always some inherent risk in owning a gun, just as there is a calculated danger in having sharp knives, cleaning fluids, and medicine accessible. And with all potentially harmful products, care must be taken in their storage and instruction must be given about their potential for injury.

Easy to say, but I realize as a mother it's not so easy to do. Having a gun for security and keeping it safe from others are mutually antagonistic. The safer the gun is, the less ready it is for emergency use; conversely, the more ready a gun is to be fired, the more opportunity there is for mishaps. In other words, an unloaded gun that is perfectly safe is perfectly useless. If you plan to have a loaded gun available, then availability in itself is going to dictate that you will have to assume some risk and make changes in your home and in your life style.

Most important, and I must stress this, if you are not a person who takes great care in all aspects of your life, you should not own a gun. That means that, if you can't acquire daily, almost ritualistic habits, a gun in your home could be more dangerous than helpful to you and your family. Boys aged ten to nineteen have the highest gun-accident death rate, so if you have teenagers think twice about having a gun in the house. Although I have acquired impeccable habits of safely hiding and retrieving my gun, I am not sure that I would own a gun if I had teenagers. But since 50 percent of all American households possess at least one firearm, it can be presumed that many of these households have children who have learned gun safety and coexist comfortably with the risks and benefits of gun ownership.

The decision to keep a gun loaded and ready for emergency use is one that must be made after a thorough appraisal of both the advantages and risks. Here are some of the things I have learned that may help you with this all-important resolution.

First, know that loading a gun in the face of danger, under the influence of adrenaline, is extremely difficult. Fear and panic, according to all police authorities and shooting experts, disable the arms and legs to some extent, as the immediate result of adrenaline in the blood. All of the shooting schools I have attended for this book provide exercises that simulate panic situations. They are timed drills; you can experience some of the results yourself at home.

Place an unloaded gun on a table, and put the ammunition on the other side of the table. Have a friend give you the signal to load and then time you. This will in no way simulate the stress of a real encounter, but you will see how clumsy you can become just from the pressure of being timed. If it is ever necessary to use a gun, you will want to eliminate any possibility of being clumsy and remove everything that interferes with or delays your readiness to defend yourself.

John Farnam offers this studied advice: "If you've got a gun in such a way that it takes more than five seconds from the time you put your hands on it to when you can get it to fire, you're probably kidding yourself. Five seconds is about the maximum you can expect that you have in an emergency, and if you have a gun locked up in a vault, and you really believe that you're going to have the presence of mind to remember the combination, open it, get the gun loaded, and use it—I suggest that you're probably better off not having a gun."

It goes without saying that, for your protection and your family's safekeeping, your gun should be loaded only when you are at home. If, for example, you come home at night and load your gun and then decide to leave, you must unload it and safely secure it again. Although there aren't any perfect solutions, there are some acceptable ways of protecting your children from a gun. As Massad Ayoob advises, instead of childproofing guns we must gunproof children.

And just how do you gunproof your children, and when? There is certainly no possibility of a baby in a crib finding a loaded gun, so that eliminates nearly two years of concern. The problem arises only during the inquisitive years (between the ages of two to four), where nothing in the house is safe from those sticky little hands. That's the time when everything is locked up, nailed down, and hidden away. I remember when my children were that age: electrical outlets were covered, knives were stored in boxes, vases and ashtrays were removed, baby locks were installed on kitchen and bathroom cabinets, bathroom doors were shut, guard gates were placed at the top of stairs, and even plants were sent to my mother-in-law. Every square inch of the house had potential to hurt my sons, but they survived. Just as your children will survive these inquisitive years, they also will survive with a gun in the house if you are careful. Again, I must emphasize that you need to be vigilant when you have a gun.

Many protective measures can be taken during these years of your child's development. One of the easiest and safest ways to secure your gun is always to carry it on you. Most women find that impractical, but I have met a few who do so, especially those who live in remote areas or feel overly insecure at night.

Most important, you should secure your gun in a place where nobody is going to locate it except you. Besides worrying about your children, you need to be concerned about an intruder's finding and stealing your gun. You have a responsibility to the general community to store your gun properly. The best method is to keep a gun and ammunition in a large safe. But this is often impracticable, and the next-best way is to keep a gun in some concealed location in a locked room or area. If you don't have a large safe, never store the ammunition with the gun when you're out of the house. Mickey Fowler advises that in the morning women put the ammunition underneath the kitchen sink in a used scouring-powder can, because intruders usually search through the bathroom for drugs rather than the kitchen.

You'd be surprised how many women I have spoken to who hide their guns in inappropriate places. One woman stashes her gun in a basket filled with dirty clothes in her closet, and another woman hides her pistol on the back of a top shelf in her kitchen. Other hiding places that I've heard of include inside a boot in a closet, the ubiquitous under-the-mattress, inside an antique vase, and in a shoebox. Even though some of these hiding places may appear to be inaccessible to a child, most kids have a knack for finding everything in the most out-of-the-way places. Just remember how, when you were a kid, you found your hidden birthday or Christmas presents or your parents' emergency money.

A number of women with whom I spoke feel comfortable about storing their gun in a locked nightstand during the day and taking it out at night. One drawback is the possibility of misplacing the key, unless it is always kept in the same place. A simpler procedure is to hide the gun in a hollowed-out book that is especially designed for a gun;

the book should be mixed with other books, yet readily accessible during an emergency.

One approach is the MagnaTrigger Safety device, which can only be used on a revolver and must be installed by a gunsmith. A rather unique gadget, the device modifies a revolver so that it cannot be fired except by someone wearing a special magnetic ring. The modification costs three hundred dollars, which may be more than you paid for your gun, and there have been reports that it does not work all of the time. A less expensive strategy that is commonly used by police officers is to lock a handgun through the trigger guard (behind the trigger) with a pair of handcuffs to some stationary object, such as a water pipe. This secures the gun from being accidentally fired or stolen, but it also makes it very difficult to use in an emergency.

An excellent device which I highly recommend is made by California gunsmith Jim Davis. For sixty-five dollars, he will take a Smith & Wesson or Taurus revolver (only K frames, L frames, or N frames) and change the inner parts creating a safety that never existed before which blocks both the trigger and hammer, but can easily be released with your thumb on the left side of the gun. The revolver can also be loaded and unloaded with the safety in the "on" position.

A number of women prefer storing their guns in the Cannon Safe, a small metal box with a push-button combination lock, which they hide during the day and keep out at night, either opened or closed. Two disadvantages are the possibilities of forgetting the combination in a crisis, or of having the box stolen by a burglar. To deter theft, some women who live in houses or in first-floor apartments install larger safes in their closets, bolted to the floor, in which they can store a gun and other valuables.

Yet none of these methods are foolproof. In the final analysis, as Ayoob says, you cannot childproof your guns. We have heard the stories about children finding their parents' guns and shooting themselves or other people. It is most unfortunate that this continues to happen, and there is no excuse for it. The culpability lies with irresponsible adults. Though the media graphically publicize these youthful shootings, they rarely espouse gun safety or report the statistics indicating that far more children die from other accidents, also caused by negligent grown-ups. The National Safety Council states that in 1987 3,500 children (ages ten to fourteen) died in auto casualties, 1,300 in drownings, 1,250 because of fires and burns, mostly from hot liquids, and only 135 from handgun accidents. Again, there is no justification for these shootings, and most of them would not have occurred if parents hadn't been so careless and ignorant of gun safety.

Telling a child not to touch a gun is not enough. Most children are attracted to guns, because the media have depicted gun users as powerful and glamorous. You and I were no different when we were growing up. A female friend of mind vividly remembers seeing the movie *Bonnie and Clyde* and rooting for Bonnie as she robbed banks and killed people. "I saw that movie three times," my friend said, "because Bonnie's life seemed so exciting and daring compared to my life. What made her life so stimulating were the guns. I just wanted to be her."

Today our youngsters see screen role models, such as Tom Selleck, Luke Skywalker, Dirty Harry, Don Johnson, and Rambo, who appear omnipotent and exciting with a gun in the hand. And according to *TV Guide,* the average child witnesses more than eighteen thousand violent deaths on television or in the movies before reaching the age of twenty-one. It is no wonder that a real gun is so enticing to a child and becomes even more attractive when a mother says, "You must never touch this gun."

Although it may sound radical at first, the ideal strategy is first to show your children how your gun works while you're cleaning it, and then, later, to go to a range and show them how to shoot a gun. You may balk at the idea, but once a child understands how a gun operates and has heard the sound of a gunshot and witnessed the potential damage, he or she will have a different view of a gun and will gain respect for it. This knowledge can have other positive effects: one woman told me that, once her seven-year-old son had shot a gun, he stopped playing war games with his friends and threw away his toy guns, including a water pistol.

From the outset, make it clear to your youngsters that they are never to handle a real gun when you are not with them, and, of course, never to point even a toy gun at anyone. At the same time, tell them that if they want to handle—not play with—a gun in your presence, they will be allowed to do so.

Teach your kids the rules of gun safety as early as possible. The most important are:

Treat every gun as if it is loaded;
Never point a gun at anything you don't intend to destroy;
Keep your finger off the trigger until ready to shoot.

At what age should children learn about guns? There is really no age minimum, but, according to Massad Ayoob, a good barometer of responsibility is the care of a family pet. A child compassionate and responsible enough to handle the feeding, medication, and cleaning chores for cats or dogs or livestock is a child who will probably prove trustworthy with guns, says Ayoob, who recommends that a child first shoot a .22 rifle, because it is small, light, and has no recoil. Of course, there are many children, as there are many adults, who are emotionally unstable and should never handle a gun.

At the age of four, Ayoob's daughter was shown how a gun worked; by five, Kathy was helping Ayoob clean his revolvers. (He finds gun cleaning to be a good learning tool, for it gives children hands-on experience, and they tend to lose their fear of the gun after learning how to safely handle one.) By six, Kathy had shot a pistol—the .22-caliber Beretta Minx—and by seven, Kathy had won her first marksmanship award, beating fifteen-year-olds in that particular match. "I would trust my nine-year-old daughter to walk behind me with a loaded gun far more than I would trust many police officers that I've had to work with on the street," Ayoob proudly says.

Ayoob's early teaching may, understandably, make some parents very uncomfortable, thinking that his daughter may have been too young emotionally to appreciate a gun's lethal force. Teaching a child how to shoot at that early age is certainly not the norm.

Dr. Richard Blasband, a former member of the teaching staff of the Department of Psychiatry at Yale University and currently in private practice, says that the average, mentally and emotionally healthy child may be safely introduced to the operation of small firearms between the ages of seven and twelve years. "This is the time that the child acquires the ability to mentally transform information about the real world so that it can be organized and used selectively in the solution of problems. This means that the child has progressed from the ability to perform simple actions or goal-directed behavior to operations where certain actions are bound up with others in an integrated mental structure," says Blasband. "By this age, the average, mentally healthy child will be able to readily differentiate between fantasy and reality and therefore know what a gun is, what it can do, and can integrate this knowledge with other internalized information and be responsible for it.

"Of course," Blasband cautions, "one must assess each child with respect to exactly when they have reached this mental integrative capacity, whether their emotional maturity is consistent with it, and whether they understand concepts relating to social responsibility. Ideally, where mental and emotional development have progressed in a healthy manner, the seven-year-old can be introduced to firearms. However, in most cases in our society, the child will not be ready until the ages of 10–12," says Blasband.

Whenever you feel that your children are mature enough to see what happens when a gun is shot, go to an outdoor shooting range or other safe area and equip them with hearing protection and safety glasses. I recommend the following exercise, which is extremely graphic and gets the point across. Place a cantaloupe or other type of melon on a box about seven yards away and have your kids watch you fire a round (preferably a hollow point, because it is more damaging) into it. If you're a good shot, the melon will be blown off the box and badly shattered, its juice and insides gushing out. With your children, examine the incredible destruction and locate where the bullet entered and exited. Since a melon is similar in size to a human head, you can easily explain what can really happen if a person is shot with just one bullet. This lesson is critical, because most children believe that a bullet only makes a small hole in the body, like the thousand or more they see every year on television. You may frighten your youngsters with this exercise, but if it takes fear to gain respect for a gun, it is worth doing.

When your children want to shoot, your next step is some kind of instruction. You can do your own teaching or, better still, contact a local club that offers firearms-familiarization programs and Junior Rifle courses, in which your kids can shoot with a team. You won't have to purchase a gun immediately, since weapons are routinely provided and turned back after each session. For nonathletic kids, this is an excellent way to learn the meaning of teamwork and the excitement of competition. For teenagers, some high schools offer riflery classes, and the Boy Scouts also offer marksmanship programs.

But your children don't have to be target shooters for you to gunproof them. What they need to know, through your own gun-safety practice and instruction, is that guns are dangerous and should be treated with great respect. If they are trained, your concern will not be that your children may take your gun but, in a world where every second house contains a gun, that your son or daughter may be in another child's home and that irresponsible child may take the family gun out of a drawer or a closet.

Mike Dalton and Mickey Fowler advise that you make absolutely clear to your children that, if they are visiting someone's home and see a firearm, short or long, they are to leave that house immediately and inform you of what happened.

Massad Ayoob goes a step further, saying that, for safety reasons, your child may have to unload the gun instantly before leaving the house; he stresses that the child should be cautioned not to run away suddenly from the youngster with the gun or yell, I'm going to tell. The kid with the weapon is obviously immature, and such a reaction could provoke him to point the gun at your child and even pull the trigger.

I have spoken to a number of children who know how to shoot. One such girl is Debby Taylor, who calls herself a speed-freak bookworm. When she was eleven, her mother signed her up for a speed-reading course; today, at sixteen, she has the uncanny ability to read nine hundred words a minute, gobbling down four books a week.

Also when she was eleven, her parents took her to a shooting range to teach her gun safety. Not at all interested in guns, Debby didn't want to know about them, but her parents insisted on it after a series of robberies in their Atlanta, Georgia, neighborhood. The senior Taylors had just purchased a revolver and were practicing when they became concerned about Debby's safety with a loaded gun in the house.

Debby enrolled in a series of Saturday-afternoon gun-safety classes especially designed for children. To this day, Debby recalls the first time she watched her instructor shooting at a filled Pepsi-Cola can, exploding it with one shot. That was lesson number one. "We all looked at this messed-up can and it was awesome! I knew that guns were incredible, because I've watched a lot of television, but I didn't know what one bullet could do. On TV, the bad guy falls down, and then it's on to the next shooting," said the exuberant teenager.

Before any of the kids even touched a gun in the class, they were drilled in the rules of safety, which Debby still remembers today, repeating them to me as if she were reciting the Ten Commandments: "Always point the muzzle in a safe direction; keep your finger off the trigger; keep the action open and gun unloaded; know how the gun operates; be sure your gun and ammunition are compatible; carry only one gauge/caliber of ammunition when shooting; be sure of your target—and what's beyond; wear eye and ear protection as appropriate; don't mix alcohol or drugs with shooting; and be aware that circumstances may require additional rules unique to a particular situation."

Debby told me how the students learned to load and unload a revolver with dummy bullets, practicing so much she joked that she speed-loads as quickly as she speed-reads. But for her and her classmates, the big lesson was learning how to shoot a .22-caliber pistol. "I guess I got into the program," admitted Debby, "because all of the kids were so up about shooting that I started wanting to learn, too, which really surprised my folks, because I was down on the whole thing from the beginning and complained about going." At first Debby was frightened to shoot and lagged behind the others, but as she watched them she realized that it wasn't difficult to do. Soon she was as spirited as the rest and was easily hitting the target.

Months later, during a tell-a-story assignment at school, Debby gave a fifteen-minute talk on gun safety, using charts from the gun club that illustrated the various parts of a handgun, and ended by distributing gun-safety pamphlets. Impressed by Debby's experience, a number of her classmates told her that their parents also had guns in their homes and they, too, wanted to sign up for the Saturday gun classes. For her work, Debby got an A +.

Five years later, Debby admits that she still isn't interested in guns but doesn't regret her training, and once or twice a year she goes out shooting with her parents. "I don't think that I could ever shoot anyone, but I don't know what I would do in a bad situation. I did learn one thing," she added. "I respect the power of a gun, yet I'm not afraid of it anymore and I know what it can do."

Ellen Wolf didn't know what to do when her ten-year-old son came home one afternoon from his friend Bobby Schiff's house and told her that he had played with a gun. She first assumed that it was a toy gun or a water pistol, but the more she thought about it the more she became alarmed, and finally called Bobby's mother. Barbara Schiff was disturbed to hear Ellen's account. Yes, she said, they did in fact keep a gun—well hidden, she added, and she couldn't imagine that the boys had played with it. Although, after thinking about it, she said that it could be a remote possibility, since she and her husband had been out in the backyard gardening and the boys had been in and out of the house all afternoon. She said that she would check with her husband to see if the gun had been moved.

That evening, Barbara telephoned Ellen to say that her husband had found the gun, but it was not in its usual position in the top drawer of their highboy dresser. They had questioned Bobby, who admitted that the two boys had pulled out the bottom drawers, using them as steps to climb to the top to "just look at Daddy's things"; it was then they had found the gun.

Ellen was concerned because she also kept a revolver, although she secured hers in a Cannon Safe underneath her bed, feeling comfortable that her son would not be able to open it. "But, still," she said, pausing, "I knew the time was coming and I was upset that I had ignored teaching him anything about the gun. Justin just seemed so young. But obviously he was old enough." Ellen now felt the need to instruct her son in gun safety and to teach him how to shoot. When she discussed her idea with the Schiffs, who were equally concerned, they immediately agreed with Ellen that it was time to gunproof their kids. They quickly developed a presentation they would give to their sons and made arrangements to take them shooting the following Saturday.

As planned, a few days later after dinner, Marty Schiff and Ellen sat down at the dining-room table with Justin and Bobby and, after making sure the revolver was unloaded and in a safe condition, the boys each held the gun, opened and closed the cylinder, and were taught to pass the gun so the muzzle didn't point at anyone. Ellen was surprised how quickly they learned gun-safety basics. Then Marty showed them a cartridge and took one apart. He explained that when the trigger is pulled the hammer falls, striking a little cap—he pointed to the back of the cartridge—that causes a spark to ignite the gunpowder, which launches the bullet out of the front of the gun. The boys were fascinated. After he demonstrated how to pull the trigger on his .38 revolver, each of the boys tried doing it, although Justin didn't have the strength to pull it back. "Secretly, I was relieved to see that Justin couldn't shoot that gun," Ellen told me.

After watching the boys repeat the basic safety rules, Marty told them that they could try practice shooting that weekend. "Justin was so excited that he couldn't stop talking about it. I think he told everyone in his class, which made me a bit nervous. I expected to get a call from some irate parent, but no calls came," said Ellen, who was as uneasy as Justin was delighted at the prospect of shooting. That Saturday morning the two families went to the Boulder Rifle Club, where they rented a .22 rifle and a .22 pistol and equipped the boys with eye and ear protection. But before the kids did any shooting, they first experienced the big gun's force. The club owners allowed Marty to arrange three filled soda-pop cans in a designated area where, according to Ellen, "Marty blasted the cans to smithereens with one shot apiece. The noise scared the kids—Justin actually jumped and Bobby swore! After Marty unloaded the gun and holstered it, we inspected the damage. The cans—if you could call them cans—were jagged aluminum strips. I think shooting soda-pop cans is one of the best ways to show a kid how powerful a gunshot is," continued Ellen. "I've even done it myself, and every time it happens I'm so stunned by the destruction that I know it makes an unforgettable impression upon youngsters."

After Marty's performance, the boys still wanted to shoot, but were more cautious when handling the borrowed .22s. As Ellen put it, "The boys lost their macho." While Marty instructed Bobby in loading the .22 rifle, Ellen watched Justin load the small pistol, and soon the kids were firing shots at the paper targets from a distance of seven yards. At first they missed the targets, but after a number of rounds they occasionally hit the paper. Ellen explained to them that accurate shooting wasn't easy, and a great deal of concentration was necessary to place shots. The parents didn't want to tire the boys, so after firing fifty rounds they called it quits for the day. But, before leaving, Ellen took her .380 autoloader out of a locked gun bag, loaded a magazine, chambered a round, and then shot from a distance of ten yards, squarely hitting the target every time.

Since then, Justin, who is now twelve years old, has come to own a .22 rifle and regularly shoots with Ellen at the range. "Sometimes I still think he's too young to shoot a gun, but he's extremely responsible, and, frankly, I feel a bit safer living alone with Justin now that he knows how to shoot and has a mature attitude about the guns. He's growing up so nicely. My biggest mistake was not teaching Justin sooner about gun safety. I kept procrastinating, because I guess I was too lazy to take the time to do it. A hidden gun is not necessarily a safe gun."

Are some handguns safer than others? Yes, certain guns have more safety advantages, especially the autoloaders, because of their slide mechanisms, which load a cartridge into the chamber. It is very difficult for a young child to pull the slide back; in fact, I know a number of women, including myself, who can't cycle the slides of some autoloaders. Furthermore, to the uneducated eye the gun doesn't look as though it even has a slide for loading a cartridge.

The safest gun in the most ready condition is an autoloader with a loaded magazine and no cartridge in the chamber. In an emergency, all you have to do is snap the slide and you're ready to fire. Equally safe but less ready for action is an autoloader that has a magazine safety, such as the Browning High-Power and most of the Smith & Wesson autoloaders. With this method, a cartridge can be chambered and the hammer cocked, but if a magazine is not inserted the gun cannot be fired. Almost a photo finish with the other two methods is the Heckler & Koch P7/9mm autoloader with the squeeze-cocking design. This is one of the finest of the imported new breed of high-tech pistols. On this gun, the grip must be depressed in order to fire a bullet. It is highly unlikely that a child would know how to do this or have the strength and dexterity to squeeze the grip safety and pull the trigger at the same time.

The revolver is the least safe and needs some external safety equipment, such as a trigger lock, a safety mechanism, or some storage container that compromises the usefulness of the gun in an emergency. A revolver must stay loaded, because it is almost impossible to load it quickly in a stressful situation.

This discussion on gunproofing your children assumes that your kids are well behaved and you have a modicum of control over their actions. If your children are emotionally unstable, it would be inadvisable to have a gun at home. Also, it goes without saying that if you or your spouse is quick-tempered or has drinking or drug problems involving violent reactions, neither of you should have the means to set up a lifetime of regret.

I wish that there were a number of methods to store a gun in a ready condition and at the same time have it absolutely childproof, but there isn't even one. Many women feel that having a self-defense gun at home is important enough to improvise a way to keep it from being accidentally discovered by their children. This can be done; it just takes some thought and careful attention to handling your gun the same way every time.

9

Buying a Gun

TO MY AMAZEMENT, selecting a suitable handgun is the most complicated, confusing, and critical purchase known to humankind. Every firearms expert, every manufacturer, every clerk in every gun store, everyone who owns a gun, and just about everyone who doesn't own a gun has an opinion about which gun is the best and which caliber of ammunition is better.

Now, please understand that I am not timid when it comes to spending money on a dress or even a pair of high-heeled shoes, and I would say that I enjoy shopping for most things and have no trouble knowing what I like and what I don't like. But the first gun I bought proved to be a mistake later, and uncharacteristically involved no shopping on my part. Because I didn't know one gun from another or a caliber from a millimeter, I purchased the first handgun the salesman recommended. Although that gun was an excellent one, it was wrong for my size and strength and actually retarded the development of my shooting skills.

After close to two hundred hours of training in the art of pistolcraft, I know now what gun I am able to handle, which calibers are right for me, and, more important, which are wrong and why. The goal of this chapter is to pass along what I have learned so you will be properly prepared to select a handgun that you will enjoy owning and look forward to practicing with, and that will provide you with the maximum degree of protection for your particular requirements and restraints.

Don't make the mistake I did when I purchased my gun. Before buying your gun, go to a target range and try shooting a number of different guns so that you can determine which kind and model you prefer. Your shopping time will be greatly reduced, and you'll get the right gun the first time.

Now, let me say that there are no bad handguns. All commercially made guns are good; some are just better. The guns that are better are better because they will last longer under the punishment of having thousands, even hundreds of thousands of rounds of ammunition shot through them, and because they are decidedly more user-friendly. They are also usually more expensive. But remember, the skill of the shooter makes the bullet hit the target, not the make, model, or price of the gun.

In the gun community, two basic arguments subsist that give license to the hundreds of differing opinions about which gun is best. Those opposing views concern revolvers versus autoloaders, and bullet size versus stopping power. These concepts must be understood before you can intelligently analyze the other variables in order to select a handgun best suited for you.

BULLETS

First, it must be understood that a bullet refers only to the tip of the cartridge that is loaded into the gun. The bullet is fired through the barrel and out the gun toward the target when the trigger is pulled. This is possible because, in addition to containing the bullet, the cartridge also holds a measured amount of gunpowder at the rear of the bullet and a sparking device known as a primer. When the tiny primer in the back of the bullet is struck with enough impact from any pointed object—in a gun this is called a firing pin—the primer ignites the gunpowder. The gunpowder does not explode; it burns slowly, causing gas to build up; the pressure forces the bullet out of the cartridge and on its way. Of course, "slowly" is only in comparison with other combustible materials such as gasoline or nitroglycerine. This whole firing sequence happens in a fraction of a second; still, the gunpowder does not explode.

It would also be good to understand at this point how the bullet gets down-range to the target with such accuracy. If you look down the barrel of any gun, you will see that the barrel is not perfectly smooth inside, as a drinking straw or water pipe is. A gun barrel has a narrowly etched groove spiraling the length of it, which causes the bullet to spin as it passes through. This groove, called rifling, spins the bullet at speeds of more than fifty thousand revolutions per minute. This extremely high rate allows the bullet to pass through the air as if it were a drill, resisting the thick atmosphere and being stabilized like a spinning top. The longer the barrel, of course, the longer the rifling, and the faster the spin of the bullet. This is why the rifle is so much more accurate than the handgun. The rifle cartridge can also be larger than the handgun cartridge, because the chamber that holds the cartridge in place for the firing pin is larger on the rifle, so the rifle cartridge holds more gunpowder and, when ignited by the firing pin's striking the primer, the extra gunpowder produces more pressure, which launches the bullet at greater speed. When the bullet comes out the end of the rifle barrel, it is going faster and spinning at a higher speed than any handgun can produce. Consequently, the rifle bullet can go farther with more accuracy.

The handgun is considered inferior to the rifle because the short barrel has only a minimum amount of rifling to spin the bullet and guarantee accuracy. Therefore, the smaller the barrel, the closer the gun must be to the target to assure a true hit. This is an important limitation of the handgun. At five yards from a target, most beginners can hit within, say, six inches. At fifteen yards, it gets harder; beyond twenty yards, it takes an expert marksman to hit her target. So, when you select your handgun, keep in mind the conditions under which you may use it. The longer the barrel, the more accurate the handgun; the shorter the barrel, the more concealable and the less accurate beyond ten feet.

There are a number of bullet shapes and weights that are necessary to know, and we will discuss them a little later, under ammunition.

CALIBERS

The word "caliber" refers to the diameter of a bullet in decimals of an inch, and, as an extension, to the inside diameter of the barrel of the handgun that uses bullets of that size. Thus, the famous .45-caliber handgun shoots bullets that are .45 inch around and are shot in a handgun called a .45; .44-caliber bullets are used in .44s; .38-caliber bullets in .38s; and .22-caliber bullets in .22s.

As the diameter of the bullet gets smaller, the hole in the barrel of the gun that shoots that bullet gets smaller, and as a consequence the ability to stop an assailant (it is called stopping power) is decreased. So the general rule is, the smaller the decimal number of the bullet and the handgun, the less effective the gun is in stopping the forward progress of an onrushing assailant. Keep in mind that all bullets will kill, but in self-defense shooting we are interested only in stopping an assailant.

The caliber story would be quite simple to understand if all we needed to know was that the bigger the decimal number, the bigger the bullet and handgun. But the ammunition manufacturers, along with the handgun makers, continually introduce new products into the market, and have managed to muddy the picture with prefixes and suffixes to the standard bullet sizes in order to come up with improvements on the theme.

As an example, the .38-caliber bullet comes in a number of different cartridges. The .38 Colt was the original cartridge designed and manufactured by Colt Firearms Company in 1875. It immediately became a very popular caliber, so Smith & Wesson, another big manufacturer of ammunition and firearms, introduced their own version of the .38, calling it the .38 Smith & Wesson. It was basically the same cartridge as the .38 Colt, but it soon captured a large share of the market and helped to position the .38-caliber as a standard in the industry. Soon Smith & Wesson designed a new .38-caliber cartridge, which was longer and more powerful. They called this cartridge the .38 Special. It was the same-size bullet in a longer case with more gunpowder, and to this day is one of the most popular calibers. Still not satisfied, Smith & Wesson designed another, more powerful and bigger .38 in 1935 and called this one a .357 Magnum, borrowing the name Magnum from champagne bottlers and using the decimal size actually closer to the real size of the .38.

Now we have extra-powerful Magnum cartridges in .22-, .32-, .357-, and .44-caliber. All the new Magnum loads required new guns to accommodate the longer cartridge, but, perhaps in an attempt not to appear greedy, Colt and Smith & Wesson chambered their new Magnum handguns to shoot the next cartridge down as well. So the .357 Magnum handgun will also fire .38 Special ammunition.

And if all that isn't enough to confuse the consumer, the Europeans designed their own version of the .38-caliber and called it by their own metric equivalent, a "9mm" followed by the maker's name, as in "9mm Luger."

Obviously there is a lot more to know about cartridges and bullet performance, but a brief summary will give you the picture.

There is a continuous, raging battle in the handgun community about which caliber bullet is the best man-stopper. The sides are drawn very clearly between the 9mm fans and the advocates of the .45-caliber. A somewhat less contentious difference of opinion exists between supporters of the .38 Special and the .357 Magnum shooters, but each side defends its caliber's ability to stop an aggressor with a minimum number of shots in a minimum amount of time. They are all arguing about the differences between a bullet's size and a bullet's speed. I am certainly not going to settle the dispute here—in fact, I am sure that it will never be settled—but here is what the ballistic engineers say about how a bullet stops a living target.

The size of the hole a bullet makes in a target is not what does the damage. It is true that the wound made from a .45 bullet will be greater than the wound made from a smaller 9mm or .38 bullet, but the real damage, the stopping power, comes from the speed of the bullet and is the result of something called hydrostatic shock.

Jim Carmichel, who has served as special adviser to the White House Crime Control Commission and is the shooting editor of *Outdoor Life* magazine, explains in his excellent book, *The Woman's Guide to Handguns,* how a bullet does its job. "Let's say you have two one-gallon plastic jugs, each filled with water. You attach a bullet from a .357 Magnum cartridge to a stick and push it into the side of one of the water-filled jugs. The bullet, which is traveling only as fast as you can push it, makes a small hole in the jug and the water leaks out. Even if you push the bullet all the way through the jug there is no sign of violent shock. Next, standing several yards back from the remaining jug you fire the same bullet at it from a .357 Magnum revolver, which hits at a velocity of over 1,000 feet per second. The jug explodes in a shower of water with such violence that the plastic is torn to shreds. This is a good demonstration of hydrostatic shock and goes a long way toward explaining why high-speed bullets result in a more immediate disabling effect."

Everyone should try this experiment. It is even more effective to shoot a filled aluminum soft-drink can or a cantaloupe or watermelon. The shock caused by hitting a liquid-filled container or a melon puts the finishing touch on your respect for the gun.

So the disabling effect of a bullet has to do with the speed with which it hits the target and the weight of the bullet, and there is, of course, a trade-off between those two.

Bullets are sized in calibers and weighed in grains. There are 437.5 grains in one ounce, and bullets range from 40 grains in a .22-caliber bullet up to 240 grains in the .44 Magnum bullet. And almost every caliber has bullets with a variety of weights to choose from. The lighter the bullet, the more room in the cartridge for gunpowder, and the faster the bullet goes. Conversely, the heavier the bullet, the slower it goes—but the harder it hits. This is called kinetic energy, and is the basis for the argument for the longer but slower .45 bullet. Think of being hit by a golf ball going 100 miles per hour or being hit by a baseball going half that speed. The golf ball would put a pretty good-size lump on your forehead, but the baseball would just as likely crush your skull.

Bullet velocity is measured in feet per second rather than miles per hour, because of their terrific speed. The .45 automatic 185-grain bullet leaves the gun going 950 feet per second, or 650 miles per hour. The .22 Magnum 40-grain bullet has a muzzle velocity (the speed at which it leaves the gun) of 1,910 feet per second, or more than 1,300 miles per hour. If it were just a matter of speed, the .22 should be a much more destructive bullet, but it isn't even close. And so the debate rages.

Combat master Jeff Cooper, who is a diehard proponent of the Springfield Armory .45-caliber autoloader, uses the symbol DVC to end the argument about bullet size and speed as far as he is concerned: D is for Diligentia, V is for Vis, and C is for Celeritas. The English translation is "Speed, Power, and Accuracy." The one who shoots the largest bullet as quickly as possible with the greatest accuracy triumphs over his opponents. And that may be all we need to know about ballistics.

Now we'll review the hardware.

REVOLVERS

The revolver is the simplest of all handguns. The variety of revolvers makes choosing one that is best suited to your characteristics and needs unnecessarily complicated, but the simplicity of its function makes the revolver the handgun of choice for most women.

The revolver, just as the name implies, mechanically revolves a cylinder that brings fresh cartridges up in place in front of the firing pin and behind the barrel. The cylinder holds either five or six cartridges, depending on the model of the gun, and each time the trigger is pulled and a bullet is fired the cylinder rotates the expended cartridge down out of the way and a new one up for the next shot. The only thing that can go wrong is that one of the cartridges may not fire when the trigger is pulled; this can happen but is very rare. If it occurs, the trigger is pulled again and the cartridge that misfired is rotated out of the way, a new one takes its place, and the trigger is pulled again. There are no safety levers to switch on or off, relatively little chance of the revolver's failing to shoot, and never any question whether the gun is loaded or unloaded—you can see the bullets in the cylinder.

Early revolver designs, and still some special hunting and target revolvers, are what is called single-action. In a single-action revolver, the hammer, which contains the firing pin or hits the firing pin, must be pulled back and cocked manually. When the hammer is cocked back, the slightest pressure on the trigger releases it to fall and fire the cartridge. Because a single-action revolver requires only a slight press on the trigger, it is often fired unintentionally.

The modern revolver is the same as the original design in almost every aspect, except that now the firing mechanism has been improved to a double-action: when the trigger is pulled, the hammer travels from its down position all the way back to the cocked position, where it falls and fires the cartridge. Double-action revolvers can also be used in the old single-action way, but it is not advised. In fact, many police departments that issue revolvers to their officers disable the single-action so that the officers are forced to use the double-action trigger pull. The safety advantage of a double-action trigger is easily understood when you know that it takes about twelve pounds of pressure to pull the trigger a distance of more than one inch to fire a cartridge with the double-action, and less than one pound of pressure to pull the trigger less than one-quarter of an inch to drop the hammer when it is locked back in a single-action condition.

If you buy a revolver, make a rule never to fire it or practice with it using the single, cocked-back hammer action. If you don't get accustomed to locking the hammer back manually, you won't even think about doing it after a while. But it doesn't seem necessary to disable the gun and prevent yourself from ever using that single-action mode of fire; remember, the handgun is an emergency piece of equipment, and there is no sense eliminating any option that might be used to save your life. A good compromise I have seen is having the thumb-cocking spur, that flat thumb plate on the top of the hammer, removed, so that it isn't easy to thumb-cock the hammer and hair-load the trigger. Removing the hammer spur is also done by undercover police and others who don't want to risk getting any part of the gun caught on clothing when it is drawn out from a place of concealment.

So the advantages of having a revolver as a personal

defense weapon are that it is dependable, easy to use, easy for you to tell if it is loaded (easy, too, for your assailant to see that the gun is loaded), safe, and versatile. The disadvantages are few, but are thought to be significant enough for many who are turning to the more streamlined, high-tech autoloading pistols.

The greatest disadvantage to a revolver, and the one that outweighs any other by a large margin, is that the revolver has a maximum of only six shots; after that, each hole in the cylinder must be emptied and then filled arduously with another six fresh cartridges before it is ready to be fired again.

The antirevolver people cite additional drawbacks to the wheel-gun, as they refer to it. They say that, although the revolver is relatively failureproof, when it does jam or have a mechanical malfunction it is virtually impossible to fix without a tool, and usually requires a tool and a workbench. The autoloader may malfunction with somewhat more frequency, but it can be cleared on the spot and ready to fire within seconds. And, they add, unless someone makes a hobby of practicing, the revolver is slow to shoot and less accurate than the autoloader.

I have received training in both the revolver and the autoloader, and the disadvantage I see in the revolver for a woman is that it takes a lot of strength to pull the trigger, which is usually harder on your hand than an autoloader. There is no question that the revolver is easier to use if you don't handle your gun very often, because it does not have a manual safety or a slide mechanism and you can immediately see if the gun is loaded.

AUTOLOADERS

The autoloading pistol is a design that has been around since the turn of the century and has recently gained a great deal of popularity with the introduction of many high-tech European products in the 9mm size.

The autoloader is an ingenious design that makes use of the cartridge's rearward pressure after the bullet is fired to move a slide on the top of the gun that ejects the spent cartridge case and feeds a fresh cartridge into the chamber, ready to be fired. It differs from a fully automatic machine gun in that with the autoloader the trigger must be pulled again for each shot, whereas the machine gun continues to fire automatically when the trigger is pulled back. You will hear the autoloader also called a semi-automatic, and sometimes improperly called an automatic. It is not an automatic-shooting pistol; rather, it is an automatic-loading pistol. It will, however, go through the process of firing a bullet, ejecting the used case, and automatically reloading and firing faster than the eye can see, and faster than you can pull the trigger again. It is truly a brilliant design.

The cartridges used in the autoloader are stacked one on top of another in a long, narrow container called a magazine or a clip. After the magazine is filled, it is inserted into the grip of the pistol, where it gets locked in. The slide on top of the gun is pulled back manually and quickly released to get the first cartridge into the firing chamber and to cock the hammer. After that first manual operation, the autoloader takes over, and all the shooter has to do is aim and squeeze the trigger ever so slightly to send each bullet down-range.

The old-style autoloader, which is still made and preferred by many, is strictly single-action and carried with a cartridge in the chamber ready to be fired, the hammer all the way back and ready to drop, and a hammer safety engaged to prevent the hammer from dropping onto the firing pin if the gun is dropped accidentally or the trigger is pressed by mistake. If you are carrying a single-action autoloader in this condition, you are carrying it "cocked and locked," the readiest condition any gun can be in for immediate use; this is why many prefer the single-action autos.

Fans of the single-action autoloaders argue that with the

double-action the first trigger pull is so different and so much harder than the single-action mode into which it changes after the first shot that the first shot usually misses the target low and the second shot is usually wasted to the side of the target in an attempt to regrip; by then the shooter has lost the fight.

The new breed of autoloaders, like the modern revolvers, have been designed with double-action triggers. A double-action works in an autoloader by allowing the shooter to carry the gun with a cartridge in the chamber and the hammer down. The first shot from this position is a long trigger pull that brings the hammer back and releases it to fall on the firing pin to strike the primer and fire the bullet, exactly as in a revolver. All the following shots are now single-action, with the hammer back and only the slightest pressure necessary on the trigger to fire the gun.

Primarily, the double-action auto was invented as a safety feature, and has quickly caught on with police departments and, most recently, as the official sidearm of the U.S. Army. Many gun experts contend that the reason for the wide acceptance of the double-action autoloaders in the public sector is that people in the police and armed forces generally lack good shooting skills, and the double-action first shot stands in the way of many accidental shootings when the police are holding guns on suspects and when soldiers are handling their weapons.

Jeff Cooper says the double-action autoloader is a brilliant solution to a nonexistent problem. With the hammer cocked and the hammer safety on, the single-action auto will not go off until the safety is released and the trigger pulled. The chance of the safety's becoming disengaged while it is stored in a dresser drawer or even carried in a holster is very remote. And if it were disengaged, the trigger would still have to be pressed for the gun to discharge; that means two things gone wrong, which is most unlikely.

I personally have shot extensively with both single-action and double-action autos. Most double-action autos that I have tested have had an extremely hard and jerky first-shot trigger pull, and, frankly, I don't like most of them. There is, however, one model made by Sig Sauer that I own and like very much, and there are a couple of outstanding autos that use neither the double nor the single action, which I will review in the section on the individual guns. Finally, the autoloader is complicated enough so that it can be stored or carried in a variety of loaded conditions, much less susceptible to accidental discharge by an inquisitive child or a playful guest who may stumble upon it. As I mentioned, when the single-action auto has a round in the chamber and the hammer cocked back and locked, it is in the readiest condition a gun can be in. But it can be almost equally ready with a full clip in the gun but no cartridge in the chamber. The hammer can be pulled back manually and the trigger pressed with no danger of its firing a bullet. Yet a round can be chambered and the gun readied to fire by pulling the slide back and releasing it —"faster," as Jim Carmichel says, "than you can look at your watch and read the time."

There are, however, definite disadvantages to an autoloader, the least of which is a lot of broken fingernails while loading it. The principal drawback is a propensity for the autoloader to malfunction, and this tendency multiplies in the hands of a woman. To explain: the recoil of the bullet being fired works the slide to eject the used cartridge casing and seat a fresh round in the chamber. This is called felt recoil, and in most of the larger-caliber revolvers it can be quite a jolt. In the autoloader, the recoil is put to work, but in order to work it must have a strong grip and a locked wrist to work against. Women like me, who have weak wrists, will experience malfunctions in autoloaders that can be fired thousands of times without any problem by most men.

A competent gunsmith can minimize this malfunctioning tendency by lightening the spring that pushes the slide so it won't need such a secure base to push against, and wrist exercises and a good shooting stance will also help, but there may always be a problem for a great many women. Manually maneuvering the slide is just about impossible for me on most of the larger-caliber autos, and not too much can be done about that without compromising the function of the gun.

Also, if you are left-handed, as I am, you are at a disadvantage, because most standard autoloaders are made for right-handed shooters. If you decide on an autoloader, find one especially made for left-handed people. There is no additional cost.

In the final analysis, whereas the autoloader may be a superior combat handgun, the gun owner must handle an autoloading pistol frequently if she is to stay current with it and have confidence in its effectiveness. Considerably more instruction and practice are required with the autoloader, and malfunction drills must be memorized and rehearsed again and again for that one chance out of many when the gun will stop working because a spent cartridge casing didn't eject or a fresh cartridge wouldn't feed into the chamber. If you plan to put in the time to learn the gun thoroughly and practice with it once a week or at least every other week, then the autoloading pistol is hard to resist.

One last point about both a revolver and an autoloader. When you go to a gun store to buy your gun, have the guns you are interested in demonstrated to you by the salesperson and then manipulate the guns yourself. If you look at autoloaders, have each one you look at taken apart and reassembled, which you will have to do each time after shooting it in order to clean it. Some autoloaders are much more difficult to assemble after cleaning, and if you don't plan on handling the gun very often, you will soon forget how to assemble it. Then it won't be long until you forget to clean it after practice, and that is the biggest cause of stoppages in an autoloading pistol.

From my experience, and from the experience of every

expert I have talked with, each handgun should be brought to a competent gunsmith to be customized with a trigger-smoothing job for a revolver and a polishing job for the insides of an autoloader. Do not trust a new gun right out of the box, and do not trust a gunsmith who hasn't been factory-trained in your particular gun. Ask your gun dealer for names of gunsmiths who have been factory-trained, or ask your local police department for the name of their gunsmith, who will either be properly trained or will know of someone who is. A gun should be chosen very personally. You should know your gun as you know your jewelry or the contents of your wallet.

Before beginning an examination of specific handguns, something must be said about shotguns and rifles as weapons for self-defense.

LONG GUNS

The rifle, as was mentioned before, is the most potentially lethal of all firearms. Most of the hunting calibers have the capacity to place a bullet a great distance with extreme accuracy. At close range, a rifle bullet will pass through your target, the wall behind your target, and quite possibly across the street and through another wall, and will not even be stopped if it hits another human target. Rifles, even small .22-caliber rifles, are far too powerful to be used for home defense. They have tremendous killing power, but the self-defense firearm needs stopping power, not necessarily killing power. You want to stop an assault right then, not kill your assailant. A rifle has a 90-percent better chance of killing, but death may result two hours later from blood loss; in those two hours your assailant can cause you a lot of damage.

Some firearms experts recommend a shotgun for home defense. Their recommendation is sound if stopping power alone is considered. Without question, the shotgun will stop the forward progress of any man, and probably kill him before he hits the ground. But the shotgun, like the rifle, is a long gun, and the length of the barrel makes it hard for you to move around in close quarters and means the gun is more easily taken away.

The shotgun is called a field gun, and is different from a rifle because it was designed to be used in the open country for hunting birds. The shotgun shell, about the size of your thumb, contains anywhere from eight round pellets about the size of the hole in a three-ring hole punch, to more than six hundred tiny pellets, each a little larger than the head of a pin. The shotgun fires these pellets in a pattern, so aiming is not critical, as with a handgun or rifle, but the recoil of the shotgun from the expended shell is almost enough to knock you down, deafen you, and temporarily blind you if it is shot inside at night. A rifle shoots a bullet.

Most experts agree that the shotgun is a tactically sound choice of self-defense weapon in an ambush situation. In other words, if you were absolutely positive that an assailant was in your house to cause you grave bodily harm, and you had the time to lock yourself in your bedroom and take a position with a shotgun behind or to the side of your bed and wait until the door was broken in, the shotgun would absolutely stop the attack, usually with one shot.

The versatility of the shotgun pretty much stops there. You cannot conceal it, as you can a handgun; you cannot store it away from the inquisitive hands of a child and still easily get to it yourself, as you can with a handgun; you cannot safely keep it loaded and be certain that it will not accidentally discharge if it falls over or is dropped; and you must always use two hands when handling a shotgun, which compromises your control and may hinder you from telephoning the police if you are able to deter a crime without shooting your assailant.

Massad Ayoob has this advice about the shotgun for home defense: "Rely on a handgun as your primary home-defense firearm, using the shotgun only as last-resort artillery to defend the final refuge where you've huddled your family . . . and if that happens, lay things out in advance so you won't have to worry about overpenetration, and then load up with buckshot that will rip through walls, furniture, and any bad guys who have breached your walls with homicidal intent."

If you are going to choose a shotgun as a second weapon for your bedroom, I have found the 20-gauge shotgun much easier to use and a whole lot kinder to your shoulder. The 12-gauge shoots a bigger load, but the bigger the load, the bigger the recoil and the heavier the shotgun. Try them both if you can, and if you choose a 12-gauge or inherit one, hold it tight to your shoulder when you shoot it or it will give you a black-and-blue mark the size of a football, if it doesn't actually knock you down.

As for ammunition, Ayoob sees the shotgun as artillery and recommends what's called #1 buckshot, which shoots twenty-four pellets the size of pencil erasers at a velocity that will penetrate walls. However, if you live in an apartment or have neighbors nearby, such penetration is foolish. Therefore, when overpenetration cannot be risked, #8 or #9 birdshot, which sends out hundreds of BB-size pellets in a wider pattern with lesser velocity, is the best choice. And if you are going to shoot a 12-gauge shotgun, Federal Cartridge Company makes what they call Extra-Lite loads, which have maximum performance and an extra-low recoil.

Finally, if you decide to keep a shotgun, there are a number of different styles to choose from. The autoloading shotgun, just like the autoloading handgun, automatically feeds a cartridge into the chamber after each shot. It is the fastest-loading of all; in fact, it loads faster than you can pull the trigger, and as a result it is less safe, but infinitely more effective, if more than one shot is to be fired.

Autoloading shotguns are usually blocked so that they cannot accept more than three shells, to comply with state hunting regulations, but the block can easily be removed so that the gun will hold five shells, and something called a

Choate extender can be installed to increase the loading
capacity to seven shells. Beretta makes the best autoloading
shotgun I have seen in a moderate price range.

The next choice in a shotgun is the pump shotgun, so
called because it is manually loaded by pumping a shell
into the chamber while the front hand pulls back the slide
under the barrel, much like a self-wringing sponge floor
mop. Most police cars are equipped with pumps, and many
of the experts who recommend shotguns recommend
pumps. The police agencies prefer them because they feel
that pumping in each new shell after expending the old one
helps avoid an accidental discharge when their officers are
under stress and adrenaline has made them excited and
jumpy. The safety advantage of a pump over an autoloading
shotgun is an excellent reason to select it. The self-
defense experts find another advantage to the pump. It
makes a distinctive ratchet sound when a shell is pumped
into the chamber, and anyone who hears it once will never
forget the sound. This may just deter an assault without
your ever having to fire a round. For a woman, however,
the pumping mechanism is difficult to operate and usually
requires that the gun be pointed away from the target if
you are to eject the spent cartridge completely and cycle in
a new one—two problems that could result in an empty
gun pointing in the wrong direction at a critical time. If
you are strong enough to pull the slide back fourteen
inches, Winchester makes an inexpensive home-defense
gun called The Defender.

The final choice in shotguns is the break-top models.
These hinge open where the barrel meets the firing pin,
above the trigger. The barrel dips downward to accept either one shell or two shells and then clicks back into position, ready to fire. These guns are obviously slow and are
usually heavier than the others. As home-defense guns
they have the added disadvantage of being able to fire only
one or two shots before they must be broken open, balanced on the forearm, reloaded with shells (which you

have taken the time to locate), and then closed up and brought back into a firing position. Not for me, thanks.

So, if the shotgun is to be used as a last-resort weapon, the primary self-defense firearm will be the handgun. Choosing a handgun, as I have said, is not easy.

THE BEST GUN FOR YOU

The difficulty in selecting a suitable handgun comes in deciding first upon either an autoloader or a revolver, then upon a caliber that will suit your needs, then upon a size of handgun that you can handle comfortably, and then upon a grip or stock that can be gripped comfortably and will allow your trigger finger to touch the trigger at the proper place. Fitting these four requirements into one gun is quite a job. *If your gun does not fit you in any of these areas, you will not shoot it well, and that is nearly the same as not having a gun at all.*

Initially you must decide between an autoloader and a revolver, and this decision may very easily come before you have tried either one. If you don't think that you will have the time or interest to take lengthy and formal instruction in combat shooting and to practice frequently, make your first handgun a revolver. Later, if you find that you enjoy the sport of shooting, you can always sell your first gun and buy another that fills your more advanced needs. But your first gun should probably be a revolver.

Next choose a caliber. The rule of thumb, as Jeff Cooper says, is, shoot the biggest bullet you can handle, fast and accurately. There is a well-accepted range to choose from. For a self-defense gun, do not go below a .32 Magnum or above a .45. The .22-caliber can be very deadly as an assault weapon, but for self-defense it is next to useless. And anything above the .45 is too powerful for most men, and has so much recoil that it must be thought of as a one-shot gun for any woman.

When it comes to choosing size, remember that the

longer the barrel, the more accurate the gun will be at distances over seven yards, and the heavier the gun will be. A heavy handgun with a long barrel is a detriment only if you plan to conceal it in a purse or in a holster or will be carrying it in the car. Otherwise a heavy gun helps by absorbing much of the recoil, to keep the gun pointed on target for a quicker second shot. It is advisable, however, not to select a barrel over four inches in a revolver or under four inches in an autoloader. The two-inch barrel on the revolver is advised by most of the experts, because it is virtually impossible to have it taken away without getting at least one shot into your assailant. Barrels of less than four inches in an autoloader result in a surprisingly inaccurate gun with a sizable recoil in the larger calibers. With the autoloaders, weight is always an asset.

For women, the size of the grip may be the single most important element. If the grip is too big, your finger will reach the trigger too close to the fingertip, which either makes it very difficult to pull or causes you to jerk the gun off target. The trigger of a revolver must be pulled by the first crease or behind the crease of the trigger finger; on the single-action autoloader, the trigger is pulled by the pad in front of the first crease, under the nail bed of the trigger finger. Most grips can be changed to make the reach to the trigger lesser or greater, but some gun frames are just too big for the average woman's hand. Be careful: a gun whose trigger can't be pulled under adrenaline-distorted conditions is worse than useless.

The price you must pay for a well-built handgun varies from $150 to $1,200. For your first gun, be prepared to spend about $200. If you are on a real budget, you will find small, so-called Saturday Night Specials under $100, but these guns will not stand up to the rigors of frequent practice shooting. They will, however, hold together for at least a thousand rounds and shoot five or six bullets when you need them, and they are better than having no gun at all. For those who don't have budget restraints, the pricing of guns is pretty much like that of most other consumer goods: the more they cost, the better they are.

Next I will consolidate the advice from the world's best gunfighting experts, people I have trained with and interviewed on the advantages and disadvantages of the various-caliber handguns. To this evaluation I will add some of my own experience with specific guns that manufacturers have made available to me to test. And I have added a very valuable "intimidation factor" from Jim Carmichel's book, *The Women's Guide to Handguns,* which he explains "has never been attempted in shooting literature because firearms writers tend to concern themselves only with the results of actually fired shots. Fortunately, far more often than not, the purpose of a self-defense handgun is served without a shot being fired because assailants are often intimidated by the sight of a gun and are frightened away. The size of the gun and, especially, the size of the hole at the muzzle is an important factor in this intimidation psychology."

.22-CALIBER

The smallest yet most popular caliber made is the .22. Almost every handgun manufacturer makes either a .22 revolver or .22 autoloader, and the number of .22 rifles just might outnumber all other rifles combined. Ammunition is very inexpensive, and comes in .22 short, .22 Long Rifle, and .22 Winchester Magnum Rimfire.

This is the training caliber and the tin-can caliber; it is not the self-defense caliber. Although the .22 Long Rifle and the more powerful .22 Winchester Magnum Rimfire are very lethal if a bullet from one hits a vital spot, they are not stoppers.

However, one outstanding feature to a .22 handgun is that there are models small enough and light enough to be carried concealed in the smallest purse or in the pocket of the lightest blazer. Many policemen carry a .22 autoloader

as a backup gun strapped to their ankles, but no professional depends on the .22 as a primary weapon except as-
sassins, who have the time to zero in on a shot to the head,
as apparently Sirhan Sirhan did to Senator Robert Kennedy in 1968. You will recall, though, that President Reagan was hit with a .22-caliber bullet by John Hinckley and
didn't even know he was shot until his motorcade had him
almost back to the White House, where his bodyguard
noticed he was bleeding.

If you can own more than a couple of handguns, a .22
Long Rifle revolver or autoloader should be the second or
third one you own. I have talked to many women who own
a .22-caliber handgun and continue to be amazed by how
many times they carry it when no other gun could possibly
be carried.

INTIMIDATION VALUE: minimal
MY FAVORITE: *Beretta Model 21*

.25-CALIBER

This caliber is continually referred to by ammunition experts as feeble and inaccurate. It is available only in autoloaders, and should be avoided because of its small bullet,
slow speed, and little stopping power. If that isn't enough
reason to stay away, the .25-caliber ammunition is also
very expensive.

.32-CALIBER

Climbing up the scale, the .32-caliber is the first caliber
that can be considered a self-defense size. Handguns in this
caliber are plentiful and are usually inexpensive.

Ammunition for a .32-caliber comes in four varieties.
The oldest dates back to a turn-of-the-century design by
Smith & Wesson, and can be thought of as a .32 short with
a lightweight bullet and slow speed. More powerful is the
.32 Smith & Wesson Long, Model 31, and the .32 Auto-

matic. And, finally, the most powerful of the .32s is the .32 H & R Magnum, which is relatively new and is the only .32 load that approaches effective man-stopping power.

INTIMIDATION VALUE: good
MY FAVORITE: *Charter Arms .32 H & R Magnum Police Undercover*

.380 AUTO

This caliber is my personal favorite. The large-caliber guys quickly dismiss the .380 as puny, but my tests have shown it to be powerful enough to do quite a lot of damage, and easy to shoot. It is a real mistake to choose a gun that isn't fun to shoot and that overpowers and hurts your hands. The .380 comes in a variety of high-tech, high-quality autoloaders. It is small enough to be carried in a purse or hidden in the hand, and lightweight enough to be concealed in the pocket.

INTIMIDATION VALUE: excellent
MY FAVORITE: *Sig Sauer Model 230*

9MM LUGER (9MM PARABELLUM)

This, as I mentioned earlier, is the European entry in the .38-caliber field, and without question the most popular caliber in Europe and gaining in the United States. It is used mainly in autoloaders and automatic weapons, has just replaced the traditional .45-caliber in the U.S. armed forces, and is quickly replacing the .38-caliber revolvers in many police departments throughout the country.

The recommended bullet weight for the 9mm is 115 grains. A bullet of this weight comes in a cartridge that propels the bullet at a very high speed with a respectable stopping power.

Most of the new breed of high-tech autoloaders are in this caliber, and 9mm ammunition is made by every cartridge manufacturer at prices that are affordable. The 9mm guns are on the expensive side, priced between $300 and $1,200.

The 9mm is an excellent choice for a home-defense gun. Though there are some small, easily concealed models, the 9mm autoloader is known for its capacity to hold a great number of cartridges; and as a result the 9s are usually pretty big.

> INTIMIDATION VALUE: excellent
> MY FAVORITES: *Glock 17*
> *Heckler & Koch P7M8*

The two guns I have chosen as favorites are unique and user-friendly of all the 9mm autoloaders I had the opportunity to test. Most of the 9s are double-action and extremely hard for me to work. The Glock is an Austrian pistol with a trigger that pulls double-action every shot. It is much like a revolver, except that it shoots straighter and faster and holds eighteen rounds of ammunition. It is lightweight and has tested to be almost indestructible. It will shoot any brand of ammunition with almost no malfunctioning. In fact, Glock has tested the pistol without any malfunctions for more than ten thousand rounds. It is surprisingly inexpensive for a pistol of this quality, and should not be overlooked if you are buying an autoloader.

The Heckler & Koch P7 is the Rolls-Royce of 9mm pistols. It is the only other 9mm that has a special trigger mechanism. This is called a squeeze-cocker, because the front of the grip must be squeezed and depressed into the grip in order to arm the trigger. If the grip is not squeezed and held in, the internal hammer will not strike the cartridge to fire the bullet. It isn't easy to depress the grip bar, which could be a problem for some women, but the safety advantage around children and in the hands of a would-be aggressor unfamiliar with the pistol is well worth the effort it may take to learn to operate it yourself. It is also one of the smallest and most compact of the full-capacity 9s, and can easily be concealed. If you can afford the price tag, and if you have any concern about your gun falling into the wrong hands, this is the gun for you, bar none.

.38 SMITH & WESSON

This is an obsolete cartridge for an obsolete revolver. It was the popular forerunner to the current .38 Special, and many used .38 Smith & Wesson revolvers are still around. It has moderate stopping power. If you are given one, take it and have confidence in it.

Its intimidation value is excellent.

.38 SPECIAL

The .38 Special is the most popular cartridge and works in a greater variety of revolvers than any other caliber in the world. It is the standard issue for law enforcement in the United States and is a cherished caliber in Europe, where the 9mm rules.

From my experience, and from the advice of all the professionals, your first gun should be a revolver and your first revolver should be a .38 Special.

Many believe that the .38 Special is the smallest of the self-defense calibers that should be considered; others believe that it is the largest that can be handled by a woman; everyone agrees that the .38 Special has the speed, accuracy, and power to get the job done.

When choosing a .38 Special revolver, remember that the longer the barrel and the heavier the weight of the gun, the more accurate it will be and the less recoil you will feel. You will enjoy practicing more with a heavier gun, and will feel a lot more confident and look more formidable with it in your hands. You will not, however, want to carry it outside the house, and on the occasion when you may feel safer having your gun with you, you will regret having such a big, uncomfortable weapon. The longest barrel you should consider is four inches. The heaviest revolver should be what they call a medium frame. A three-inch barrel is a good compromise and will allow you to conceal the gun in the house better and carry it if you absolutely have to.

The small, lightweight .38 Special revolvers are numerous and are relatively inexpensive. The smallest have two-inch barrels and hold only five cartridges. These are called small frames. Their advantage in maneuverability and concealability is countered by their inaccuracy at a distance beyond twenty feet, man-size recoil, and ability to hold one less bullet. If you plan to carry your gun concealed—and a gun should never be carried otherwise—the small-frame .38 Special is ideal.

INTIMIDATION VALUE: excellent
MY FAVORITE MEDIUM FRAMES:
Rossi Model M851 (stainless)
Ruger Speed-Six Model 738 (stainless)
Smith & Wesson Model 10 (blue finish)

MY FAVORITE SMALL FRAMES:
Smith & Wesson Model 49 Bodyguard
(two-inch barrel, blue finish)
Charter Arms Undercover
(two-inch barrel, blue finish)
Taurus Model 85
(two-inch barrel, blue finish)

.357 MAGNUM

The .357 Magnum is a beefed-up .38 Special—in fact, the .357 revolver can also use .38 Special cartridges, but not the other way around—and is the first of the really high-power rounds. The FBI made this caliber famous and still uses it. It is a tremendous man-stopper, almost too good. It has the bullet speed and power to kill large game, including bears.

The .357 Magnum is an overkill caliber for home defense. It will power a bullet through walls, appliances, car doors, and people. And for home defense or self-defense on the street it is a liability.

Shooting a .357 revolver with a .357 cartridge is a singular act of courage. The noise and the recoil are enough to make you want to drop the gun after the first shot, and anyone standing alongside a .357 on a shooting line moves away from the compression each shot produces; it is a horrible caliber.

However, the revolvers built to handle the .357—there are some autoloaders for real masochists—are excellent guns that are made hefty enough to withstand the tremendous power of the .357 cartridge and are also able to handle the wide range of .38 Special ammo, which has more than adequate stopping power and is far more inexpensive for practice.

If you will be buying a revolver to keep in the house, you are better off buying a .357 and loading it with .38 Special ammunition. For an emergency piece of equipment, it is always better to have as many options as possible. With a .357 revolver, you have the option of practicing with .38 Special cartridges and upgrading to the .357 Magnum whenever you find a need. You will not, however, find this medium- or large-frame gun easy to carry concealed.

INTIMIDATION VALUE: excellent
MY FAVORITE: *Smith & Wesson Model 13 (three-inch barrel)*

.41 MAGNUM

This caliber is designed for big-game hunters. More powerful than the .357 Magnum, the .41 Magnum is unmanageable in the hands of anyone but experts, and even they have no reason to choose this caliber unless they live around alligators or rhinoceroses. Its intimidation value is very high.

.44 SPECIAL

Another of the overkill cartridges. It would not be recommended except for a fine revolver made by Charter Arms in this caliber called the Bulldog.

> INTIMIDATION VALUE: maximum
> MY FAVORITE: *Charter Arms Bulldog .44 Special (blue finish)*

.44 MAGNUM

A favorite of outdoorsmen, this is one of the world's most powerful handguns. It is far too powerful for a home-defense weapon, and even the most compact models weigh close to three pounds. The weight of the revolvers in this caliber makes the .44 Magnum relatively easy to shoot and exceptionally accurate. If you have an opportunity to shoot one, take a good stance and try it. It is so powerful, it is actually fun to shoot.

> INTIMIDATION VALUE: maximum
> MY FAVORITE: *Smith & Wesson Model 629 (six-inch barrel, stainless steel)*

.45 AUTOMATIC

This may just be the most famous caliber in handgun history. It has been the official handgun of the U.S. military since 1911, and is considered by many to be the epitome of self-defense weapons.

If you have the hand strength to work the slide and have the interest to stay current with an autoloader, the .45 is my choice for a self-defense gun.

There are a number of manufacturers of quality .45 autos, and a number of different sizes and weights to choose from. Remember that the smaller and lighter the gun is, the less accurate it will be and the more recoil it will have. With a caliber this large, recoil is a definite consideration. My suggestion is that you find a shooting range with rental guns and try the .45 auto in a small frame and in a large frame. I found the large-frame models a little too difficult to manipulate, and the small-frame models a little too jumpy to be fun. They both, however, are very impressive.

INTIMIDATION VALUE: maximum
MY FAVORITE SMALL FRAME: *Star PD*
MY FAVORITE LARGE FRAME: *Springfield Armory,*
                         1911-A1 Combat
                         Commander

Used Guns

All guns, handgun and long guns alike, wear out after having a certain number of rounds fired through them. They do not wear out from disuse, and rust is the only thing that can ruin a steel gun. Stainless-steel guns, of course, don't rust, and are almost a necessity if you live around water or in an exceptionally humid area. With the better-known and well-made guns, it may take a hundred thousand rounds of ammunition to wear them out, but with the cheaper handgun the life expectancy may extend to only a few thousand rounds or less. So be careful if you find a used gun from a private source. Have it inspected by a competent gunsmith, who should measure the tolerances of the barrel and chambers and check for cracked frames and worn parts.

Buying a used gun from a gun dealer should be safer than buying one from a friend or out of the newspaper, but you may find that a used gun from any source is not that much less expensive than a new one. And if all you can save is thirty or forty dollars, don't take the chance on a used gun.

CUSTOMIZING YOUR HANDGUN

New guns are made on assembly lines with no special features or adjustments for any particular shooter. All new guns should be taken to a gunsmith trained by the factory for that specific gun, to be customized for you. Some experts say that it is absolutely imperative to have a new gun worked on by a gunsmith; others say it is recommended but not necessary unless the gun is not performing the way it should; I have to think it is a safety measure that should not be overlooked for any reason. Gunsmiths' services are surprisingly inexpensive; everything they must do to tune up your gun will probably not cost more than fifty dollars for a revolver and less than a hundred dollars for an autoloader. That has to be money well spent.

Massad Ayoob will not own a handgun unless it is first worked on by a gunsmith. He says *In the Gravest Extreme:* "Too hasty a pull on a standard Smith & Wesson revolver's trigger which may require a 14-pound pressure on the two-pound weapon, through 'hesitation points' that occur in the mechanism where the moving parts may not have been finely hand polished—can make the difference between a shot that misses or perhaps goes through the flesh of the attacker's arm, and one that strikes center and instantly stops the threat he is presenting to innocent life."

The trigger on a revolver must be smoothed out to get rid of the inevitable hesitation points, and must be lightened to accommodate a woman's weaker hand strength. Be careful, though, about having the trigger lightened. If it is lightened too much, the hammer will not have the power to strike the cartridge with enough force to fire the bullet. Again, a competent gunsmith must be found to do any work on a gun. Ask around, and don't be embarrassed to ask to see their work and try squeezing a few triggers they have worked on.

The next and perhaps the most important after-market customizing that must be done to almost every revolver, and especially to a woman's gun, is the installation of the proper-size grips.

The single most important component of shooting any handgun straight is the position of the gun in the shooting hand and the position the shooting finger has on the trigger. Not only are a strong and proper grip of the handgun and trigger control the key to accurate shot placement, but improper grip and trigger control are the least-detected mistake by shooters, whose poor performance with a handgun may be blamed on a myriad of other problems.

In preparation for shooting, the handgun is grasped by the stock of the gun frame. The stock is enclosed by grips, usually made of either wood or plastic. On a revolver, the grips determine the size of the stock and the distance of the shooting finger to the trigger. For most people, factory grips on a revolver are uncomfortable and make holding the gun awkward; for many women with small hands, factory grips not only are clumsy but do not distance the trigger finger properly.

On the single-action autoloader, you must press the trigger with the tip of your shooting finger. This is usually learned and practiced until it becomes natural for most people with large hands, and it is why even the largest single-action autoloader can be easily handled by women with small hands—the shooting finger reaches the trigger with the tip naturally.

With double-action autoloaders it is quite a different story. The first shot is a double-action trigger pull, just as with a revolver. The first joint of the shooting finger must pull the trigger to fire the first shot; then you must reposition your hand so that the fingertip fires all the rest of the shots. This repositioning is a problem for everyone, and especially difficult for a woman. Like many people, I do not like most double-action autoloaders for this reason. You can almost count on missing your first shot, because the double-action trigger on almost all of the double-action autos is stiff and jerky, and you can bet you will miss your second, single-action shot if you don't reposition your shooting finger. It is a lot to think about even in practice, and I'm sure it will mean two wasted shots and a loss of precious moments in the heat of combat.

Grips don't usually help size the reach to the trigger in most autoloaders, and in fact most cannot be changed. But in revolvers it is almost mandatory that you find grips to replace the factory issue. There are many after-market grip makers. Pachmayr Gun Works makes unique rubber grips in many sizes and shapes for every revolver and all of the autos whose grips are replaceable. These rubberized and textured grips afford a very secure hold on the stock of the gun, and dampen the recoil somewhat. Many of their models, however, increase the size of the stock and lengthen the distance between the shooting finger and the trigger— exactly what you don't want—so, if you find Pachmayrs that feel comfortable, have the salesman put them on your gun and pay close attention to where your shooting finger touches the trigger, then practice firing the gun unloaded in the store many, many times before you purchase them.

Besides the commercial grip makers like Pachmayr, there are a number of custom shops throughout the country that make the most beautiful pistol grips out of exotic hardwoods. One custom grip maker I am familiar with by reputation is Jim Hoag in Canoga Park, California. Craig Spegel from Hillsboro, Oregon, is another. An excellent grip maker who actually makes them specifically for women is Russ Maloni of Russwood Custom Pistol Grips in East Aurora, New York. I have used Spegel's grips and Russwood grips on a number of the guns I tested for this book, and I can report that they are not only marvelously comfortable and have improved my shooting, but are sculptures of the most fascinating swirls and patterns of wood, so that I want to display them as I would other works of art in my home. As I have said, it is important to develop an intimacy with your handgun, and custom-made grips will help you accomplish that quickly.

AMMUNITION

After you have selected the caliber of revolver or autoloader you want, you must next decide upon one kind of ammunition to use for practice and another kind to keep in your gun for a defense load.

Ammunition is expensive, especially for the larger calibers. It is not uncommon to spend as much as fifteen dollars for a box of fifty rounds of .45-caliber ammo. And at that price either you don't practice with your gun very often, or you spend a lot of money keeping current with your shooting skills and become painfully aware with each shot that you just spent thirty cents or more. Practicing at thirty cents a shot quickly takes the fun out of shooting, even if you can afford it. So you will find target loads to practice with, and high-quality ammo to keep in your gun when you are at home or traveling.

Target loads are usually soft lead bullets called wadcutters or semi-wadcutters. They are square in front so that they make nice, sharp holes in your paper targets. Semi-wadcutters have a smaller flat leading edge and then are stepped into a larger flat surface. Both are soft lead bullets used for target shooting, but the semi-wadcutters also make an acceptable defense load, and are the choice of many police departments.

For target practice you will want to find reloaded ammunition. Every gun shop sells reloads, and the more shooting you do, the more people you will find who reload their own ammunition and will reload yours for less cost than the stores. The key to reloads is that you gather up your spent cartridges, or brass, after you shoot and give them to the gun shop or reloader, who will either exchange them for reloaded cartridges or reload your brass and give them back to you. You can expect to pay somewhere between four and six dollars per box of fifty cartridges for reloads in the larger calibers of .38, 9mm, and .45. Smaller calibers are not usually reloaded.

Ammunition to be kept in your defense handgun is made by a number of manufacturers in a variety of styles. American ammunition manufacturers make the finest ammo in the world, so the brand name doesn't matter when it comes to safe, reliable cartridges. The differences in brand names are important when it comes to bullet design and performance.

From all the shooting schools I have attended in preparing for this book, and all the ballistics experts I have interviewed, there is a clear picture of the best design for a self-defense bullet and the most respected manufacturer. *Hollow-point bullets* are the recommended choice of every expert, and Federal Cartridge Company is one of the most respected makers of ammunition.

Hollow-point bullets are hollow from the leading edge of the bullet back almost to where the brass case encloses it. They look something like a cookie cutter, and perform so much better than standard round-nose bullets that they are not even in the same class. The hollow bullet is designed to spread and more than double its size after it enters the body. It has tremendous stopping power because it wreaks such enormous damage, and is less likely to pass right through your target and endanger someone in the background. Hollow points also ricochet less than standard bullets, which again minimizes the likelihood of wounding an innocent person who may be within range. Following are the Federal cartridges recommended for the various calibers:

CALIBER	BULLET STYLE	BULLET WEIGHT IN GRAINS
AUTOLOADER		
.380	JHP	90
9mm	JHP	115
.45	JHP	185
REVOLVER		
.32 Magnum	JHP	85
.38 Special	SWHP	158
.357 Magnum	JHP	125
.41 Magnum	JHP	210
.44 Magnum	JHP	180

JHP—Jacketed Hollow Point
SWHP—Semi-Wadcutter Hollow Point

Bullet selection for an autoloader is much more critical than for a revolver. All home-defense loads should mushroom or spread when they hit the target, as a hollow point does, but in an autoloader the cartridge must also automatically feed into the firing chamber. Autoloaders are designed to use smooth, round bullets so they won't get snagged on the way to the chamber. Because hollow points are not smooth and round, they have been designed with a metal jacket surrounding the hollow bullet, enabling them to slide smoothly into place to be fired. With revolvers, bullet shape cannot interfere with the function of the gun, which means the jacket is unimportant. Federal jackets most of its bullets, so the lead is covered and won't foul the barrel as much after prolonged shooting.

There are two other styles of cartridges for the handgun. One is called shot loads, designed much like a shotgun shell, whose dozens of tiny balls of lead shot are fanned out toward the target. Unlike the shotgun shell, which is very lethal, the shot loads for a handgun are relatively harmless, causing many painful punctures of the skin but having no stopping power unless the target is at point-blank range. You wouldn't want to bet your life that shot loads would stop an assailant.

Finally, there is a relatively new cartridge now available for almost every caliber called Glaser Safety Slugs. Glasers are really the first new design in cartridges in one hundred years, and they seem to be the ultimate in a self-defense load. The bullet in the end of a Glaser cartridge is not lead like all the others. It is a brass cup that is filled with minute, irregular-shaped metal fragments. After the cup has been filled with the fragments, it is sealed with a round plastic plug to hold the fragments in the cup and shape the cup in the form of a regular bullet. The cup-bullet is then forced into a gunpowder-filled cartridge case, just the way a lead bullet is fitted, and the result is a cartridge that looks like any other but has a blue plastic tip. Upon impact, this plastic tip is forced into the cup, which expands the cup and disperses the hundreds of fragments. These dispersed fragments and the expanded metal cup are more damaging and have more knockdown power than any other bullet ever made for any particular-caliber handgun.

Actually the Glasers have been around for some time. It is just within the last few years that they have been perfected to the point where they will expand every time and reliably feed through the autoloader. The design of the Glaser has been worked out and the quality control upgraded, placing the Glaser Safety Slug at the top of the list of ideal self-defense ammunition. They do not ricochet. They will not overpenetrate a target to go through a wall or another person. And they shoot straight. They just can't be counted on to go too much farther than thirty yards.

To give you some idea of the destructive power Glasers have, I tested them along with round-nose and hollow-point bullets on watermelons. I used .380, 9mm, .38 Special, and .45-calibers.

The conventional round-nose lead bullets put a nice

crisp hole in the front of the melons, and exited with just about the same-size hole. In some cases the round bullets cracked the melons because of the speed at which they passed through, but mostly they just made holes.

The hollow-point bullets in all the same calibers cracked every melon going in, and took out large pieces from the back when they exited. The larger the caliber, the greater the damage—although the Federal .380 auto hollow point surprised me with its impressive power.

But whereas the hollow points impressively broke up every melon into more than five or six pieces, the Glasers, in every caliber, made juice out of every melon. I am astounded at the effectiveness of this cartridge. There were no malfunctions and no misfires in more than two hundred rounds.

Now here is the bad news. The Glaser Safety Slug costs more than two dollars per cartridge. You do not practice with Glasers. But if you are going to load your self-defense handgun with them, you should at least shoot a dozen of them, to feel the difference from your practice ammo. They are a hot load; that is, the cartridge contains an extra amount of gunpowder, to launch the bullet at a very fast rate, to assure that the plastic tip gets forced into the cup when it hits the target. And it is a light bullet, so it may shoot higher than the heavier, lead bullet in your practice ammo. Try Glasers out on melons. You will want to feel these differences before you load your gun with them and keep them in your gun for an emergency situation.

CLEANING YOUR GUN

When you purchase your gun, also buy a cleaning kit specifically designed to clean the kind of gun and caliber you possess.

Cleaning your gun is mandatory. Every shot leaves a residue of powder and lead fragments. Worse than that, your hands leave perspiration salts and body oils, which permeate and corrode gunmetal.

Once, I didn't bother cleaning a revolver after shooting one hundred rounds, and during the next practice session I had so many repeat malfunctions that I had to quit for the day.

Cleaning takes only about ten minutes and is simple to do. Some people even say it's a relaxing chore. Since gun mechanisms vary, follow the gun manufacturer's cleaning instructions. One of the mistakes many people make is applying too much oil; most guns don't need it.

Before you begin cleaning, remember all safety procedures and assume the gun is loaded. Don't proceed without checking to make sure that it is unloaded.

Gun Leather

There is no satisfactory way to carry a handgun concealed. Period. Every holster, every method to conceal a handgun is flawed more ways than it works, and this is especially true for women.

If you carry a handgun, not only do you want to conceal it from view, but it is of utmost importance that you get to it as quickly as possible when you need it. The two goals, it seems, are mutually incompatible.

In self-defense, time is working against you and working for the aggressor. If a gun is needed outside the home for self-defense, it is needed without a fraction of a second to spare. The better concealed it is, the longer it takes to present. And the longer it takes to have the gun in your hand and pointing at your target, the more ineffective, even useless it will be.

For a woman, the handbag is the best and easiest place to conceal a handgun. It is also the most difficult place of concealment from which to retrieve a gun hastily, and presents the easiest way for you to lose your weapon in a scuffle or a purse-snatching. If you only occasionally carry a gun and have no obvious or identifiable threat to face regularly, the handbag will probably be the only carry method to consider. Safariland of Monrovia, California, makes a number of leather purses designed with special compartments to conceal a handgun that can be reached without opening the purse. This is faster than fumbling around inside a normal purse, when you must first find and then produce the gun. The Safariland purses offer the option of grasping the gun while it is still concealed, should trouble come toward you. Many experts say, incidentally, that the shoulder strap of any purse in which you carry a gun should be reinforced with a thin wire cable inside, so that the bag cannot be torn from the strap by a purse-snatcher. Not a bad idea.

There are all kinds of holsters: holsters for the belt on the strong side, whereby you just drop the shooting hand and draw the gun; holsters for the belt on the weak side, whereby you reach across and cross-draw the gun; holsters for the small of the back, the ankle, the shoulder, the thigh, for around the waist under a blouse, inside the waistband, and wallet holsters. For anyplace leather can be attached to the body, a holster is available. And I daresay that nobody who wears a holster to conceal a gun is happy either with the way it conceals or with the time required to get the gun out of it. All holsters have problems.

If you carry a gun professionally, or if you choose to carry a gun all the time, you must find a holster to carry it in. For women, I think the shoulder holster is the most adaptable to fashion and the easiest to reach. You must always wear a blazer, heavy sweater, or coat to conceal it, but the shoulder holster is just about your only choice. All the belt holsters and inside-the-waistband holsters require at least a 1.25-inch-wide belt tightly buckled, and that is just not possible for a woman unless she wears jeans and a mid-length jacket.

If your choice of handgun is one of the large autoloaders or a medium-frame revolver with a four-inch barrel, there may be no successful way to carry it concealed except in a purse. Even men have a difficult time concealing the big guns.

Bianchi and Safariland, both of California, are the top commercial manufacturers of quality gun leather. Both offer a great variety of holsters that can be seen at most gun stores, and both have excellent catalogues, in which you can see all the styles and how they work before you go out to sample them yourself. The president of Bianchi, by the way, is a woman.

There are a number of custom leather manufacturers who make the gun-leather equivalent of fine English saddles. I'm not familiar with all of them, but I can recommend four whose work I have found to be extraordinary.

Andy Arratoonian of Horseshoe Leather Products in Great Britain makes excellent gun leather. His holsters are especially suited for women, if you can find a place to wear a holster, because Arratoonian uses only English saddle leather, which is lighter in weight than most American gun leather, and not so thick and bulky.

Ken Null of Hanover, Pennsylvania, provides about the most beautiful custom-made holsters I have ever seen; especially impressive is his shoulder holster. Then there is Milt Sparks of Idaho City, Idaho, Bruce Nelson of Tucson, Arizona, and Davis Leather Company in Walnut, California. All are true craftsmen, and if you carry a handgun frequently, good gun leather is as important as the gun you carry.

So, you see, there is a lot to consider and a lot to know about handguns, ammunition, and equipment. Once you get started shooting, you will absorb a lot of what I have just discussed. And don't be afraid to ask questions at the shooting range or in the gun stores. Just be wary of the answers until you have tested them for yourself. Everybody and his brother has an opinion about which gun and what ammunition is best, and most of those opinions are dead wrong.

10

Gun Defense

WHEN THE DUST settles from the debates about the pros and cons of handgun ownership and the politics and morality of using lethal force to defend against lethal threat, and the proper handgun is purchased for a confirmed need, becoming proficient at gun defense immediately becomes the most important issue of all.

Handling a handgun in a self-defense situation is called combat shooting. It is, after all, a combat situation if you must defend yourself against an aggressor who may be stalking through your home or waiting in ambush with criminal intent. "Combat," however, being mostly a military word, has been replaced by the word "practical" for civilian functions. So, if you own a gun for self-defense, you must learn "practical shooting," which includes reloading, marksmanship, and tactics.

There are many practical-shooting schools throughout the country. I have attended all the major ones and throughout this book have quoted most of the directors, who have offered to share their knowledge and specialized skills so that American women can feel safe and continue to enjoy all the freedoms granted to every citizen. What follows comes from more than two hundred hours of training with the top combat masters of the country.

Each school has a slightly different emphasis to its training, and some techniques are even contradictory, but everything I have learned has been carefully thought out and researched by each of these talented and caring teachers. I have attempted to take the best of what applies to women, and offer differing opinions where they apply.

There is no substitute for having hands-on instruction, but if this is not available it is my intention to give you enough information in this chapter to become a competent practical shooter, if you want to and are willing to do the necessary exercises and practice. I must warn you at the outset, however, that it is not easy to shoot well under pressure, and shooting under pressure is what you must be trained and prepared to do.

GUN HANDLING

Tactics are far more important than marksmanship in any encounter where a handgun is to be used. However, good, accurate shooting builds confidence in the shooter and influences greatly the tactical advantage in a gun-defense situation. So begin your training by aspiring to become an exceptional marksman; the rest will come easily.

When you first purchase a gun, have a salesperson at a gun store show you all the features on the gun you plan to buy; if you already own a handgun, take it to a gun store for an update. Have the salesperson show you all the safeties, how to work all the features, and how to disassemble and reassemble your gun. Even if you didn't buy your gun from him, most gun salespeople will be happy to give you instructions on what they know best. Have the salesman show you everything your gun does; then take the gun from him and show him everything you've just learned. Take the gun apart and put it back together two or three times in front of him; if you have to, go back the next day or the next week and do it again, if you have trouble at home by yourself. You must learn your gun inside and out to be a confident and competent shooter.

All the experts agree that practicing with an unloaded gun is what really develops a good marksman. This is called dry-firing, and its importance begins the day you take home your first gun and ends only on the day you decide that you will never touch a handgun again.

When you buy your handgun, or if you own a gun now and have never had formal instruction in shooting, your training starts by resisting the temptation to go out and shoot immediately. At least a week or two of familiarization and dry-firing before shooting live ammunition will help you develop dependable shooting skills. In fact, shooting without a groundwork of sound preparation will most likely retard your progress, or may even fix habits and reactions that forever keep you from becoming competent.

To begin with, following the instructions in the manual that comes with your gun, clean the gun thoroughly. New guns are coated with oil, which must be cleaned off. This is especially important if you have purchased an autoloader. Heavy oil on the parts of an autoloader will attract dust and particles of dirt, and represents a sure way of causing the gun to misfire. In addition to cleaning your gun, this exercise is the beginning of becoming familiar with your equipment, and being familiar and comfortable with your gun is vital to you in becoming a competent shooter.

It is necessary to point out right here that concerns for safety are primary every time you pick up any gun. It seems that anyone ever shot by accident has been shot with a gun thought to be unloaded. There is an easy way to prevent an accidental discharge: *consider every gun to be loaded; check to see if the gun is loaded when someone hands you one and every time you walk away from a gun that you have been handling; never allow the muzzle—the business end of the barrel—to cover anything you are not willing to destroy; and keep your finger off the trigger and outside the trigger guard until your gun is pointed at your target and you are ready to fire.* If you are meticulous about adhering to these rules, you will never have an accident with any gun.

You may feel a little silly checking the condition of a gun that was just checked by someone who passed it to you, but do it. You may feel overly cautious inspecting your gun to verify that it is unloaded after you have been sitting alone on the couch practice-firing with an empty gun for the last twenty minutes before getting up to answer the telephone, but do it. Open the cylinder of a revolver and see light through every chamber. Stick a finger up the magazine well of an autoloader to be certain that the magazine is not inserted, and carefully pinch the slide back to see through the ejection port that there is no cartridge in the chamber.

There is protocol among handgunners, and it has to do mostly with safety. You will be respected as a responsible practitioner if you check the condition of every gun whenever it is handed to you and always pass a handgun with the muzzle pointed up in the air or down-range, never crossing or sweeping anybody. Practice these until they become habits and you will never have an accident or be in the way of someone else's negligence. And if someone you are around is handling a gun unsafely, it is your responsibility to instruct him or her in the proper procedure—or to leave the area.

When you bring the gun home, make sure it is unloaded and then clean it. For the autoloader owners this is not so easy, one of the drawbacks to the autos, as I have said before. Some are easier to disassemble than others, but they all require a series of steps that must be followed exactly the same way each time, and must be done often enough to be etched in your memory. So, if you own an autoloader, disassemble and reassemble your gun every day for at least a week, or until you can do it as agilely and quickly as you can brush your hair.

Both autoloader and revolver owners should spend at

least one half hour each day just handling the unloaded gun. While you are watching television in the evening is a perfect time. Again, always make sure that your gun is unloaded each time you pick it up; while you are sitting comfortably watching television, get to know your weapon. Aim it at the TV or at lamps around the room and pull the trigger; pull the slide back on an auto and lock it back if your gun has that feature, then unlock it and slide it forward again—slowly. Never let the slide snap forcefully closed unless there is a round in the chamber, and always let it snap forcefully forward when a round *is* in the chamber. More about that later. Switch hands, aim, and fire at the television. Handle your gun as much as you can for the first few days, until it feels like part of your hand and at least one spot on your hand is sore from the unaccustomed contact with the strange piece of metal.

Since you will be dry-firing hundreds of times just in the first week you own it, and thousands upon thousands of times during your ownership of the weapon, check with the manufacturer (not a gun store) to make sure that dry-firing doesn't hurt the mechanism. As a general rule, auto-loaders can be dry-fired without any problems, but some revolvers cannot stand the continuous crash of the hammer falling on an empty chamber. Gun stores sell a plastic disc that can be placed in the back of the cylinder of a revolver and will act as a cushion for the falling firing pin, preventing any damage from dry-firing.

After a session or two a day for the best part of a week handling your gun, you will begin to feel comfortable with the gun in either hand; if you are anything like me, you will actually find yourself liking the shape, weight, and texture of the instrument. Now we can move on to the next step in becoming a competent practical shooter, the proper techniques for loading and unloading live ammunition.

During this first week of familiarization, there was no ammunition in or around your gun. Now live ammunition will be used for the first time, and will continue to be available as long as you own the gun. You are going to get sick of hearing it over and over, but attention to safety becomes vital at this point. From now on you must assume that your gun is always loaded, and you absolutely must keep your finger off the trigger and outside the trigger guard until you have pointed the gun at your intended target and are ready to destroy that target. At first you will have to be very deliberate about these rules, but soon they will be second nature. Now is the time to be compulsive.

LOADING THE REVOLVER

The cylinder release is on the left side of the revolver, behind the cylinder. To load the revolver, the cylinder release is pushed in the only direction it can go, and the cylinder is nudged out of its locked position in the frame of the gun by the two middle fingers of your weak hand, while the trigger guard rests in the palm just behind the backs of the knuckles. The two middle fingers that pushed open the cylinder maintain pressure on the cylinder to keep it from returning.

With the cylinder open and the revolver held firmly in the weak hand, tip the muzzle on the barrel of the gun downward as far as your wrist will allow and load the cartridges one at a time. You might as well start out loading your revolver the most advanced way right from the beginning. First of all, when you are loading cartridges one at a time, as you will be for a while, you should put all the cartridges that you are going to load in the palm of the hand that is holding the gun. It is a lot to have in one hand, but having the cartridges anyplace else only necessitates another step, reaching into your pocket or bending over to get the shells out of a box on the floor, and in practical shooting time is of the essence.

Every move, every action, every reaction must be pared of all excess time and be done the same way every time. It has been found in study after study that, under the highly

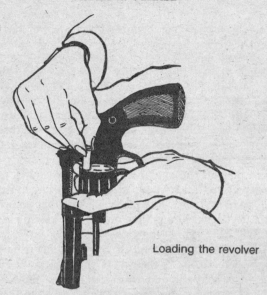

Loading the revolver

stressful conditions of a gun-defense incident, the shooter will do only that which he or she has been trained to do. In other words, if you handle your gun the same way each time you handle it, you will handle it that way when you actually need it. And, conversely, if you set no pattern, establish no efficient methods of putting your gun into action, you will not have the time or the clearness of mind to think your way through to success.

In addition to holding all the cartridges along with the gun in the weak hand, there is another very smart tip you should follow. Before loading a single cartridge, dry-fire your revolver a few times, to learn the direction the cylinder revolves. Smith & Wesson revolvers turn counterclockwise as you look at the cylinder from over the hammer. Other makes revolve clockwise. As you hold the gun in your weak hand with the cylinder open ready to load, and after you have loaded a cartridge, use your thumb to rotate the cylinder in the opposite direction than it revolves when

it is being fired. After loading each new cartridge, rotate
the cylinder again in the opposite direction, to bring the
next empty chamber up to the top for the next round to be
loaded. If in an emergency you could not finish loading all
the cartridges, you could snap the cylinder closed and have
those fresh cartridges rotate up under the hammer to be
fired. This little trick has saved the lives of many police
officers. And since you are training to be competent in gun
defense, you may as well learn and practice everything that
may contribute to the success of that defense.

Now that all the chambers are loaded, slowly snap the
cylinder closed and rotate it slightly in either direction,
until you hear it click into place. Be sure that your finger is
not on the trigger at any time during this loading sequence,
especially now, when you close the loaded cylinder. Start
right away to make a habit of keeping your trigger finger
straightened out along the side of the gun on the frame. If
you always hold the gun with your trigger finger straight
until you have the gun aimed at your target and are ready
to pull the trigger, you will eliminate any possibility of the
gun's discharging accidentally.

UNLOADING THE REVOLVER

To unload the revolver, the cylinder is opened in the same
way it was when the gun was loaded. Now, instead of the
thumb's rotating the cylinder as it did when you placed
successive cartridges in the chambers, the thumb of the
weak hand moves up to the tip of the rod that runs
through the cylinder. Holding the gun in the same position
in the hand as you did when loading, tilt the muzzle skyward and, using the thumb at the end of the rod, push the
rod downward or back into the cylinder, to eject all the
cartridges at once.

This will be easy to do with live, unshot cartridges, because they will still be heavy from the bullets in them, but
spent casings may be a little harder to eject. After a car-

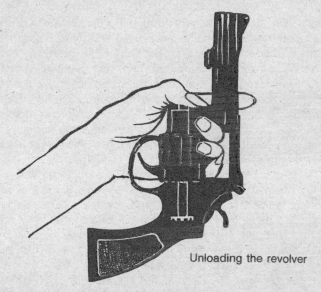

Unloading the revolver

tridge has been fired, besides being lighter, it expands just a little and sticks in the chambers, anywhere from slightly to almost jammed. You will want to thrust that rod with your thumb to be sure that all the casings come out at once. Each spent shell will require a different amount of thrust to be dislodged, so the push on the rod must be strong enough to eject the tightest one, and they all must come out with one stroke of the rod.

The mechanism that pushes the shells out of the cylinder is called the ejector rod. It is a star-shaped precision piece of steel that is fitted into the back of the cylinder. When you load cartridges into the chambers of the cylinder, they come to a stop and rest on top of the ejector star. When you push the front of the ejector rod, it pushes the star away from the cylinder, and with that go the shells. If the rod is not thrust with enough power to lift and eject the one or two shells that inevitably don't want to leave, one or more of the casings may slip under the ejector star and back into the chambers. If that happens, the star comes down on top of the shells that slipped back, and it requires a good deal of time and perhaps a tool to get them out. This is not very common but also not very uncommon and, as I have mentioned before, is the cause of great concern among police departments and others who have had years of experience with revolvers. If the ejector star comes down on top of even one empty shell, the gun cannot be loaded or fired, and in an emergency gun-defense situation you might as well throw it at your assailant.

If you take a practical-shooting course, you will be taught how to speed-load. In speed-loading, instead of inserting the cartridges one at a time, you use a device called a speed-loader to load all the cartridges at once. A speed-loader is round, like the cylinder of a revolver, and is exactly the same dimensions as the cylinder. Almost like the cap of a jar, the speed-loader holds all the cartridges and fits directly over the back of the cylinder. Once all of the bullets have found their chamber holes, the top of the speed-loader is twisted to release the cartridges, which fall into place all at once. A skilled revolver shooter can reload his gun in just about the same time as an autoloader shooter can push the magazine release button and insert another magazine.

Always keep an entire reload with your gun at all times. If not a speed-loader, you can use a device that Bianchi makes, called a speed strip. This is a rubber strip a few inches long with round circles cut out of it to hold all the bullets firmly in place in a row. It is easy to carry if you move your gun from location to location within the house, and takes up almost no room in a pocket or purse. The one disadvantage of the Bianchi speed strip compared with the bulky speed-loader is that it can only load two cartridges at a time, so it takes much longer to reload.

Practice loading and unloading exercises with your revolver until you can do them in the dark; if you ever have

Loading the autoloader

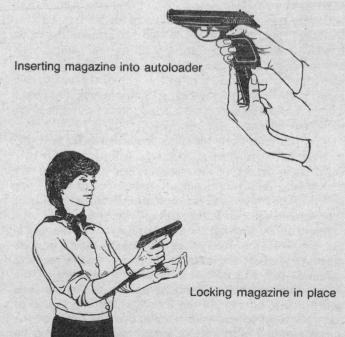

Inserting magazine into autoloader

Locking magazine in place

to reload your revolver in a hurry, it will probably be in the dark.

It is important with all gun-handling techniques that you do them the same way each time, for safety and for reliability. I will say this again, more than a few more times, but it is important to know that in an emergency you can only count on reacting the way you have been trained. It is therefore to your benefit to handle your gun the same way every time you handle it. If you create habits, you will not make mistakes.

LOADING THE AUTOLOADER

To load an empty autoloader, grasp the gun in your strong hand as you would if you were to fire it one-handed, but with your trigger finger straight alongside the frame above the trigger guard. Grasp the loaded magazine in the weak hand with the forefinger straight along the leading edge and the fingertip touching the first bullet. Insert the magazine into the magazine well in the grip of the pistol, and thrust it upward until you hear it click and lock into place. Thrust it with the heel of your hand; don't push it in place with your fingers.

Next you must cycle the slide, or move it as far as it will go, then let it go sharply, so that it will pick up the first cartridge in the top of the magazine you just inserted and load it into the firing chamber. Remember to keep your finger off the trigger and pointing straight along the side of the frame of the gun during the slide release.

Manually cycling the slide its full distance to the rear is not easy. Some autoloaders are easier than others, but none are easy. The best way to cycle the slide is first to cock the hammer—this will take at least half the pressure off the move—then grasp the serrations on the rear of the slide with the first knuckle of the forefinger and the thumb of the weak hand so that your palm is over the slide and the gun is pointing more or less under your weak elbow. Be muzzle-conscious: you should always know where the muzzle is pointed, and that it is pointed in a safe direction.

With the weak hand grasping the serrations of the slide over the top of the gun, as opposed to grasping the serrations from the rear of the gun, the gun will be close to the body, a short distance above the waist. From this position you can exert rearward pressure on the slide with the strength of the whole side of the body plus the arm and shoulder of the hand holding the gun. The position looks something like an isometric exercise in which you push both palms together in front of the chest to strengthen and firm the bust.

Once you have found the grip and the position, the slide is cycled to the rear, very deliberately and strongly, then released. Do not help it forward, guide it forward, or interfere with it in any way. Just let it go. The spring inside the slide is very strong and will snap the slide closed; by doing so, it will load a cartridge into the chamber and put the firing pin in the proper place to strike the primer when the trigger is pulled and the hammer drops.

After the slide has slammed into place, always make a visual check to see that a cartridge is in the firing chamber. This is called a pinch-check. You wouldn't take the time to do it in an emergency, but if you have time do not miss the opportunity to verify visually that the gun is loaded.

The pinch-check can be accomplished in a number of different ways. One way, taught by Jeff Cooper, is to hold the gun in the strong hand with the one-hand shooting grip —finger straight alongside the frame—then grip the front of the slide from underneath the gun with the thumb and the first three fingers of the weak hand. Use the opposing forces of both hands again and move the slide to the rear about one half-inch, or until the opening on top of the slide, or the ejection port, is opened enough so you can peer in and see the cartridge in the chamber.

After you verify that the shiny brass casing can be seen, release the pressure on the slide and let it slip back into its

Removing the magazine

closed position. You may occasionally have to use the heel of your weak hand to smack the slide closed. The reason you released the slide when you chambered a round, instead of gently helping it forward as you do when the pistol is empty, was to ensure that the slide closed forcefully, all the way. Now that you have just cracked the slide open again to peek inside, it may not close all the way. This will not happen often, though, but check to see that the slide is closed after verifying that the gun is loaded.

Use the thumb on your gun hand either to put on the safety if your autoloader is a single-action, or to operate the lever that safely lowers the hammer if you own a double-action. And, finally, before you put your gun away, remove the magazine and refill the cartridge that you have just released into the chamber. Now the job is done, the gun loaded and ready for an emergency. If you own a double-action, it is vital that you make a habit of returning the hammer drop lever to its original position after lowering the hammer, or your gun will not fire when the trigger is pulled. Again, training by a certified instructor is the best way to learn all these techniques.

Once your gun is loaded, don't think of it as a bomb. It will not go off by itself, and most modern handguns have internal safeties that prevent them from accidentally discharging even if they are dropped on a cocked hammer. Always handle a gun with respect, but handle it and understand it well enough to dispel any fear you may have of it.

UNLOADING THE AUTOLOADER

Depressing the magazine release button on the side of the autoloader frame or on the heel of the grip will disengage the magazine from its locked position inside the grip of the pistol. Most of the autoloaders I tested will actually drop the magazine out when the button is depressed; some magazines have to be pulled out, especially if they are filled with cartridges that haven't been used and ejected out of the top of the gun.

To unload the autoloader fully, you must take the magazine out first. Then the gun is held in the strong hand in front of and close to the body, with a twist of the wrist that points the ejection port on top of the slide down toward the ground. The trigger finger is, of course, off the trigger and pointing straight along the side of the frame of the gun, and the muzzle is pointed in a safe direction. Now

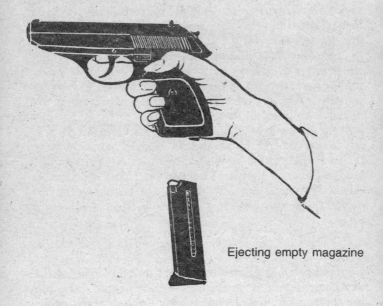

Ejecting empty magazine

grab the slide of the gun, which is now upside down, with
your weak hand cupped over the ejection port. Push on the
grip with the web of your strong hand at the same time
that you push in the opposite direction with the weak
hand, which is holding the slide and cupped over the ejection port. This double pushing will move the slide rearward to allow the chambered cartridge to fall into the
cupped palm of your weak hand.

The autoloader should be fully unloaded at this point.

Your final step is to move the slide back so that you can see into the chamber and visually confirm that there is no round in the gun. Then point the gun in a safe direction and pull the trigger. This will test your confidence that you have properly disarmed the gun, and will assure that, if you have missed a step or are unsure of the procedure, the accidental discharge is spent in a harmless direction.

Speed and ease of reloading are two of the design features of the autoloading pistol. You must have a fresh magazine with your autopistol when your gun is in combat-ready condition. If you ever have to respond to an emergency situation with your handgun, take the spare magazine with you. Tuck the spare into your waistband, rather than putting it in a pocket when you are responding with your gun at home, so that you will have it in position to retrieve it with speed and an economy of motion—the two key ingredients in emergency gun handling.

It should be noted at the outset that every expert in the field considers it unacceptable and inexcusable to shoot an autoloader until it is empty of cartridges. The pistol must be reloaded before all the bullets have been fired. At the schools I have attended, anyone found with an empty autoloader on the firing line was ridiculed. In practice, it isn't important if you shoot all your bullets, but in a real-life gun-defense situation, emptying your pistol would mean you were defenseless while you took the gun and your attention off the target, reloaded a fresh magazine, and cycled the slide to put a cartridge in the empty chamber. And as I have pointed out, under the stress of a real incident you will do what you have been trained to do. If you don't practice either counting the shots you have fired or arbitrarily finding opportunities to reload after more than four shots have been fired, you may fire your gun dry when the heat is on.

Stoppages

Unfortunately, the autoloader is prone to more malfunctions than a revolver. This is particularly problematic during emergency use, so you need to know how to quickly correct stoppages. Four types of stoppages are common to the autoloader. Two of them are more frequent in the hands of a woman.

The autoloader is an ingenious, rather complicated machine. A number of lightning-fast steps have to be completed in just the right order to fire a cartridge, eject the empty case, recock the hammer, and chamber a new round. If anything interferes with the sequence, the gun will not fire more than the first cartridge before it stops working. Failing to fire and jamming are called stoppages or malfunctions. Every conceivable stoppage, short of losing parts to the gun, is curable on the spot.

You may shoot five hundred rounds of ammunition in your autoloader without a single stoppage, or you may have two stoppages in the first ten shots. You must learn how to clear every form of stoppage, practice the clearing drills, and treat every stoppage as if it were an emergency.

The most common stoppage results from not seating the magazine all the way into the magazine well. To see what this would look like and why it would prevent the pistol from firing, unload the gun, making sure that the cartridge is removed from the chamber as described earlier, and lock the slide back so that you can look through the ejection port on the top of the slide right through the magazine well and down to the floor. Then slowly insert the magazine into the magazine well while you watch through the open ejection port. Seat the magazine with a strong thrust just before it reaches the top. Then push the magazine release button, holding the magazine so that when it releases it isn't allowed to slip out too far. You will be able to see that, when the magazine is even as much as one-sixteenth of an inch out of place, the bullet isn't lined up to be snapped into the chamber when the slide goes forward.

Because women are usually not as strong as men, they often have difficulty thrusting the magazine forcefully enough into the magazine well to ensure a good seating every time. The remedy is practice, and the place for such practice is at home, with an empty gun and a full magazine. The magazine always needs to be fully loaded when you are practicing to give you the feel of its weight and the strength required to click it into place. Just be sure that you do not cycle the slide while you are practicing this drill, because you will load a cartridge into the chamber and have one of those I-thought-the-gun-was-empty loaded guns. The possibility of loading your gun while you are practicing changing magazines is remote, but stranger things have happened, and this is a perfect example of why experienced handgunners inspect their guns with what seems like unnecessary frequency whenever they handle them off the shooting range, to be absolutely certain of their condition.

Another pointer that will help you get the magazine seated well every time is that you should buy magazines that have a rubber pad attached to the heel. This pad will give you a little extra to push against, and at the same time will keep the hard metal of the base of the magazine from digging into the skin of your palm and occasionally causing a blood blister.

The other most common stoppage in the autoloader, especially for women, is called a stovepipe. It is caused by the expended cartridge casing's not being fully ejected as the slide recycles a new cartridge into the firing chamber. The result is an empty cartridge shell sticking straight up out of the ejection port and a new cartridge partially chambered. This malfunction is cleared by sweeping the weak hand back across the top of the slide and ejection port, catching the stuck case by hooking it with the crook of the little finger, and throwing it over the shoulder.

Some schools teach that the sweep should also include recycling the slide, in case the stovepipe prevented a new round from being chambered at all. I have practiced this clearing procedure dozens of times both ways, and I can report that, when I did nothing more than hook the stovepipe and sling it over my shoulder, there was always a hot round in the chamber ready for the next shot. When I have hooked the stovepipe and recycled at the same time, I have always ejected a live round. It hurts to waste a live round in a combat pistol, but it would be horrible to clear a stovepipe in an emergency and find that there was no live round in the chamber ready for the next shot.

This stovepipe stoppage is common to women because they have a tendency to hold their handguns with a weak grip and a loose wrist. The loose wrist especially contributes to stovepipes, since the powerful spring that recycles the slide that ejects the spent case doesn't have a firm enough base to push against. It is sort of like trying to get a running start on sand, as compared with the powerful jump you can achieve on a paved surface.

The solution is to develop a consistently good shooting stance with a strong grip on the gun and a locked wrist. If improving your stance doesn't seem to help, the only other solution would be to have a factory-trained gunsmith replace the recoil spring in the slide with a weaker one.

The next most common stoppage is the autoloader's failure to feed a new cartridge into the firing chamber. This is an infrequent problem, but a big one. It is usually caused by two cartridges' coming out of the magazine at the same time. Often called a double-feed, it is the most time-consuming and troublesome to remedy. To clear a double-feed, the magazine has to be removed and the slide has to be cycled to the rear while the gun is upside down and the chamber is pointed toward the ground. The gun is then shaken back and forth so that the round or rounds that are not feeding are removed.

Clearing a double-feed doesn't sound too hard, but the difficulty comes in trying to remove the magazine. The double-feed usually clutches the magazine in the gun, and most of the time the slide must be locked back in order to free it. Some autoloaders, like my favorite Sig Sauer, Model 230, offer no method for locking the slide back, so the gun has to be muscled against the body or leg so that you can cycle the slide and remove the magazine at the same time. You can practice this by manually placing a single cartridge in the chamber, then putting the magazine in and slowly releasing the slide so that another cartridge is brought up to be loaded.

Set up the double-feed a few times and see if you can rip out the magazine without locking back the slide. If you have the strength it can be done, and is certainly the best and fastest way to clear the problem. After you get the magazine out, all you have to do is pull back the slide and shake the gun. The jammed cartridges will fall out, either through the inverted, open ejection port or through the empty magazine well. The ideal way to handle a double-feed is to minimize the chances of its happening by using high-grade commercial ammunition from reputable manu- facturers like Federal Cartridge Company, and to have your pistol's feed ramp and barrel polished by a gunsmith.

The final stoppage you may see, especially if you prac- tice with reloaded ammunition, is a failure of the slide to close fully. This can be caused by a dirty gun or by a cartridge case that is slightly oversized or out of round. To clear this stoppage, either place both thumbs on the back of the slide and push, or use the heel of your left hand to whack the back of the slide to force the slide closed, as you would after a pinch-check.

One other problem that can occur with autoloader and revolver alike is a cartridge that fails to fire the bullet out through the barrel. Most of the time when this occurs, you will pull the trigger and hear nothing. If this happens with a revolver, all you have to do is pull the trigger again to bring up another cartridge. But with the autoloader you must manually work the slide to eject the defective round and load a new cartridge to continue to shoot. Moreover, if you hear only a faint pop when you pull the trigger, you may have a cartridge with little or no gunpowder, which may result in the bullet's traveling only partway down the barrel. If you hear only a pop, you must unload the magazine, cycle the slide to eject the chambered case, and look into the barrel to make sure that a bullet is not lodged. If a bullet is stuck in the barrel, a special clearing rod or a dowel or pencil that can fit into the barrel can be used to push the bullet out. Do not overlook this procedure if you have a partially fired cartridge. To fire another bullet through a barrel in which a bullet is lodged will certainly destroy your gun, and may possibly injure you or anyone standing beside you.

This procedure for handling any and all stoppages in the autoloader should be memorized and practiced before you spend the time addressing any of the specific malfunctions. This three-step, high-speed tactical procedure for handling all stoppages in the autoloader should be practiced in sequence for every stoppage.

1. Release and press the trigger.

2. TAP—RACK—BANG: tap the magazine to seat it in case it is not fully seated, rack or cycle the slide to assure that there is a live round chambered, and shoot.

3. LOCK—RIP—WORK—TAP—RACK—BANG: If the other two clearing techniques don't work, this is the final procedure: lock the slide back, rip the magazine out, work the slide back and forth to get the rounds out of the gun, tap the magazine back into the grip, rack or cycle a new cartridge into the chamber, and shoot.

After you have discovered that your gun does not fire, release and press the trigger to make sure that you haven't inadvertently forgotten to release the trigger after firing the last round. If this does not cure the problem, then check visually to see if you have a stovepipe; if you do, sweep it over your shoulder and continue to shoot. If you still have no function, go through step two described above. If still nothing happens, go to the third procedure. If the third drill produces nothing, either you have gone through all of this with an empty magazine or you have lost some parts to your gun, probably the firing pin, in which case your gun has just turned into a club.

I mentioned earlier that the autoloader is more complicated and can be more difficult than the revolver. And I will say again that your first gun should be a revolver. If, however, you own or purchase an autoloader, you must spend more time with it to learn all the above safety measures in addition to the marksmanship and tactics that follow.

EXPERT SHOOTING

Jeff Cooper, unquestionably the world's leading authority on combat techniques, began his six-day course by telling us that poor gun handling, rather than poor marksmanship, is responsible for more bad hits than any other component of shooting. Mind-set, Cooper continued, determines the winners and the losers in any confrontation. "In defense we do not initiate violence. We must grant our attacker the vast advantage of striking the first blow, or at least attempting to do so," Cooper told his class of wide-eyed students from all over the country, England, and Mexico, including physicians, businessmen, police officers, commanders of elite military forces, and four women. "But thereafter we may return the attention with what should optimally be overwhelming violence. 'The best defense is good offense.' This is true," he continued, "and while we cannot apply it strictly to personal defensive conduct, we can propose a corollary. 'The best personal defense is an explosive counterattack.' "

Massad Ayoob, world-famous combat instructor and ballistics authority, introduced his six-day course in threat management that I attended by saying, "The mind is the weapon; the gun is only the tool. What they fear is not the gun; rather, it is the resolutely armed man."

Mike Dalton and Mickey Fowler, combat masters and perhaps the most decorated practical-shooting competitors in the world, begin their weekend course and their fine book, *Handguns and Self-Defense: Life Without Fear*, with this: "Survival is not a subjective grey area to be discussed in an intellectual arena with morals, religious beliefs, and psychological theories intertwined. It might make for good cocktail party conversation but that never saves anyone's life. Survival is a simple, cold fact. You either want to survive, believe you have the right to survive, or, in a life and death situation, you will likely die."

Ray Chapman, one of the first combat masters and competitive shooters in the country, emphasizes in the course I attended in Columbia, Missouri, that in order to be a competent combat shooter you will have to train against a natural instinct—an instinct to run away from something terrible.

What all these teachers are saying is that your state of mind, including your will to win and your confidence to apply your skills decisively, determines the outcome in a self-defense situation. Marksmanship—your ability to place your shots consistently where you intend—contributes least to winning in gun defense. The significance, however, is in the confidence good marksmanship builds and the high-quality gun handling it develops. You must develop a solid shooting platform or launching pad in order to defend yourself effectively with a handgun.

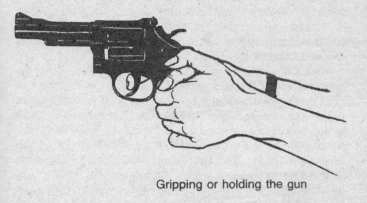

Gripping or holding the gun

GRIPPING OR HOLDING THE GUN

The modern way to hold or grip a handgun is with two hands. The strong or dominant hand grasps the grip of the handgun comfortably as high as possible without interfering with the hammer. The back of the grip should line up with the long bone in your forearm, and fit in the web of your hand between the thumb and forefinger. If your gun is a revolver, the trigger finger should be able to reach the trigger at some point between your first and second joints —closer to the second joint, if possible. If your gun is an autoloader, the forefinger should reach the trigger at the pad of the fingertip. There should be no problem reaching the autoloader with the pad of the fingertip, but if you cannot reach and pull the trigger of a revolver close to the second joint of the forefinger you will need to get smaller grips for your gun or get a new, smaller gun.

I had this problem during Massad Ayoob's course. I just

didn't have the strength to pull the trigger smoothly after more than a few shots with a small Smith & Wesson revolver. As a result, my shooting was terrible and my confidence to do better was becoming dashed with every shot. At lunchtime we changed the grips on my revolver to smaller ones, and my scores and confidence for the rest of the week soared.

With the strong hand firmly in place as high as it can go on the grips of the gun, the three bottom fingers wrapped tightly around the grips, the thumb presses against and on top of the middle finger to lock your grasp. In this position, squeeze almost as hard as you can. Now the weak hand encircles the strong hand, with the forefinger on top of the middle finger of the strong hand, the middle finger over the third finger, the third finger over the little finger, and the little finger of the weak hand on top of the little finger of the strong hand. The thumb of the weak hand goes on top of the thumb of the strong hand and presses firmly to lock the two hands together. In single-action autoloaders, the thumbs are always on top of the thumb safety. Do not place the weak-hand thumb around the back of the gun. It will interfere with the hammer on a revolver, and will get cut badly from the slide on an autoloader.

The reason for the two-hand grip is to better manage the recoil the gun produces after each shot. With a one-hand grip, the recoil forces the muzzle of the gun skyward. With the two-hand grip and the proper stance, the recoil comes straight back and repositions the gun for another shot. This is a tremendous advantage in self-defense shooting, because you will later learn to take two shots instead of only one, and the two-hand grip returns the gun to the target fast enough to allow the second shot to be aimed and rapid.

The secret to a good hand grip, whether it is the preferred two-hand grip or a one-hand grip, is the positioning of the back of the gun exactly in the "v" of the web of the hand, and the strong squeeze. If the gun is off to either side, you will always shoot to one side or the other, and perhaps never know why; if it is held weakly, the trigger pull will exert enough movement to influence the path of the bullet. Until you get used to the feeling of the gun properly placed in the hand, spread the thumb and the forefinger of the strong hand and position the gun exactly in that "v" directly in front of the wrist bone and parallel with the long bone on the top of the forearm. Overemphasize the placement each time you pick the gun up for the next week or so, until you put the correct grip into your muscle memory.

Although you will hold your gun with the two-hand grip every time you shoot from now on, you must feel comfortable and learn to shoot with a one-hand grip from both the strong side and the weak side. While you are handling your gun at home, and later, when you practice live-firing, spend some time dry-firing and live-firing from both one-hand grips. In an emergency, you may have to shoot from less than ideal positions, and now is the time to have a feel for some of those positions.

THE STANCE

Two stances accommodate the two-hand shooting style: the isosceles and the Weaver. Either can be used for both autoloaders and revolvers, but the Weaver stance has the edge for autoloaders.

The isosceles is, as the name implies, made by thrusting both arms out straight in front of the body in the secure shape of a triangle. The feet are spread about shoulder width apart and squared with the shoulders to the target. The hands come up in the two-hand grip to eye level, with the arms fully extended and the elbows locked. The weight of the body is directly over the feet, or perhaps shading a little forward. If your weight is back on your heels, you

The isosceles stance

will be pushed off balance by the recoil when you fire each shot.

At this point it is a good idea to determine which of your eyes is dominant. Right-handers usually have a right dominant eye, while a good many lefties are left-eyed. If, however, your dominant eye is opposite from the hand with which you control the handgun, you must know that, so you can either bring the gunsights over to the opposite eye or close that eye and use the weak eye to aim.

To find your dominant eye, make a circle with your forefinger and thumb, as if you were flashing the okay sign. Hold the circle at arm's length in front of your face, and with both eyes open place the circle over an object across the room. Then, without moving the circle, close one eye. If the object is still within the circle when one eye is closed, the eye you see it with is your dominant eye. Swap eyes and you will see that the other eye puts the circle a good distance to one side of the object. You can see what a terrible shot you would be if you were aiming with both eyes open and seeing the target with the wrong eye.

Whether to close your weak eye when you shoot is an issue that should be settled now, before you begin dry-firing practice with your new hand grip and stance. The combat masters almost all recommend that you shoot with both eyes open, because that way you will have a wider field of vision and see more of the scene of combat in case there is more than one assailant or perhaps help coming from the wings. This is excellent advice, but as a beginning shooter you may find it disconcerting to see so much when you are doing your best to concentrate on your fundamentals. At this stage it would probably be best to squint the weak eye instead of closing it, and plan to use both eyes later, when all the other components fall into place. Ray Chapman, however, makes a very convincing argument that a closed-eye shooter brings the gun up on target much faster than the shooter with two eyes open.

Begin now to practice the two-hand grip in the isosceles stance. You will find the isosceles more natural than the Weaver, but as you become more skilled at shooting you will find that the Weaver stance gives you more control over the gun and allows you more mobility and faster and more accurate shots.

In the Weaver stance, which was named after its creator, San Diego County deputy sheriff Jack Weaver, the feet are again at shoulder width, but the feet and the shoulders are

The Weaver stance

at a forty-five-degree angle to the target. To find this position, pick a target on your wall at least ten feet away and lay a string or a yardstick on the floor, parallel to the wall. Place the toes of both feet on the line at approximately shoulder width apart, as you would if you were going to use the isosceles stance. Now step back with your strong-side leg so that the toes of your strong leg are on a line with the heel of your weak leg. Your feet are still shoulder-width apart. You will not be facing the target. Then twist on the balls of your feet so that you blade about forty-five degrees to the target.

The same two-hand grip is used, but now, when the gun comes up, instead of both arms' being locked in front, the strong arm is locked and the weak arm is bent about forty-five degrees, with the elbow pointed toward the ground. The weak hand is pulling back toward the body while the strong hand is pushing forward to lock the arm, wrist, and gun isometrically into the shoulder. The head is tilted over the strong arm so that the eye is looking straight down the arm, right over the sights.

The Weaver stance is superior to all others because, with the handgun being pushed and pulled at the same time, the recoil goes straight back and is absorbed by the body rather than by the muzzle of the gun as it flies up into the air. Another advantage is that the forty-five-degree angle of the feet makes your stance more secure and your balance more sure; you can swing your aim more easily to either side; less time is needed to sight follow-up shots, because the muzzle of the gun hardly moves, and if your target is armed there is less of a target for him to hit with you standing at an angle.

Mike Dalton and Mickey Fowler advise that the shooter lean slightly forward with approximately 60 percent of the weight on the balls of the feet, knees slightly bent, and leg muscles flexed. Jeff Cooper teaches a more erect stance, with weight evenly distributed over the center of the legs; Chapman teaches a squarer position, with less angle in the weak arm; and everyone cautions that you not lean backward, which comes naturally at first.

The key to the Weaver stance is to lock the wrists and the strong-side shoulder. If you do this correctly, the tension from the two locked joints will cause a muscle burn down the left side of your back if you are right-handed. It is not comfortable, and feels unnatural for quite a while, but it is proved to be the best in controlling the gun.

Practice both of these stances for a couple of days at

home. During your practice sessions, don't dry-fire; work on the stances alone, to find the one you prefer. Begin by facing a target on a wall in either the isosceles or the Weaver stance. The gun is held in the correct two-hand grip at what is called the low-ready position, with the arms extended and the gun pointed at a spot about three feet in front of you. This position, incidentally, is the combat-ready position that you will use before you have identified your target.

So from now on you will be bringing your gun up on target from this low-ready position every time you practice without using a holster or other carrying device. You will be learning about trigger control after learning how to use the gunsights, so try both stances until you feel comfortable with one and can quickly bring the gun up on target before adding another element, perhaps the most important element.

It is worth mentioning Ray Chapman's ready position, in which the gun is held almost under the chin, with the elbows bent and close to the body. Chapman asserts that this high-ready is superior to the low-ready because the gun can always be seen by the shooter, and can therefore be thrust out in front with more speed and accuracy than if you bring it up from the low-ready. He has also demonstrated to me that the high-ready leaves you less vulnerable to being pounced on by an assailant as you walk through a doorway.

THE SIGHT PICTURE

Using the sights on the handgun is somewhat different from using the sights on a long gun. With the handgun, the hands bring the gun up to find the target; then the focus is on the front sight only. The target and the rear sight are seen as a blur.

Getting used to this takes some practice, but it is absolutely essential for consistently accurate shot placement. In

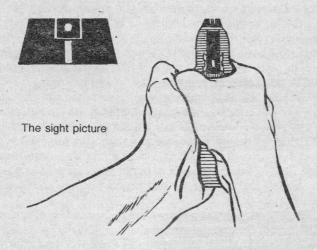

The sight picture

the handgun, the front and rear sights are so close together that, if you move the muzzle of the gun a fraction of an inch, your shot can be off target by feet. If you focus on the target and see the sights peripherally, you will miss, just as you will miss if you focus on the rear sight and try to see the front sight and the target in the distance. Seeing the front sight in focus while the target is out of focus is called a sight picture. And a good sight picture is one of the four primary components of marksmanship.

Once you have the sight picture, the front sight should be in the center of the notch or tunnel in the rear sight. The top of the front sight is in line with the top of the rear sight.

The next step is known as hold. Once you have the sight picture with the sights properly aligned, you must hold that front sight on the spot on the target you are aiming. No one can hold perfectly still, but if you find at first that your front sight is trembling, relax your grip on the gun just a little and check to see that you are not leaning backward. You should be including the hold with your practice sessions at home now.

If you begin to tremble, lower the gun, take a deep breath, and try to get in a few five- or six-second holds before you relax, or practice loading and unloading, or do something else that doesn't require so much muscle tension. It will take you a while to build up the strength and coordination to feel natural with many of these exercises, but this will come more quickly than you may think at first. It is precisely to build up such strength and coordination that you are practicing at home now rather than wasting bullets and developing bad habits with the excitement of live fire.

Once you bring the gun up from a low-ready position, or straight out from a high-ready position, and find your sight picture and hold, you are ready to press the trigger. And think of it as pressing the trigger, not pulling the trigger. Poor trigger control is alone responsible for more bad shots and complete misses than all other components combined. The trigger must not be pulled, but pressed or squeezed with a steady pressure until the hammer falls. When the gun fires, it should surprise you every time. This is called a surprise break, and all good shooters, no matter how fast they can shoot, get a surprise break with every shot or they don't remain good shooters very long.

The experts call poor trigger control mashing the trigger or jumping on the trigger, and this almost always produces a shot low on the target or off the target to the weak side. If you anticipate the gun's firing, you will flinch every time. Instructors on the shooting ranges at the schools I attended could walk down the line and identify each shooter who made his gun go off deliberately; they were always proved right by seeing the target hit low or missed entirely.

The final component necessary to marksmanship skill is the follow-through. It consists of holding the sight picture after the shot and releasing the trigger, both in preparation for the next shot.

After the gun has been shot, or at home after the hammer falls in dry-firing exercises, you must concentrate on keeping the front sight in focus and on the target while you release the trigger and ready it for the next shot. The follow-through actually helps get the shot off more accurately, in addition to preparing for the next shot. When you build the follow-through into your stance, you build the habit of keeping the gun up on the target; as a result, you won't have a tendency, as many shooters do, to drop the muzzle before the shot is away. The follow-through will also help with trigger control. Again, by developing the habit of holding on target after the shot is gone, you will be schooling yourself not to rush the trigger, because the shot will not be complete until the sight picture is again regained and held for three or four seconds.

Mike Dalton and Mickey Fowler use a technique to help the trigger squeeze and the hold in their courses at International Shootists, Inc. With this final step added to your stance, you are ready to put all the pieces together and cement the sequence with dry-fire practice at home. After you have assembled all the steps, from the two-hand grip, low- or high-ready, step into a Weaver stance, sight picture and hold, surprise-break trigger squeeze, and follow-through, Dalton and Fowler suggest that you balance the flat side of a coin on the front sight of your gun to practice trigger control and follow-through. If you press the trigger smoothly and hold the sight picture, the coin will stay balanced. If you jerk the trigger, the coin will fall. It is a good exercise to do from time to time.

If the coin falls too frequently and you are convinced that your trigger control is good and produces a surprise break, you may want to check to make sure that, as your trigger finger is tensing to press the trigger, all the fingers on that hand are not also tensing. If you tighten your grip as you press the trigger you will, as it is called, heel the gun, driving your shots high on the target and probably over the target.

There is a lot to proper shooting, and if you are going to keep a handgun around the house and depend on it in emergencies, you must know how to handle it safely and hit what you shoot at.

Right now is the time to pay your dues. Build a strong foundation before you ever fire your gun, and you will always have confidence and feel secure in your ability to protect and defend yourself. Dry-fire, assembling the whole sequence, every day for one week before you make your debut on the range with live ammunition.

Dalton and Fowler recommend that you practice not more than five to eight minutes a session, but have three to five sessions per day. Cooper advises one twenty-minute session a day. All the experts recommend that dry-firing sessions last only as long as your concentration holds up and your muscles don't tense. Remember, dry-firing is what will make you an expert marksman and keep you expert. The top combat shooters dry-fire a hundred times for every live shot they fire on the line. And most of the top competitors fire more than a thousand rounds a week.

POINT SHOOTING/INSTINCT SHOOTING

Shooting with the sight picture and the hold is known as aim firing, and is your primary method of putting a handgun into action and hitting your target. There may conceivably be times, however, when you will not have the time or see the gun or target well enough or have sufficient distance from the target to set up in a Weaver or an isosceles stance. Your proficiency in aim firing will nevertheless prepare you for effectively using your handgun in any number of gun-defense situations.

As an illustration of your ability to adapt to conditions that vary from the norm, try this exercise. Stand a distance across a room with a target on a far wall or table, just as you have been doing during your dry-firing exercises. Assume your Weaver or isosceles position with the gun at the low- or high-ready. Now, instead of going through the usual dry-firing drill, close your eyes. Stand there, don't move, with your eyes closed. Then, with your eyes still closed, go through the first part of the drill, quickly bringing your gun into place for the sight picture and hold. Then open your eyes while your gun is on hold. You will see that you are either right on target or off by only a small margin. This is the muscle memory the experts talk about. It is why we must handle the gun the same way every time we handle it. Our body learns the procedure even without the assistance of our eyes.

When there isn't enough light for you to see your front sight, you will not be able to get a sight picture. But as you just demonstrated, you can hit your target by simply bringing the gun into your familiar stance and pointing your arms and the gun at your target. This is called point shooting, and though it isn't as accurate as aim shooting, it is fast and effective.

Point shooting is used only when conditions are such that you cannot see your front sight for a sight picture. You should focus on the target and take multiple shots to ensure at least one hit.

Throughout the country, there are a number of custom gunsmiths who can arrange to equip your gun with night sights. These are radioactive tritium dots that are installed in the existing sights to glow in the dark. They are terrific, and since we know that most gun-defense encounters take place in dim light, they are almost indispensable. They cost approximately a hundred dollars. If you can't find a gunsmith who can arrange night sights for you, Self Powered Lighting in Elmsford, New York, is licensed by the Nuclear Energy Commission to install tritium, and you can send your gun directly to them.

You must be prepared for one final situation in which you may have to use what is called instinct or hip shooting.

In this situation, you are too close to your target to extend your arms or take the time to use the two-hand grip. Your target will have to be closer than five feet, and probably closer than that. You may even have one hand occupied in pushing an assailant off or protecting yourself from battering.

Instinct shooting is unsighted fire. The gun is held in one hand, more or less at the waist, and forward enough to be seen peripherally. The elbow is bent about ninety degrees and slightly behind the back. The forearm is parallel to the ground and held close to the body, the wrist locked.

There are no surprise breaks with instinct shooting; the trigger is pulled sharply straight back. It is extremely inaccurate and is used only if an assailant is right on top of you, or if you have to cover an assailant standing at arm's length while you telephone the police.

Instinct shooting is used in situations in which I hope never to find myself. It is actually not being taught or practiced in any of the shooting schools I have attended except Ray Chapman's. It should be practiced by women, I believe, because a woman's assailant in a robbery, rape, or burglary sooner or later gets around to her body. Crimes against women are more intimate crimes, closer crimes, hands-on crimes, and they are defended against with little warning and at arm's length all too often.

OTHER SHOOTING TECHNIQUES

One-hand shooting—both strong side and weak side—should be practiced during your dry-firing at home and your live-firing exercises later at the range. They employ the same bladed Weaver stance as two-hand shooting, with one exception. The free hand, which usually supports the gun in two-hand shooting, should be bent at a forty-five-degree angle and held firmly to the side of the chest with the fist clenched. This position will give you added balance and, as in karate, will direct your strength into the thrusting arm with the gun. Note also that, by cocking the free arm at the side and clenching the fist under the breast, you will keep the free hand from wandering into the line of your own fire in the confusion, heat, or pain of the battle.

It goes without saying that, whenever it is possible, you should shoot from behind cover or concealment. Cover is any kind of barrier that a bullet cannot penetrate, like a cement wall or the engine of a car. Concealment hides you from view but does not stop bullets, like furniture or plaster walls in the house.

Your shooting technique behind barriers is the same two-hand Weaver or isosceles adapted for shooting over, around, or under something. At this point in your training, you know how to shoot properly, so shooting behind a barrier is only a matter of not exposing too much of yourself. The two-hand grip should always be used whenever possible, especially behind a barrier where you will have compromised your stance and balance. If you are behind a door frame, use the knuckles of your weak hand to press against the wood to give you added support, and don't be afraid to shoot your gun sideways or upside down if that position gives you better aim.

Kneeling and lying prone on your stomach are the two other positions you may want to use. The experts say that the prone position is the steadiest of all the stances from which to shoot. My experience is that it takes a lot of time to get into a secure prone position, and I for one cannot hit 50 percent of my shots lying on my stomach at twenty-five yards from a target.

Kneeling, however, is quite close to ducking, which is about the most natural thing to do when the pressure is on and you have a gun in your hands. I know this from the simulators I practiced in at the shooting schools I have attended. In these simulators, both inside and outside, we were asked to move through a maze with our handguns at the low, combat-ready, looking for armed and dangerous combatants among innocent people at every turn and around every corner. These people were drawings placed on steel targets concealed under stairways or inside dark bedrooms or behind trees or in ravines. Once we saw a potential target, we had to identify it as either an innocent bystander or an enemy, and either quickly continue to search past the bystander or shoot the enemy with enough solid hits to knock down the thirty-pound steel plate behind him. These were just games, but our hearts were pounding and our hands were sweaty, and my instinct was to duck into a crouch whenever I identified an enemy.

It didn't take long to learn that shooting from a crouch results in a lot of bad shots. And it didn't take much longer to figure out that dropping into a crouch was just my cowardly way of trying to get closer to the ground to become a smaller target—even in front of a paper bad guy. But it did take a while to figure out that dropping into a kneeling position with the strong-side knee on the ground and the weak knee up and used as a brace for the weak elbow to rest on not only got me closer to the ground, but also produced very accurate shooting.

Kneeling is a very natural position to be in if someone is shooting at you or throwing things or swinging a club. It is assumed by stepping back with the strong leg, which is back to begin with in a Weaver stance. The leg then collapses under you as it might if you were to plop into the fluffy cushions of a couch to read a book sitting on one leg. If you can, sit on your rear leg. If you can't get down that far, sit on your heel. The front leg is close to you, with the knee high. The weak elbow rests on the front knee, just as it would rest on a table. You now have a low profile and a steady platform from which to shoot.

Include barrier shooting and kneeling in your dry-firing practice at home. Use your furniture and doorways for barriers. If you have a mirror at the end of a room, position a chair in front of it and take a position behind the chair, then shoot into the mirror to see how much of you can be seen. Pick out your target on a wall and practice dropping quickly into a kneeling position with a good two-hand Weaver upper-body stance, propped up securely by the front knee. Drop into a kneeling position from your low-ready, bringing your two-hand grip up or out as you fall on the back leg so that the target is covered before you hit the ground and prop the elbow. That way you will get used to covering your target quickly when necessary, no matter what else is happening, even if you are falling to the floor.

You are getting closer to taking your newfound skills to the range to practice with live ammunition. Now is the time to incorporate one more habit into your gun handling. Whenever you are not aiming and ready to shoot at a target, your trigger finger should be outside the trigger guard and alongside the frame of the gun. You should have that down by now; it is something you cannot afford to be lax about. Beginning at this point, every time you are on target your finger should be on the trigger, and if there is any slack in the trigger it should be squeezed out. Practice this until it is as automatic as all the other pieces of the puzzle.

Before moving on to the shooting range, be sure that you have spent at least a couple of weeks practicing your grip, stance, sight picture, hold, and then your trigger control, follow-through, reloading, and barrier and kneeling techniques. If you practice at least fifteen minutes every day without any distraction, you will develop these skills and build necessary concentration, without which you may just as well point your gun and close your eyes and pull the trigger.

THE SHOOTING RANGE

Well, the time has come to see what those weeks of practice have produced and have some real fun.

Before you go to the shooting range, you need to find

one that is ready for you. Most outdoor ranges and virtually every indoor range will not permit you to practice
most of the practical-shooting drills you have been working on at home. Commercial ranges are generally untrusting of their customers—as well they should be, you will
find—and do not allow drawing from holsters or hand-
bags, or kneeling, or taking multiple shots, or barrier
shooting, speed-loading, etc. Self-defense shooting is not
permitted. The owners of most public ranges want you to
shoot holes in paper targets and nothing more.

So, if you can find an International Practical Shooting
Confederation Association (IPSCA) club or some other
practical shooting group, contact them and join. IPSCA is
the best, and they have affiliate clubs throughout the country. Also, if you have the opportunity, go out in the country to set up your own targets and make your own rules
about the safety procedures you will follow and the drills
you will practice.

For the first few times it might be advantageous to find a
commercial shooting range, just to practice your fundamentals with the added pressure of live fire and real recoil.

For live fire you will need some kind of eye protection
and ear protection. For the eyes, regular glasses will do just
fine. If you don't wear glasses, buy some shooting glasses
in any gun store. They are inexpensive and shatterproof.
You can use regular sunglasses when shooting outside. Eye
protection is not to prevent eye damage from the gun's
firing or the possibility of parts flying into your face but,
rather, to protect the eyes from small pieces of lead or tiny
particles of debris that may ricochet from your target
when it is hit or from the person alongside you at the
range. If you stand alongside someone who is shooting,
there is a good chance that you may occasionally get splattered with powder ashes. Usually nothing that might
splash in your face is serious enough to cause injury, but
even the slightest object flying into the eye can be serious

trouble. So never shoot, even alone, without eye protection.

Most of the old-timers in the shooting community have significant hearing losses. They were shooting before the advent of effective hearing protection. There is no excuse for that to happen anymore. Excellent hearing protection is available in a number of different styles at a cost ranging from fifty cents for the plugs you insert in your ears to five hundred dollars for earphones with tiny speakers that enable you to hear better than you can normally while deadening the high-pitch decibels of gunshots. I like the earphone types and use Bilsom Comfort ear muffs, which are lightweight and designed for women. If you stop shooting for a while, you can slip them down off your ears; if you're outside, they keep your ears warm in the cold. Other people swear by the plugs. Either way, don't shoot without some kind of ear protection that shields against as much as twenty-five decibels.

You will also need targets, which you can buy at any commercial range, and target tape, which you usually cannot buy at the range. I suggest that you use silhouette targets, which are amorphously shaped like the torso of a man, rather than bullseye targets. Not only will you have rings or areas for scoring your shots, but the symbol of the silhouette will keep the shape of a man in front of you, and your hits cannot help being seen as hits to the body, which is certainly good mental conditioning. The tape—masking tape will do—is used to cover the holes you put in the target.

The holes in your target, by the way, must be taped after every gunful. These holes, or the lack of holes, are the only indicators of your progress and problems. Read your target. You might need some expert help to learn how to read a target, but, basically, holes on the lower weak side of the target suggest that you are mashing the trigger or that your grips are too large for the size of your hand and you are having to reach for the trigger, which always points the gun to the off side and low. Holes grouping to the top of the target mean that you are heeling the gun or pulling the trigger with all the fingers on your trigger-finger hand. And there are a number of signs the target gives about your use of the sight picture.

If you are on an outdoor range, walk up to your target after every gunful, talk to it, ask questions of it, and listen to the answers; then tape the holes and do it again—only better.

At the beginning you should be shooting your target at a distance of four yards. After the first practice session start at four yards again, and then move back to seven yards. Practice only at four and seven yards the next few times you go to the range; when you feel up to a new challenge, move back to nine yards. Most of your practice should be at seven yards, occasionally moving back to nine, fifteen, and twenty-five yards. If you take a practical-shooting course, you may shoot as far back as fifty yards from a prone position, but for the kind of shooting you may ever be forced to do, four to nine yards will be your range.

On your first time out you will be nervous; everyone is a little apprehensive. So use that time at the range just to get used to the gun's noise and its recoil. Work on your stance, grip, and sight picture, but never mind any of the other exercises you have been practicing at home. The first time or two should be short and end on a good shot. On the first outing you even may want to quit for the day after only twenty shots. Never, never shoot more than you feel like shooting. Always end all your practice sessions feeling positive and only after you have achieved a good group of shots in the middle of the target, or after you feel exceptionally good about your trigger control or follow-through or any new accomplishment.

The experts all recommend that you practice with live ammo once a week. If you practice once a week and dry-fire at home every day or two, you will quickly become expert. Many of you, I know, will not practice so often. I mentioned before that the average handgun owner fires fewer than fifty rounds of ammunition per year, which averages out to one or two practice sessions each fifty-two weeks. I would like to think that I have inspired you to apply yourselves and become expert shooters—your life, after all, may depend on it. If you can, practice at the range once a week for at least a few weeks, and practice at home every night or two for at least ten minutes. That much will give you some confidence and develop some skills, even if you cannot practice as often as you should later on.

When you fire at a target, just as when you fire at an enemy, you aim for the center of mass. You do not try to wound or disable or kill; you shoot for the center of mass to stop your assailant. Think of this when you practice. Aim for the center of the target. After you feel comfortable firing live ammunition, which should be the second or third time on the range, begin shooting two shots at once. Jeff Cooper teaches that firing two shots rapidly in succession gives four times the chance of hitting the target. This is called a double tap. You need a sight picture for both shots; however, with the second shot all you need is what is called a flash sight. The eye can pick up the front sight at one one-hundredth of a second. So, after your first shot, wait until you see the flash of the front sight in focus on your target before you shoot the next round.

After two or three times at a commercial shooting range, it will be time for you to find another range or shooting club or isolated area to practice your practical skills. Even if such a place is far away, make the effort to practice all of your combat skills at least once a month; after you break in at the commercial range, you can practice everything you need to practice at your combat range.

All the schools teach and advise that you practice engaging multiple targets staggered at distances of five yards, seven yards, and ten yards. In this case you would not want to shoot double taps at each target—if you missed one or two shots, you would not have enough ammunition to hit the last target. So, for multiple targets, shoot single shots at all three and then come back with second shots after you are absolutely sure that each target has been hit once.

Mike Dalton and Mickey Fowler recommend that you practice all three styles of shooting during your range sessions—aim, point, and instinct shooting—as well as breaking down each range session into the following order:

Fifty percent standing, two-hand position.
Thirty percent from behind cover and concealment.
Ten percent strong hand and ten percent weak hand in both standing and barricaded positions.

And, based on my experience at the various shooting schools, I strongly recommend that you spend one-quarter of your time shooting from a kneeling position.

Finally, you will want to practice quickly bringing your gun into action from a place of concealment if you ever plan to carry it. I have spent in excess of a hundred hours learning and practicing quick draws from a holster. Since, in my opinion, you will probably never use a holster around your waist to carry your gun, I will not go into the procedure for quick drawing. If you do carry your gun, you will carry it either in your purse or in a shoulder holster. Drawing from both of these is slow, and none of the schools I attended taught either way. So, if you are going to carry your gun occasionally (and legally), practice drawing it from a purse. If you are going to carry it all the time, Safariland makes purses with hidden compartments that are easily accessible, and all the commercial and custom gun-leather manufacturers offer at least one shoulder holster.

This chapter is intended to give you the fundamentals in marksmanship, but there is no substitute for hands-on training. If you are not able to take a course from one of the combat masters I have referred to, look around or ask your local police for a shooting course in your area. There is bound to be someone teaching practical shooting. If all you can find is an NRA course in hunter safety or basic pistolcraft, enroll in one or both. But realize that you must develop combat skills that are beyond the scope of any of the NRA courses I am familiar with.

The instruction in this chapter will develop your shooting skills if you practice. And if you have the opportunity to take a course in practical shooting, the information in this chapter will supplement your instruction and give you a framework for evaluating it. As you will learn, practical shooting classes are challenging and the exercises can help you develop better concentration, as well as improve your hand/eye coordination. Also, you will be widening your circle of friends by meeting men and women who have similar interests in learning self-defense.

11

Tactics for Home Defense

INDISPUTABLY, A LARGER percentage of violent assaults occur outside the home. Having a gun available to deter or stop criminal aggression on the streets, in parking lots and garages, and in parks, shopping malls, and public buildings can be just as effective as having a gun to defend your home. I have not, however, discussed gun defense outside the home because of the myriad of situations where a gun could be useful. Also, it would be next to impossible and inadvisable to discuss out-of-doors gun defense due to the complexities of state and local laws restricting the carrying of a concealed weapon. And though it can be argued that a handgun is needed more beyond the security of the locked doors of your home, the skill necessary to use a gun in public requires extensive training beyond the scope of this book, and the penalties for displaying or using a gun in public can ruin your life. Even a justified shooting in public will result in an elaborate police investigation followed by a criminal-court trial.

In addition to the immense responsibility and legal risk of using a gun in public, carrying a weapon concealed and yet having quick access to it is quite difficult. And carrying a pistol in a handbag—which is usually where it winds up —just begs to be stolen by the common purse-snatcher.

SECURING YOUR HOUSE

The foremost tactic for defending your home against intrusion from crime is fortifying your house to prevent or discourage illegal entry. Just having a handgun ready and available is not the whole answer, and certainly not the first solution to being safe in your home.

There are some simple precautions and some inexpensive security devices you will want before you design your plan for defending your home with a firearm. The first should be an increased awareness when going to and from your residence. In large metropolitan areas this might be called urban survival, but just about everywhere crime has risen to the extent that we all must be alert to the possibility of danger.

This means that you should make a habit of anticipating and avoiding situations in which a threat to your safety may develop. Just as you should never get into your car without first looking into the back seat to see if anyone is hiding there, you should never allow anyone entrance to your house for any reason if you do not expect or do not know the person. So the first security device you will want is a peephole for your outside doors. They are easily installed and should either be rotating or fixed to view a 180-degree picture outside the door. Some home-security designers even advocate installing a small door through which you can talk and listen to someone who has come to the door.

It is not easy to refuse entrance to someone who has come to your door claiming an emergency, but there are countless stories of rapes and robberies that began at the door with an appealing cry for help. If a stranger comes to your house, you should be able to see him without opening the door, then offer to telephone for whatever help he may need, but do not open your door to anyone you do not expect or personally know.

Outside lighting should be another major priority when securing your house. The deterrent effect of exterior lighting was mentioned over and over again by the prisoners I interviewed. They all emphasized that first and foremost on their minds when they committed a crime was escaping detection and apprehension by the victim or the police. A well-lit house exterior increases the criminal's chance of being seen, and unless a particular house has been targeted for some specific reason, most intruders will choose to victimize a dark house where their approach and entry can be concealed.

There are some very sophisticated security lighting systems available, and then there is the old-fashioned high-wattage light bulb over all the outside doors. It would be irresponsible not to beef up your outside lighting in some way. Most hardware and home-improvement stores sell spotlights that have a motion sensor for an on-off switch. Installed over the front door or on the corner of the house or over the garage door, the spotlights are activated by any movement within a twenty-foot range or so. What a surprise that would be to some burglar creeping up to the house, and what a natural alarm it would be for you inside to see the outside lights suddenly go on.

Speaking of natural alarms, experts from self-defense instructors to insurance underwriters all agree that the best early-warning alarm you can own is a dog. Even a small dog will alert you to unusual noises outside and give you time to prepare to defend yourself. A large dog, of course, has the added advantage of being a formidable opponent that most intruders would choose not to confront.

Next are electronic alarms. Few new houses are being built without prewiring for alarm systems, and it won't be long before all houses will have alarms on their doors and windows. This is the fastest-growing segment of the industrial community, with new applications, products, and technology coming along every day. Consult a licensed alarm installer for an explanation of his products and services. You will find that some kind of alarm system can be installed to conform to almost any budget. The best systems automatically call for a response from the alarm company and/or the police. Remember, though, an alarm is only good if it gives you enough time to prepare a defense. Premises alarms—sensors on doors and windows, and movement detectors within the house—are really only for alerting authorities to the break-in of an empty house. You should not rely on these burglar alarms to protect you and your family inside—they are a late-warning system, though certainly better than no warning system at all.

The final prevention measure, and possibly the most important, is the installation of dead-bolt locks on all your outside doors and on your bedroom door. You should also have someone check to see that your outside doors cannot be removed by the hinges. If the hinges on these doors are on the outside, have them pinned permanently so that they cannot be disassembled and the door cannot be opened from the hinge side.

The dead-bolt lock for the bedroom door is part of a concept of making a safe room, where final refuge and defense take place. The ultimate safe room will be equipped with a telephone that is not part of the telephone system throughout the rest of the house, and an exit. The idea is that, if an intruder enters your house, you can retreat to this safe room, dead-bolt the door, call the police from a phone that cannot be compromised by having the receiver on an extension phone removed, and exit the house through the door in the safe room if that is possible. If an exit is impossible, locking yourself in your safe room gives you the time to set up a gun defense from behind cover and wait for your assailant to break down the door. With good timing, the police will arrive before you have to confront a life-or-death scene.

The most natural place to establish a safe room is in your bedroom, where you spend most of your time at night. If you have children, however, it may be better to make one of their rooms a safe room: it would save time, when responding to the sounds of someone breaking in, to gather up your children and wind up with everyone in the one child's room. If you have children to protect, take your gun and spare ammunition with you as you assemble everyone in the safe room before you call the police. You cannot always depend on the police to arrive in time; when responding to an emergency, make certain that, wherever you move in your house, you have with you the necessary emergency equipment to defend yourself and your family.

This means that you do not move in an emergency situation without your gun, spare ammunition, and a flashlight, and though it may sound trivial, without being clothed. It is worth the extra few seconds to put on blue jeans and a sweater or a warm-up suit, and always put on shoes before you respond to any emergency situation. You will feel more confident, and as a result your reactions will be sharper and you will handle the problems with more concentration and capability.

Rehearse the evacuation of yourself and your children to the safe room. In fact, you must lay out your house to make the best use of furniture for concealment and cover in case trouble enters through any door or window, and rehearse your response to the various scenarios that may evolve.

I have stressed over and over again the importance of learning and practicing the various components and stages of gun defense. If you have heeded my advice, you will have devoted a good deal of time to gun handling by now. If you have not put in the time—and, believe me, I know it is hard and monotonous time—you will not be a competent gunwoman, but you will probably be able to point your handgun at an assailant at close range and shoot him at least once.

If you are not a self-motivated student and have only familiarized yourself with your handgun enough to feel confident that you could deploy it in the unlikely event that you would ever need it, you may be lucky enough to be right. But one thing is for sure: if you don't study your house for tactical advantage and rehearse gun-defense tactics in dark rooms, the stress of a real-life confrontation will put the advantage clearly on the side of the assailant. Surprise has the tactical advantage over every defense, and fumbling around a dark house with a gun in your hand, after having just been awakened by the noises of an intruder somewhere in a house you have never moved through in the dark, will turn you into a statistic almost as certainly as being surprised in your own bed.

Almost all the women I interviewed for this book who had been assaulted said they had found themselves amazed, initially disbelieving what was happening or about to happen to them. Massad Ayoob also talks about the victim's initial reaction of wanting to "change the channel" when confronted with violence. This delayed reaction, while the victim tries to wake up from a bad dream, is all the assailant needs to turn surprise to a deciding advantage.

With the proper training in threat management, this immediate paralysis can be minimized or eliminated. Preparation is key, and knowing the layout of your house and the positions of tactical advantage within your environment is vital to a successful defense. *Never forget: tactics beat marksmanship.*

MAPPING YOUR HOUSE

You know the layout of your house (or apartment) better than anybody, isn't that true? You can walk through every room in the pitch dark without tripping over furniture or knocking over lamps. Well, that's probably close to true. Certainly you know the contents of your own house better than any stranger, and you are probably capable of feeling your way through the living room to where you know candles are stored should you have a power failure. But you would be amazed to see how many places in your house a stranger could hide, and how quickly someone could enter your house and move through it behind the cover of furniture or appliances.

It will take only a few minutes to sketch the floor plan of your residence with furniture and fixtures in place, and only another few minutes to study the layout for places of cover where you would be able to conceal yourself and take aim on an intruder who was entering your house or moving through a room. After you have studied the floor plan for each room, noting how the furniture aligns and offers concealed angles from which to shoot toward doors, windows, and hallways, go to those rooms and crouch alongside or behind the barriers to experience first-hand the cover they offer and the angles afforded.

Select one spot in each room that will provide the best vantage point for seeing all entries to the room at the farthest distance from each. This may be hard to find, and you may have to move some furniture around to construct such a spot. You may think this is extreme, but without a secure, concealed point of defense you will lose the tactical advantage in your own place. And without tactical advantage, you may be forced to defend against a surprise attack from an unknown direction, so that the attack may well overwhelm you and cause you to react with panic and recklessness. Luck becomes your weapon at that point.

Find your vantage point in each room of your house. It must provide you with cover and a shooting angle to every door and window in the room. It must also be a position from which, if you had to shoot, you would not risk the lives of innocent family members or neighbors behind where your target would be moving. Always think of the background before you shoot any gun; that's the primary rule of gun safety and is stressed over and over again in every training course in gun handling. As you study and adjust the layout of your rooms, you have the advantage of preplanning the direction in which you might have to shoot. Find a spot for the living-room couch or reading chair such that, when you hide behind it, you will have a view of entrances to the room and angles to shoot from that will not permit a stray bullet to penetrate a wall into a bedroom or family room or possibly go through a window headed directly for your neighbor's kitchen door. If you cannot find a spot from which every shooting angle would be safe, you must absolutely load your handgun with Glaser Safety Slugs, which will not penetrate walls.

Locating a position of tactical advantage in your bedroom is a little more difficult and a lot more critical. More critical because bedrooms are usually grouped in one section of a house, so the shooting angles from within your bedroom can easily lead to penetration of your children's bedrooms. And more difficult because in a bedroom there is usually a minimum of furniture from which to find concealment.

In most bedrooms the bed will be used for a shooting barricade, and must therefore be positioned in the room to give you tactical advantage from a crouch that will provide concealment from and shooting angles to all the doors and windows in the room. And that position of the bed must be such that a shot toward the bedroom doors or windows will not have as a background the walls or doors of other, occupied bedrooms. It may take some research and rearranging, but if you have children or family members in the house you must be absolutely sure that your tactical positions within your residence will not compromise the safety of anyone.

After you have studied your floor plans and gone into each room to establish your vantage points, take a few more minutes to rehearse getting into position in each room at night, with no light coming in except through the windows. You will only have to do this rehearsal once, so make it good. In fact, you may want to run through your home tactics one night with your empty gun in hand, so you can really see the angles and learn the positions.

Again, you will do in an emergency only what you have been trained to do. Think of this practice as training; take it seriously. The object is to learn tactics, eliminate confusion, and reverse the surprise advantage your opponent has. Do it once under simulated conditions and you will not forget it should the time come to defend yourself in your home.

LOCATION OF YOUR HANDGUN

The only thing that all the experts agree on about where to keep your handgun is that it should be close to you. Notwithstanding the safety considerations if youngsters are in the house, a gun in the home for self-defense must be accessible in a ready condition to be of any use at all. And by all accounts, when a self-defense gun is needed, it is needed immediately, usually without much warning.

Some women I interviewed keep their handgun with them all of the time, inside the house and out. Some have more than one gun in the house, so they will never be too far from one wherever they may be. Others have only one weapon but move it from room to room as they change activities. Most people, however, locate their gun in a place where they spend most of their time, and play the odds.

Mike Dalton and Mickey Fowler recommend that two guns be kept in different areas of the house, so that an intruder can never come between you and your gun; they further emphasize that a gun should not be located between you and an area of entry to the house, such that you would be forced to pass a door or window to get to it. They also advise that a gun be kept at least one step away from your bed, and not under a pillow or mattress or on top of the night table. Other experts concur, all citing examples of people who have reached under the mattress or into the nightstand drawer to produce a gun in reaction to a nightmare, or in sleepy response to a noise in the house that a more awake person could easily identify as one of the children opening the refrigerator door.

Find a place to keep your gun that makes you feel comfortable, but whatever place you prefer, even if it is under your bed or in the night table, against the advice of many, put it there every time you put it anyplace in that room. Again, consistency will save you precious moments in an emergency, when you are not thinking so clearly. Of course, wherever you keep your gun in the house or in the car or on your person, always keep it out of sight. It would be more than terrible if an intruder or an assailant saw your gun before you planned for him to see it.

One of the more interesting places I have seen for concealing a handgun in the house and still having it very accessible is, as I've mentioned, in a hollowed-out book mixed in with another book or two. Other clever hiding places, as suggested earlier, are in a tennis shoe or boot on the floor of the closet close to the bed, in the pocket of a bathrobe in the closet, and in an empty detergent box under the kitchen or bathroom sink.

When you leave home, your gun must either be taken with you or unloaded and hidden well enough that in the event of a burglary no criminal will find it, to steal it or use it on you when you return. It is the obligation of every gun owner to see to it that her weapon does not fall into the hands of the wrong people. Stolen guns account for a great percentage of weapons that are used for criminal purposes. If criminals can buy on the black market guns that have been easily stolen along with televisions and VCRs, we will in effect be arming the very people we are arming ourselves to resist. Before leaving the house, unload your gun and hide it and the ammunition in very different places in remote areas of the house. An empty detergent box in the laundry room is a good place for the gun, or a large pot mixed among other pots in the kitchen—both unlikely places for a burglar to look. If you buy a hollowed-out book, you can keep it in your bedroom at night and place it on a bookshelf where it looks like any one of a dozen or more books during your absence.

Upon returning home, reload the gun and place it back in the location you have decided is most accessible. This means that you will be handling your gun at least twice a day, loading and unloading it each time. This habit actually is good practice. It will keep you comfortable with your weapon, and keep your hands accustomed to the fine details of arming and disarming your life-support system. And, once again, routine makes this work and keeps you safe—do it the same way every time and you will always have a safe gun and will never have to wonder about where or in what condition it is.

ENCOUNTERING AN INTRUDER

The first rule advised by the police and self-defense professionals alike is, do not search your house for a possible intruder. Searching a house for a criminal—always assumed to be armed and dangerous—is called clearing a house, and it is a job for the police only. Most police agencies have special teams that clear houses—that's how specialized and dangerous a job it is.

So, if you come home and find your door is open or has been tampered with or a window is ajar, leave immediately and call the police. That's the easy situation.

But what do you do if you are awakened in the middle of the night by unusual noises in another room? Do you call the police after barricading yourself with your gun under the cover of your preselected vantage point, and wait? Or do you take your gun and stealthfully go to investigate? And how is that different from clearing your house?

First of all, common sense dictates that, if you called the police and barricaded yourself ready to shoot anyone coming through your bedroom door every time you heard a strange noise in the house, you would never get any sleep and would never get the police to respond to your calls after a few times. So you will have to go investigate noises that awaken and concern you, but just to the point of identifying the source of the noise, and, it is to be hoped, far short of confronting an intruder should you discover one. The tactics you use to investigate an unidentified noise in the house are almost identical to those the professionals use to search, or clear, a house. The way you carry your gun, the use of cover as you move through the rooms, and the importance of identifying the target are identical and critical. The danger in clearing a house is the same. I have been trained by John Farnam at Executive Security International (ESI) to clear a house, and by Jeff Cooper at The American Pistol Institute (API). At ESI we used guns that shot paint balls and practiced searching the simulated house for real enemies armed with paint guns. At API we used live ammo to clear simulators with pop-up targets. In both courses, everyone came away with either paint splotches or points deducted because they had not seen hidden intruders—everyone.

In the past—for me, anyway—when I heard those suspicious noises in the other room or outside in the black of night, I curled up tight in bed and pulled the cover up and hoped that it was just the heat causing the creaking or a stray cat in a tree doing the rustling outside. And that's all it ever is, usually. But after you buy a gun and take a course in practical shooting and experience the confidence that comes with a learned skill, no longer must you hide under the covers and shiver. In fact, when you feel secure in your ability to defend yourself with your gun, many of those late-night noises will be dismissed easily as regular house sounds, and you will shed the concern and wakefulness you once had about them. You will know when to investigate, after you know how to investigate.

Let's say you are awakened by what you think is someone in the kitchen. After only a moment or two you are fully awake and hear the sound again; this time you can almost make out the sound of a kitchen drawer closing. You are still a little fuzzy about the noises, but they were enough to awaken you and frighten you. What do you do?

Here is what I would do. First I would assume that, if there is an intruder in the kitchen, he either wants nothing to do with me or doesn't know I am there. In either case— still not knowing for sure that anyone is in the house—I will quietly get out of bed, take my handgun, and put on the jumpsuit I have hanging on the back of my closet door for emergencies. Then I will go to my bedroom door to listen more closely and attempt to identify the noises I heard. If I again hear the sounds of drawers or cabinets opening and closing, I will dead-bolt my bedroom door if it wasn't already bolted, retreat with my handgun to the side of my bed that I have established as a vantage point, and call the police.

This will all be done in the dark and under a lot of pressure; I already know that and am prepared to operate in such conditions. When I telephone the police, I will first identify my problem by saying that there is an intruder in my house. Next I will give my name, address, and telephone number, then repeat the address and add directions or a cross street. I will explain that I am locked in my bedroom behind a barricade with a loaded gun trained on the bedroom door. If I am in a position to pass the keys to the house through my bedroom window to the police when they arrive, I will offer that information, along with the location of my bedroom, describing it in a way that some-one facing the house or apartment can follow. I will then wait for instructions or questions.

Sometimes, if possible, the police will want to keep a caller on the line until a patrol car arrives. In other com-munities the police are unable to tie up a telephone line that long, and will only repeat your instructions and assure you that help has been dispatched. In either event, it is I who have the final responsibility to defend myself should the situation escalate to that; no matter what assurances the police have made, my primary focus is over the sights of my gun aimed at my bedroom door. The police know I am armed, and if they come to the door before the intruder, they will be certain to identify themselves and will probably instruct me to lay my gun down and open the bedroom door. Before I give up my vantage point, however, I will make absolutely sure that it is the police who have asked me to surrender my position, even if I have to call the department again to verify names and badge numbers.

If, however, when I get to the bedroom door to listen for more sounds I hear nothing, or hear occasional sounds that I can't identify, I may choose to investigate.

Beside my bed I always keep a high-powered flashlight —the kind with a halogen bulb that directs a piercing pinpoint beam rather than a flood pattern. I will use the flashlight in my barricaded position, quickly turning it on and off to make a positive identification of and momentarily blind someone coming through my bedroom door if it is not bolted, and I will depend on the flashlight even more to identify anyone I may find in my investigation. However, there is still a remote possibility that someone I find in my house uninvited and unannounced in the middle of the night might be a playful, intoxicated friend or neighbor. I must identify every target before I put my finger on the trigger—this is the cardinal rule in the gun community. It is so important to identify the target before shooting that I am willing to give away my surprise advantage and my concealment to use my flashlight or turn on a room light to make sure my intruder is a threat.

Having decided that I will investigate the source of the occasional sounds coming from the kitchen or elsewhere, I prepare by quietly opening my bedroom door while standing up against the wall next to the door so I can see out as soon as it opens a crack, and won't be in a position behind the opening door to be knocked over if the intruder is waiting to burst in. The gun is held in the strong hand, by the side, close to the body, so the weak hand is free to open doors and carry the flashlight. If it was daytime and the flashlight wasn't necessary, the gun could be carried in low- or high-ready position.

After the bedroom door has been opened, a quick peek down the hallway will clear that area for me to move into. Then, moving down the hallway with my back to the wall that affords me the best angle to see the most of the up-coming room, I will check each bedroom or bathroom as I come upon them by moving to the wall opposite each doorway to increase the angle of view and, finally, by ducking into each room to see the blind spot.

If I am moving toward a possible threat in a house, I assume that there may be more than one assailant. I must, therefore, investigate all the rooms in my path and be certain that the area left behind is safe and clear.

As I get closer to the target room, using doorjambs and anything else as cover along the way, I must be alert to everything around me in every direction. If I cannot identify the source of the sounds I heard a while ago, I must assume that the source may indeed be an intruder who may be anywhere in the house except the area I have just cleared. I must therefore not find myself in the middle of a room with no cover or concealment. I will want to keep walls behind me as much as possible, to minimize my exposure to rooms or sections of rooms. In looking around a corner, I'll look at knee level first, then again at another level if I need a second look. I know not to turn on house lights unless I can light a room and remain in the dark. And I will not use my flashlight to light my path; I must work my way through a dark house and use my flashlight only to identify and temporarily blind a target when I see one.

One word about using a flashlight with a handgun. There are a number of methods of holding a handgun and a flashlight aimed at a target at the same time. All the methods are awkward, and the really secure methods are almost too complicated to remember and do well if you don't practice them frequently. Perhaps the best method for home defense is the old FBI style recommended by Mike Dalton and Mickey Fowler at International Shootist Institute. In this method, the gun is held at arm's length with the strong hand, and the flashlight is held with the weak hand off to the side and slightly above the head. You will want to practice this a few times to get the correct twist of the wrist holding the flashlight, so the beam will be directed along with the gun toward the target. The most important thing to remember is that the illuminated part of the flashlight must always be in front of your body, or you will be bathed in enough light to be seen clearly, while at the same time destroying your night vision for when you turn the light off.

SHOOT OR DON'T SHOOT

The moment of decision is when you have your front sight over a target identified as hostile. Do you shoot?

Shoot/don't-shoot scenarios are practiced more by police and other law-enforcement agencies than almost any other gun-handling technique. It is of critical importance to law enforcement on the street that a policeman wait until the last possible moment before deciding to shoot a suspect; when a police shooting does occur, departmental investigations dissect and reconstruct the incident to determine cause and justification.

What it comes down to is that the police must do everything in their power to disarm and arrest suspects, but the homeowner has no such obligation. So what do you do now that you have investigated suspicious noises and found an intruder in your kitchen or in your living room rummaging through your drawers and cabinets?

Massad Ayoob says that an intruder coming up the stairs in a two-story house, or anywhere in a single-story house, is in what he calls a free-fire zone. Ayoob contends that it is not practical to call out a challenge, such as "Don't move," or "Freeze," or "Drop that gun," when you and an intruder are within sight of each other, even if his back is turned to you. They don't call it a challenge for nothing, many experts say. Ayoob is adamant that fair play in a life-or-death situation is a myth of the Old West; that "Hold it right there" command doesn't freeze thc bad guy in his tracks, as it has so many times on the big screen. An unexpected challenge to an intruder who is already a bundle of nerves produces a reflexive response. He whirls around to meet your challenge, and, as Ayoob paints the picture, if he does not pull the trigger automatically as he faces you, it will be the first response that occurs to his hair-trigger nervous system when he sees you.

Now is a good time to review. Before you can be legally justified in shooting someone, your intruder must have the ability, the opportunity, and the intention to cause you death or grave bodily harm. You cannot shoot an intruder who has just come for your television set. But how do you decide if this real-life intruder you have stalked down the hall to find rummaging through your belongings is intending only to take your flatware and serving pieces and dash back out the broken window he used to come in?

You can reasonably assume that, if you find an intruder in your house in the middle of the night, he has automatically put you in jeopardy, one of the three criteria for using lethal force in self-defense. You may also assume that, because he is a man, there is enough disparity of force that he has the power and strength to kill you. Finally, if you are close enough to see this intruder, you are probably close enough to be attacked by him. This man in the kitchen has the ability and opportunity, and has placed you in enough jeopardy for you to use justifiably any means necessary to prevent your death or serious injury.

Under these conditions, Massad Ayoob says to shoot him and keep shooting him until he is unable to harm you. The other experts agree: expect the intruder to attack, and the average armed homeowner is no match at close range for the average criminal, who probably learned his skills in prison. You must be prepared to shoot.

Distance from an intruder is the only edge you have against being attacked, and attention to the gun-handling basics is your defense against an assailant's making a grandstand play to disarm you. You cannot break down. You cannot show weakness in your resolve to defend yourself. You must control the scene, and only the confidence that comes from practice will make that possible.

Preparation for this night is the key to success. Mike Dalton and Mickey Fowler say that coolness is not a part of mental skills, they say it is only a by-product of preparation. Everyone says that a lethal confrontation is the highest form of stress the mind and body can experience, and they all agree that you will do the right things and survive only if you prepare yourself to do them.

What to do should you find an intruder or identify an assailant depends on so many variables that it is truly outside the scope of this chapter. Again, it is inadvisable to search your house. So, if you are alarmed by the sounds of an intruder, try your best to verify his presence from the end of a dark hallway or from behind your locked bedroom door. The tactical advantage of having a gun in the house for self-defense resides in using it to surprise or ambush an intruder from behind cover or concealment in the event that his presence becomes a lethal threat.

If, however, you are forced to leave your hiding place for any one of hundreds of reasons, you must be prepared and able to shoot if necessary or safely immobilize an intruder—who at the time of his discovery immediately becomes a bonafide threat to your life—and call the police. This is not easy to do, and all I can say is that the most immobile position to put someone in without the aid of restraining devices is face down on the floor with the hands clasped behind the head and the ankles crossed. Do not under any circumstances attempt to tie an intruder up or allow him to talk.

DEADLY TIPS

If there is even a remote possibility that you may someday wind up having to defend yourself with a gun, there are a few tips you should know.

As I mentioned before, you do not ever attempt to shoot to wound, disarm, or scare an assailant. You shoot to stop an attack, and you shoot at the center of mass in the body. That means that you aim for the center of your target—the chest.

If you are facing one assailant, always shoot two shots in quick succession. Unless your first bullet hits the head or the spinal column, you will probably need at least two shots to stop the attack, especially if your assailant is under the influence of drugs, and the odds are he is. Do not shoot one shot and then wait to see the results. Shoot two quick shots to the center of the chest.

When facing multiple assailants, the one representing the most immediate threat must be shot first. This may not always be the closest assailant. If two men are standing in front of you, one with a knife ten yards away and one with a gun at twenty yards, the man with the gun is your most immediate threat. If there is an assailant just five yards away coming toward you with only his hands as weapons, and another man at fifteen or twenty yards with a gun, the closer man is your most immediate problem: as soon as he reaches you he will disable you, so he must be stopped before the man with the gun is addressed.

If you face two assailants, fire two quick shots at the immediate threat first; then, without hesitation, redirect your attention to the secondary target and again fire two quick shots. If you are using a revolver, that gives you only one or two more shots. After firing at your secondary target, you must direct your aim to your primary threat again. If you have managed to stop him with your first two shots, go back to the secondary target to make sure that he is disabled. With only one or two shots left, you must be very careful how you use them.

Should you be in absolutely the worst place at absolutely the worst time and be facing more than two murderous assailants, you must fire single shots at each target, beginning with the most immediate threat. The only situation I can think of where you could face more than two assailants is if you are confronted by a street gang carrying weapons. My brother used to say that you should always pick out the leader, or, as he used to say, the big-mouth, to hit first. The theory is, of course, that the rest of the gang will be frightened away by the loss of their strongest member. I'm sure that if I find myself facing five or six street warriors, I will remember that advice and shoot the boss first.

One thing to keep in mind from time to time is that it takes less than 1.5 seconds for the average out-of-shape person to run twenty-one feet from a complete standing start. Couple that with the fact that the average gunfight takes place at less than five yards (fifteen feet) and is over in approximately three seconds. You will have to be fast and first to be the victor in a firefight. It is worth a pound of practice for a ton of protection.

Use silhouette targets for practice shooting instead of the bullseye targets. Get used to the shape of the assailant you may someday face, and practice shooting at the center of mass. Practice shooting at no greater distance from your target than seven yards, and spend at least 25 percent of your practice shooting at three to five feet, using the hip-shooting technique. Also practice shooting at close range from a crouch position. Ray Chapman is the only one of the well-known instructors in this country whose school I attended that teaches or even allows shooting from a crouch. It is just a natural position to find yourself in when you are threatened.

And, as a final piece of advice, do not show your gun to too many people or even let it be known that you own a gun for self-defense. You will have plenty of gun talk at the shooting range. Showing your gun to houseguests is a dangerous practice, and letting it be known that you own a handgun will attract attention that you may not want. If you carry a handgun, never display it unless you plan to use it. A handgun is very personal and very lethal. Resist imitating the foolish gun handling you see on television, and respect and trust your gun.

12

Gun Laws

OUR COUNTRY HAS a federal law governing the sale, purchase, and transportation of guns. The McClure-Volkmer Firearms Owners' Protection Act took effect on November 15, 1986, amending the Gun Control Act of 1968, and is governed by the Bureau of Alcohol, Tobacco and Firearms, a division of the U.S. Department of Treasury. Although some of the Act's rules may not interest you because they govern licensed gun dealers, other stipulations dictate who cannot possess firearms.

The following classes of people are ineligible to possess, receive, ship, or transport firearms or ammunition: (1) those convicted of a crime punishable by imprisonment for over one year which is not a state misdemeanor punishable by two years or less; (2) fugitives from justice; (3) unlawful users of certain depressant, narcotic, or stimulant drugs; (4) those adjudicated as mental defectives or incompetents or those committed to any mental institution; (5) illegal aliens; (6) citizens who have renounced their citizenship; and (7) those persons dishonorably discharged from the armed forces.

Handguns may be purchased only within your state of residence. Transporting a gun from state to state has its problems, and there is no such thing as a federal permit that allows you to carry a firearm while vacationing or taking a business trip. If the possession of the firearm is lawful in your state of destination, you can, however, transport any legally owned firearm through a state that otherwise might make such transportation illegal. Some states require that firearms be unloaded and stored in a trunk, while others allow you to carry a gun openly on your car seat or dashboard. Since the laws vary so much, it's difficult for me to help you other than to advise that, if you plan to take a firearm into another state, you should phone that state's highway patrol to learn how you can legally transport your gun through that state.

If you're traveling by air, never put a gun in your carry-on luggage. You'd be stopped while going through the electronic screening monitors, and you could go to jail. Federal law requires that airline passengers traveling with firearms pack them unloaded in locked luggage and have the luggage stored in the baggage compartment. Each airline, however, has its own rules, so, before traveling with a firearm, check with your carrier.

Some airlines, after verifying that your gun is empty and locked in your luggage, will put a bright-colored tag on the bag with the word "firearms" on it. This is certain to get your luggage stolen, either by the bag handlers or at the airport luggage claim. An excellent way to avoid this unnecessary advertising is to have your gun in a briefcase or other lockable box. Then, after it has been inspected and tagged by the airline personnel, the whole locked briefcase or box goes into your regular bag, which is locked and checked. No one along the route will know your luggage contains valuable firearms, and you will only risk losing the bag through normal channels. Also insure your bag with the gate personnel for extra value, to cover the cost of your gun and the other contents. Excess-valuation insurance is very inexpensive and well advised, especially since the carrier already knows your bag contains an expensive firearm.

If you're going to a foreign country, *do not* pack a gun in your luggage; it is illegal to bring firearms into most countries. I have been advised by many experts that, if you feel a need to have a gun in a foreign country, you should buy one there and leave the gun behind when it's time to depart. Don't even try to sell it.

Also, firearms are not permitted in "natural and historical areas and national parks," unless they are unloaded and cased or packed in such a way as to prevent their use while in the parks. You can carry a firearm into certain "recreational areas" (hunting areas) of a national park; however, inquire with the park superintendent where those sites are located.

Although the McClure-Volkmer Act is important, the purchase, sale, and possession of firearms is also regulated by many state and city laws. There are so many different gun laws that it would be next to impossible to describe them all. Our country has in excess of twenty thousand laws regulating firearms, and some of them change each year. What all the gun laws try to accomplish is to keep guns out of the hands of criminals, emotionally disturbed people, illegal aliens, and minors. We can also assume that these laws were made to help the majority of people, for the good of the American populace.

Yet all of these laws are highly political and controversial. Millions of dollars a year are spent lobbying for or against proposed legislation. Gallup polls are usually taken after an attempted assassination of a political figure or celebrity to determine the people's sentiments on stricter gun-control laws. The so-called gun issue is perhaps one of the most emotional political issues we have in America, and at this point neither side is really winning.

Our strictest gun laws are in the cities of New York, Detroit, Washington, D.C., and Chicago (except for three Chicago suburban towns that have absolute bans on firearms), with the largest populations and the greatest law-enforcement problems. The most lenient state laws are found in rural areas in the Northeast, such as Maine and

Vermont, and in the West, in Arizona and Idaho, where hunting is legal and there is little crime. Most states do not have uniform state laws but, rather, have city and county laws whereby sheriffs and chiefs of police can arbitrarily decide whether a person is granted a permit to carry a concealed weapon.

In California, for instance, each of the fifty-eight counties has authority to issue concealed-weapons permits, which allows holders to carry a weapon concealed anywhere within the state. The inequity in this system is that only eleven people in San Francisco County have carry permits, whereas in nearby Kern County 5,157 carry permits have been issued. To make things even more ridiculous, the punishment for being discovered carrying a concealed weapon without a permit is the same as that for running a red light—a misdemeanor.

Well, you might think that California's laws are confusing because it's California, but Florida used to have the same jumble of laws and inequities. Prior to 1987, Florida had more than four hundred local gun-control laws. To rectify the confusion, the legislature passed two state laws that preempted the regulation of firearms and ammunition to the state and established a statewide system for issuing concealed-weapons permits. The new law eliminated local county or city concealed-weapons laws, which were controlled by politically minded police chiefs and sheriffs, and the requirement for a citizen to show special need such as threats to life or the carrying of large amounts of money. Before the passage of the new law, for example, in Broward County, which includes Fort Lauderdale, applicants for a concealed-weapons permit were required to pay five hundred dollars, pass a stiff background check, get a mental examination, be endorsed by the police chief, obtain approval of a hearing officer at an interview, and have an approved reason for carrying a gun. In a county of 1.2 million people, there were only twenty-two gun permits.

Under the new law, a permit costs $146, and an appli-

ARMED & FEMALE 267

cant must be twenty-one and a Florida resident for six months and must take an approved gun-training course. In addition, an applicant can't have been convicted of a felony or have been labeled a habitual user of drugs or alcohol. There are a few areas where firearms can't be carried, such as police stations, courts, bars, and college campuses, although students and faculty can get permits to carry stun guns.

Dade County, which includes Miami, had the highest violent-crime rate in the United States in 1986, according to the FBI. Proponents of the new law contend that it will enable residents to protect themselves against the state's rampant crime. Opponents say that it will only make the crime worse. Florida, and especially Dade County, will certainly be a good testing ground to prove or disprove that a legally armed citizenry can responsibly defend itself and deter violent crime.

For many Americans the issue is the ability to carry a concealed weapon legally. If you feel that you need to carry a gun, know the rules as well as the penalties in your city, county, and state. If you don't like the rules, write letters to your city or state elected officials, or join a political organization that you feel represents your views, and it will lobby for your interests on a local, state, or federal level.

The following chart, compiled by the NRA Institute for Legislative Action, lists the main provisions of state handgun laws. It does not include cities that may have their own handgun ordinances. Although the chart is a good guide, check with your local police before you purchase a gun to find out your city and state laws as well as to get advice on the interstate transportation of weapons.

STATE	PURCHASE				CARRYING				OWNERSHIP	
	Application and Waiting Period	License or Permit to Purchase	Registration	Record of Sales Sent to State or Local Govt.	Carrying Openly Prohibited	Carrying Concealed Prohibited	License to Carry Openly	License to Carry Concealed	Owner Licensing or I.D. Cards	Constitutional Provision
ALABAMA	x			x			x	x		x
ALASKA						x				x
ARIZONA						x				x
ARKANSAS					X[2]	X[7]				x
CALIFORNIA	x			x		x		x		
COLORADO						x		x		x
CONNECTICUT	x	x		x				x		x
DELAWARE		x						x		x
FLORIDA	X[1]			X[1]				x		x
GEORGIA	x						x	x		x
HAWAII	x	x		x		x	X[5]	x		x
IDAHO			X[3/12]			x	x	x	X[6]	x
ILLINOIS	X[1]	X[11]	X[11]	X[11]	X[4]					x
INDIANA	x			x		x		x		x
IOWA				x		x		x		x
KANSAS						x	x			x
KENTUCKY						x	x	x		x
LOUISIANA						x	x	x		x
MAINE	x			x		x	x	x		x
MARYLAND		x		x			x	x		x
MASSACHUSETTS		x		x				x		x
MICHIGAN	x	x	X[6]	x			x	x	x	
MINNESOTA		x					x	x	x	x
MISSISSIPPI			x			x				x
MISSOURI	x	x		x		x				x
MONTANA						x	x	x		x

HANDGUNS

STATE									
NEBRASKA									×
NEVADA			×			×	×	×	×
NEW HAMPSHIRE			×			×	×	×	×
NEW JERSEY	×		×	×			×		
NEW MEXICO						×	×	×	×
NEW YORK		×	×	×			×		
NORTH CAROLINA				×		×		×	×
NORTH DAKOTA			×	×			×		
OHIO	X[9]			×		×		×	×
OKLAHOMA	×			×		×	×	×	×
OREGON	×		×	×		×	×	×	×
PENNSYLVANIA			×	×			×	×	×
RHODE ISLAND	×		×	×	X[4]		×	×	×
SOUTH CAROLINA	×		×	×			×	×	×
SOUTH DAKOTA			×	×	×		×	×	×
TENNESSEE	×			×	X[4]	X[2]	×	×	×
TEXAS	×			×	X[10]	×	×	×	×
UTAH			×	×		×	X[1/4]	×	×
VERMONT						X[10]	×		×
VIRGINIA	X[15]		×			×			×
WASHINGTON	×		×	×					×
WEST VIRGINIA			×	×				×	×
WISCONSIN	×			×			×		
WYOMING			×			×		×	×
DISTRICT OF COLUMBIA	X[12]	X[12]			X[12]	X[12]		X[12]	

[1] License to carry in a vehicle either openly or concealed.

[2] Arkansas prohibits carrying "with a purpose to employ it as a weapon against a person." Tennessee prohibits carrying "with the intent to go armed."

[3] Chicago only.

[4] Loaded.

[5] Effective 10/1/87 repealed.

[6] Handguns must be presented to the city chief of police or county sheriff to obtain a certificate of inspection.

[7] Permission to carry concealed may be granted by county sheriff on written application.

[8] Handguns prohibited in Evanston, Oak Park and Morton Grove.

[9] Some municipalities control the possession, sale, transfer or carrying of handguns; e.g. Cleveland and Columbus require a police permit for purchase; Toledo requires a handgun owner's I.D.; Cincinnati requires application for purchase.

[10] Prohibits carrying a firearm "with the intent or purpose of injuring another."

[11] Certain cities or counties.

[12] Applies only to pre-registered firearms. No new handguns can be brought into the city.

Resources

PRACTICAL SHOOTING SCHOOLS

The American Pistol Institute
Jeff Cooper
P.O. Box 401
Paulden, Arizona 86334
(602) 636-4565

Chapman Academy Practical
Shooting
Ray Chapman
Route 1, Box 27A
Hallsville, Missouri 65255
(314) 696-5544

Chelsea Gun Club of New York
City, Inc.
James D. Surdo
c/o West Side Range
20 W. 20th Street
New York, New York 10011
(212) 929-7287

Defensive Training, Inc.
John Farnam
P.O. Box 665
Niwot, Colorado 80544
(303) 530-7106

or
Executive Security International
500 Main Street
Aspen, Colorado 81611
(303) 920-2323

International Shootists Inc.
Mike Dalton and Mickey Fowler
P.O. Box 5254
Mission Hills, California 91345
(818) 891-1723

Lethal Force Institute
Massad Ayoob
P.O. Box 122
Concord, New Hampshire 03301
(603) 224-6814

EXECUTIVE PROTECTION SCHOOLS

Executive Security International
Bob Duggan
500 Main Street
Aspen, Colorado 81611
(303) 920-2323

Richard W. Kobetz & Associates, Ltd.
Richard Kobetz
North Mountain Pines Training Center
Arcadia Manor, Route 2, Box 100
Berryville, Virginia 22611
(703) 955-1128

G. Gordon Liddy Academy of Corporate Security and Private Investigation
G. Gordon Liddy
7630 Biscayne Boulevard, Suite 204
Miami, Florida 33138
(305) 758-0146

MODEL MUGGING DEFENSE COURSES

Impact Model Mugging of Los Angeles
Lisa Gaeta and Al Potash
13550 Roscoe Boulevard
Van Nuys, California 91402
(818) 509-8166 or (800) 541-KICK

Bay Area Model Mugging
Sheryl Doran
3410 Devon Way
Redwood City, California 94061
(415) 342-BAMM or 368-8932

Subsidiary Chapters of Model Mugging:
San Luis Obispo, California: (805) 544-KICK or 995-1224
Boulder, Colorado: (303) 444-6994
Chicago, Illinois: (312) 338-4545
Boston, Massachusetts: (617) 730-4129

Honolulu, Hawaii: (808) 735-7598
New York, New York: (212) 650-9546
Washington, D.C.: (301) 589-1349

GUNSMITHS

Andy Cannon
P.O. Box 357
Victor, Montana 59875

Jim Davis Gunsmithing
7636 Tampa Avenue
Reseda, California 91335

James Hoag
8523 Canoga Avenue
Canoga Park, California 91304

Judy's Comp & Carry
Specializing in Competition and Defense Handguns for Women
Box 640
Plains, Montana 59859

John Lawson
1802 Columbia Avenue
Tacoma, Washington 98404

John Mahan
The American Pistol Institute
P.O. Box 451
Paulden, Arizona 86334

Wayne Novak
P.O. Box 4045
Parkersburg, West Virginia 26102

Armand Swenson
P.O. Box 606
Fallbrook, California 92028

Lance Weber
4535 Highway 82
P.O. Box 367
Basalt, Colorado 81621

ACCESSORIES

Andy Arratoonian (custom gun leather)
Horseshoe Leather Products
The Cottage, Sharow
Ripon HG4 5BP
England

Bianchi Gunleather
100 Calle Cortez
Temecula, California 92390

Bilsom International Inc. (ear protection)
11800 Sunrise Valley Drive
Reston, Virginia 22091

Cannon Safe Company (gun safes)
9358 Stephens
Pico Rivera, California 90660

Gordon Davis (custom gun leather)
3930 Valley Boulevard, "F"
Walnut, California 91789

E-A-R (ear protection)
7911 Zionsville Road
Indianapolis, Indiana 46268

Bruce Nelson (custom gun leather)
Box 8691 CRB
Tucson, Arizona 85738

Ken Null (custom gun leather)
678 Green Springs Road
Hanover, Pennsylvania 17331

Pachmayr Gun Works (rubberized grips)
1220 S. Grand Avenue
Los Angeles, California 91352

Peltor Inc. (car protection)
East Providence, Rhode Island
02914

The Pro Timer III (reaction timer)
Competition Electronics, Inc.
753 Candy Lane
Rockford, Illinois 61111

Rogers Holster Co. (gun leather)
1736 St. Johns Bluff Road
Jacksonville, Florida 32216

Russwood Custom Pistol Grips (grips)
P.O. Box 460
East Aurora, New York 14052

Safariland (purses and gun leather)
1941 S. Walker Avenue
Monrovia, California 91016

Self Powered Lighting (sights)
8 Westchester Plaza
Elmsford, New York 10523

Shotgun News (weekly guide to wholesale prices)
Box 669
Hastings, Nebraska 68901

Milt Sparks (custom gun leather)
Box 187
Idaho City, Idaho 83631

Craig Spegel (custom handgun grips)
Route 4, Box 974
Hillsboro, Oregon 97123

T.M. Industries (silhouette targets)
P.O. Box 68
Santa Monica, California 90406

COMPETITIVE SHOOTING ORGANIZATIONS

United States Practical Shooting Association/IPSC
P.O. Box 811
Sedro Woolley, Washington 98284

SPECIAL INTEREST ORGANIZATIONS

Citizens Committee for the Right to Keep and Bear Arms
Liberty Park, 12500 N.W. Tenth Place
Bellevue, Washington 98005

The Firearms Coalition
P.O. Box 6537
Silver Spring, Maryland 20906

Guardian Group International
21 Warren Street, #3-E
New York, New York 10007
(Assists qualified people in obtaining handgun permits in New York City)

Gun Owners of America
8001 Forbes Place, Suite 102
Springfield, Virginia 22151

Handgun Control, Inc.
1400 K Street N.W., Suite 500
Washington, D.C. 20005

Handgun Information Center
1400 K Street N.W., Suite 500
Washington, D.C. 20005

National Coalition to Ban Handguns
100 Maryland Avenue, N.E.
Washington, D.C. 20002

National Rifle Association of America
1600 Rhode Island Avenue, N.W.
Washington, D.C. 20036

Second Amendment Foundation
James Madison Building
12500 N.E. Tenth Place
Bellevue, Washington 98005

VIDEOTAPES

A Woman's Guide to Firearms
Lyon House Productions
Starring Lee Purcell
Available through gun stores or sporting-goods stores.
(800) 854-8545
(800) 826-8192 (California)

Gun Wise
A safety-education film.
(213) 240-9300

Gunfight, USA
A Public Broadcasting Service documentary.
(800) 424-7963

Gun: Pro and Con
Correspondents Howard K. Smith and John Scali argue for and against handgun control.
(212) 997-6572

Choose Your Weapon
A guide to selecting the self-defense handgun.
With Sergeant Dennis B. Tueller
(801) 571-8757

Principles of Home Defense
A Wild Wing Production
(818) 994-4955

Bibliography

ANDERSON, JERVIS. *Guns in American Life.* New York: Random House, 1984.

ARNOLD, DAVE. *Shoot a Handgun.* Canyon County, Calif.: PVA Books, 1984.

AYOOB, MASSAD. "Combat Shooting: Suggested Positions and Techniques." *The Sentinel,* Spring 1974, pp. 51 ff.

———. *Gun-Proof Your Children.* Concord, N.H.: Police Bookshelf, 1986.

———. "The Eight Dangerous Myths of Self-Defense." *The Gun Digest,* 40th ed., 1986, pp. 14–17.

———. *In the Gravest Extreme.* Concord, N.H.: Police Bookshelf, 1980.

BANKSTON, WILLIAM B.; THOMPSON, CAROL Y.; and JENKINS, QUENTIN A. L. "Carrying Firearms: The Influence of Southern Culture and Fear of Crime." Paper presented at the annual meeting of the American Society of Criminology, October 1986, Atlanta, Ga.

BARTHEL, JOAN. "Women and Guns." *Woman's Day,* September 1, 1983, pp. 84 ff.

BEARD, MICHAEL K. "Showdown with the Gun Gang at Gun Control Corral." *Business and Society Review,* no. 23 (Fall 1977): 67–71.

BECK, ALLEN J. "Recidivism of Young Parolees." Bureau of Justice Statistics, Special Report, U.S. Department of Justice, Washington, D.C., May 1987.

BENDIS, PAUL, and BALKIN, STEVEN. "A Look at Gun Control Enforcement." *Journal of Police Science and Administration,* no. 7 (1979): pp. 439–78.

BENEDICT, HELEN. *Recovery.* New York: Doubleday, 1985.

BENEKE, TIMOTHY. *Men on Rape.* New York: St. Martin's Press, 1982.

BENNETT, GEORGETTE. *Crime Warps.* New York: Anchor Books, 1987.

BIANCHI, JOHN. *Bluesteel & Gunleather.* Temecula, Calif.: Bianchi International, 1986.

BIGELOW, STEVE, and GILKISON, TIMM. "Proactive Protection." *Law and Order* 34, no. 3 (March 1986): 40–43.

BLACKMAN, PAUL H. "Carrying Handguns for Personal Protection: Issues of Research and Public Policy." Paper presented at the annual meeting of the American Society of Criminology, San Diego, Calif., November 13–16, 1985.

———. "Firearms and Violence, 1983/84." Unpublished paper.

———. "Flaws in the Current and Proposed Uniform Crime Reporting Programs Regarding Homicide and Weapons Use in Violent Crime." Paper presented at the annual meeting of the American Society of Criminology, October 1986, Atlanta, Ga.

BLAKELY, MARY KAY. "Could You Feel Safer Carrying a Gun?" *Ms.,* May 1982, pp. 16–18.

BORDUA, DAVID J. "Firearms Ownership and Violent Crime: A Comparison of Illinois Counties." In *The Social Ecology of Crime,* James M. Byrne and Robert J. Sampson, eds. New York: Springer-Verlag, 1986, pp. 156–207.

BORDUA, DAVID J., and LIZOTTE, ALAN J. "Patterns of Legal Firearms Ownership: A Cultural and Situational Analysis of Illinois Counties." *Law and Policy Quarterly* I (1979): 147–75.

BROWNE, ANGELA. *When Battered Women Kill.* New York: Free Press, 1987.

BROWNMILLER, SUSAN. *Against Our Will.* New York: Random House, 1976.

CARMICHEL, JIM. *The Women's Guide to Handguns.* Indianapolis: Bobbs-Merrill, 1982.

CARR, PATRICK, and GARDNER, GEORGE W. *The Gun People.* New York: Doubleday, 1985.

COBB, C. G. *Bad Times Primer.* Los Angeles: Times Press, 1981.

COLEMAN, KATE. "Women in Arms." *Savvy,* September 1981, pp. 34–39.

COOK, PHILIP J. "The Effect of Gun Availability on Violent Crime Patterns." *Annals of the Academy of Political Science* 455 (1981): 63–79.

COOPER, JEFF. *Principles of Personal Defense.* Boulder, Col.: Paladin Press, 1972.

"Crime of Rape." *Bureau of Justice Statistics Bulletin.* U.S. Department of Justice, Washington, D.C., March 1985.

CRIUT, RONALD L. *Intruder in Your Home.* New York: Stein & Day, 1983.

DALTON, MIKE, and FOWLER, MICKEY. *Handguns and Self-Defense: Life Without Fear.* Mission Hills, Calif.: ISI Publications, 1984.

DUGGAN, BOB. "In a Mexican Prison." *Gung-Ho,* December 1984, pp. 26–33.

ELLIOTT, CHIP. "Letter from an Angry Reader." *Esquire,* September 1981, pp. 33–37.

FINE, RALPH. *Escape of the Guilty.* New York: Dodd Mead, 1987.

FLYNN, GEORGE, and GOTTLIEB, ALAN. *Guns for Women: The Complete Handgun Buying Guide for Women.* Bellevue, Wash.: Merril Press, 1988.

FRAZIER, PATRICIA, and BORGIDA, EUGENE. "Rape Trauma Syndrome Evidence in Court," *American Psychologist* 40, no. 9 (September 1985): 984–93.

GARRISON, WILLIAM, JR. *Women's View on Guns and Self Defense.* Bellevue, Wash.: Second Amendment Foundation Monograph Series, 1983.

GELB, CONNIE. "Women and Gun Clubs: Make Their Day." *The West Side Spirit* (New York), June 9, 1986, pp. 3 ff.

GORDON, MARGARET T.; RIGER, STEPHANIE; LEBAILLY, ROBERT K.; and HEATH, LINDA. "Crime, Women, and the Quality of Urban Life." *Signs,* Spring 1980 Supplement, pp. S144–S160.

GOTTLIEB, ALAN. *The Gun Grabbers.* Bellevue, Wash.: Merril Press, 1986.

———. *The Rights of Gun Owners.* Ottawa, Ill.: Green Hills Publishers, 1983.

HAGEDORN, ANN. "Shoppers Beware: Malls May Look Safe, But Some Lure Crooks As Well As the Crowds." *Wall Street Journal,* September 10, 1987, p. 1.

HALBROOK, STEPHEN P. "Firearms, the Fourth Amendment, and Air Carrier Security." *Journal of Air Law and Commerce* 52, issue 3 (1985): 585–680.

———. "What the Framers Intended: A Linguistic Analysis of the Right to 'Bear Arms.'" *Law and Contemporary Problems* 48, no. 1 (1986): 151–62.

HARLOW, CAROLINE. "Robbery Victims." Bureau of Justice Statistics, Special Report, U.S. Department of Justice, Washington, D.C., April 1987.

HAZELWOOD, ROBERT R., and HARPOLD, JOSEPH A. "Rape: The Dangers of Providing Confrontational Advice." *FBI Law Enforcement Bulletin,* July 1986, pp. 1–5.

HEATH, LINDA. "Gleaning Accurate Crime Risk Estimates from the Mass Media." Paper presented at the meetings of the American Psychological Association, August 27, 1985, Los Angeles.

HEATH, LINDA; GORDON, MARGARET T.; and LEBAILLY, ROBERT. "What Newspapers Tell Us (and Don't Tell Us) About Rape." *Journal of Newspaper Research* 2, no. 4 (1981): 48–55.

HEATH, LINDA, and SWIM, JANET. "Perceived Control and the Genesis of Fear." Paper presented at the meetings of the American Society of Criminology, November 14, 1985, San Diego.

HOLMSTROM, LYNDA L., and BURGESS, ANN WOLBERT. "Rape: The Husband's and Boyfriend's Initial Reactions." *The Family Coordinator,* July 1979, pp. 321–30.

HORAN, JAMES D. *Desperate Women.* New York: Bonanza Books, 1952.

HOWARD, MARGARET. "Husband-Wife Homicide: An Essay from a Family Law Perspective." *Law and Contemporary Problems* 49, no. 1 (1986): 63–88.

JACOBS, JAMES B. "Exceptions to a General Prohibition on Handgun Possession: Do They Swallow Up the Rule?" *Law and Contemporary Problems* 49, no. 1 (1986): 5–34.

JONES, ANN. *Women Who Kill.* New York: Fawcett Columbine Books, 1980.

JONES, JAN. *Self-Defense Requires No Apology.* Phoenix, Ariz.: Security World Publications, 1985.

KATES, DON B., JR. "The Battle Over Gun Control." *The Public Interest,* no. 84 (Summer 1986): 42–96.

———. *Firearms and Violence.* San Francisco: Pacific Institute for Public Policy Research, 1984.

———. "The Second Amendment: A Dialogue." *Law and Contemporary Problems* 49, no. 1 (1986): 143–150.

KATES, DON B., JR., and ENGBERG, NANCY JEAN. "Deadly Force Self-Defense Against Rape." *Law Review* (Davis, Calif., University of California) 15 (1982): 873–906.

KATES, DON B., JR. with KLECK, GARY; BORDUA, DAVID; MAGADDINO, JOSEPH; and MEDOFF, MARSHALL H. *Why Handgun Bans Can't Work.* Bellevue, Wash.: Second Amendment Foundation, 1982.

KATES, DON B., JR., and VARZOA, NICOLE. "Aspects of the Priapic Theory of Gun Ownership." Paper presented at the Popular Culture Meetings, 1987, Montreal, Canada.

KATES, DON B., JR., ed. *Restricting Handguns: The Liberal Skeptics Speak Out.* Croton-on-Hudson, N.Y.: North River Press, 1979.

KELLERMAN, ARTHUR L., and REAY, DONALD T. "Protection or Peril? An Analysis of Firearm-Related Deaths in the Home." *The New England Journal of Medicine* 314, no. 24 (June 12, 1986): 1557–60.

KENNEDY, EDWARD M. "The Handgun Crime Control Act of 1981." *Northern Kentucky Law Review* (1983): 1–11.

KENNETT, LEE, and ANDERSON, JAMES LAVERNE. *The Gun in America: The Origins of a National Dilemma.* Westport, Conn.: Greenwood Press, 1975.

KLECK, GARY. "Crime Control Through the Private Use of Armed Force." *Social Problems* 35, no. 1 (February 1988): 1–21.

———. "Policy Lessons from Recent Gun Control Research." *Law and Contemporary Problems* 49, no. 1 (1986): 35–62.

KOPEL, DAVID B. "Foreign Gun Control in American Eyes: An Essay on American Popular Culture." Paper presented at the 17th annual meeting of the Popular Culture Association, March 28, 1987, Montreal, Canada.

KOPPEL, HERBERT. "Lifetime Likelihood of Victimization." Bureau of Justice Statistics, Technical Report, U.S. Department of Justice, Washington, D.C., March 1987.

LAKE, PETER A. "Shooting to Kill." *Esquire*, February 1981, pp. 70–75.

LANGAN, PATRICK A., and INNES, CHRISTOPHER A. "Preventing Domestic Violence Against Women." Bureau of Justice Statistics, Special Report, U.S. Department of Justice, Washington, D.C., August 1986.

LAVRAKAS, PAUL J., and HERZ, ELICIA J. "Citizen Participation in Neighborhood Crime Prevention." *Criminology* 20, nos. 3 and 4 (November 1982): 479–98.

LAVRAKAS, PAUL J., and LEWIS, DAN A. "The Conceptualization and Measurement of Citizens' Crime Prevention Behaviors." *Journal of Research in Crime and Delinquency* (July 1980): 254–72.

LEONARD, GEORGE. "The Warrior." *Esquire*, July 1986, pp. 64–71.

LIZOTTE, ALAN J. "Determinants of Completing Rape and Assault." *Journal of Quantitative Criminology*, forthcoming.

LIZOTTE, ALAN J., and BORDUA, DAVID J. "Firearms Ownership for Sport and Protection: Two Divergent Models." *American Sociological Review* 45 (1980): 224–44.

MACK, TONI. "Looking Out for Number One." *Forbes*, December 31, 1984, pp. 28–29.

MAHONEY, REV. R. J. "The Morality of Home Defense." *Guns for Home Defense* (1975): 54–56.

MALAMUTH, NEIL M. "Rape Proclivity Among Males." *Journal of Social Issues* 37, no. 4 (1981): 138–57.

MALCOLM, JOYCE LEE. "The Right of the People to Keep and Bear Arms: The Common Law Tradition." In *Firearms and Violence*, ed. Don Kates. San Francisco: Pacific Institute for Public Policy Research, 1984, pp. 385–416.

MCDERMOTT, JOAN M. "Rape Victimization in 26 American Cities." U.S. Department of Justice, Washington, D.C., 1979.

MCGEORGE, HARVEY J. II, and KETCHAM, CHRISTINE C. "Protection of Senior Executives." *World Affairs* 146, no. 3 (Winter 1983–84): 277–83.

MCGRATH, ROGER. *Gunfighters, Highwaymen, and Vigilantes: Violence on the Frontier*. Berkeley, Calif.: University of California Press, 1984.

MILLER, SHARI. "Women & Self-Defense." *Vogue*, March 1985, pp. 499 ff.

NADELSON, CAROL C., and NOTMAN, MALKAH T. "Emotional Repercussions of Rape." *Medical Aspects of Human Sexuality*, March 1977, pp. 16 ff.

NADELSON, CAROL C.; NOTMAN, MALKAH T.; ZACKSON, HANNAH;

and GORNICK, JANET. "A Follow-Up Study of Rape Victims," *American Journal of Psychiatry* 139, no. 10 (October 1982): 1266–70.

NEWTON, GEORGE D., and ZIMRING, FRANKLIN E. *Firearms and Violence in American Life.* Washington, D.C.: U.S. Government Printing Office, 1969.

POLSBY, DANIEL D. "Reflections on Violence, Guns, and the Defense Use of Lethal Force." *Law and Contemporary Problems* 49, no. 1 (1986): 89–124.

POYER, JOE. "G.I. Jane: Should Women Be Allowed to Fight?" *ICA,* November 1986, pp. 54 ff.

"Prisoners in 1986." *Bureau of Justice Statistics Bulletin,* U.S. Department of Justice, Washington, D.C., May 1987.

RAND, MICHAEL; DEBERRY, MARSHALL; KLAUS, PATSY; and TAYLOR, BRUCE. "The Use of Weapons in Committing Crimes." Bureau of Justice Statistics, Special Report, U.S. Department of Justice, Washington, D.C., January 1986.

Rape Victimization Study. San Francisco: Queen's Beach Foundation, 1975.

RHODES, RICHARD. "Why Do Men Rape?" *Playboy,* April 1981, pp. 112 ff.

RIGER, STEPHANIE, and GORDON, MARGARET T. "The Fear of Rape: A Study in Social Control." *Journal of Social Issues* 37, no. 4 (1981): 71–92.

RIGER, STEPHANIE; GORDON, MARGARET T.; and LEBAILLY, ROBERT K. "Coping with Urban Crime: Women's Use of Precautionary Behaviors." *American Journal of Community Psychology* 10, no. 4 (1982): 369–86.

ROSE, DEBORAH S. " 'Worse Than Death': Psychodynamics of Rape Victims and the Need for Psychotherapy." *American Journal of Psychiatry,* July 1986, pp. 817–24.

ROSENBERG, TINA. "The Female Persuasion." *Regardie's,* July 1985, pp. 36–39.

RUSSELL, CARL. *Guns on the Early Frontiers.* Berkeley, Calif.: University of California Press, 1957.

SAUNDERS, DANIEL G. "When Battered Women Use Violence: Husband-Abuse or Self-Defense?" *Victims and Violence* 1, no. 1 (1986): 47–60.

SCHNEIDER, ELIZABETH M.; JORDAN, SUSAN B.; and ARGUEDAS, CRISTINA C. "Representation of Women Who Defend Themselves in Response to Physical or Sexual Assault." New York, Center for Constitutional Rights, 1978.

"Sentencing and Time Served: Federal Offenses and Offenders." Bureau of Justice Statistics, Special Report, U.S. Department of Justice, Washington, D.C., June 1987.

SHENK, J. FREDERICK, and KLAUS, PATSY A. "The Economic Cost of

Crime to Victims." Bureau of Justice Statistics, Special Report, U.S. Department of Justice, Washington, D.C., April 1984.

SHIELDS, PETE, with GREENYA, JOHN. *Guns Don't Die—People Do.* New York: Arbor House, 1981.

SILVERMAN, DANIEL C. "Sharing the Crisis of Rape: Counseling the Mates and Families of Victims." *American Journal of Orthopsychiatry* 48, no. 1 (January 1978): 166–73.

STRAUS, MURRAY A. "Domestic Violence and Homicide Antecedents." *Bulletin of the New York Academy of Medicine* 62, no. 5 (June 1986): 447–61.

SWANSON, GERALD, and TABBUSH, VICTOR. "The Economics of Crime and Punishment." *Contemporary Economic Issues,* Summer 1988.

TESORO, MARY. "Model Mugging: The Rape You Prevent May Be Your Own!" *Black Belt,* May 1986, pp. 32–37.

TIMROTS, ANITA D., and RAND, MICHAEL R. "Violent Crime by Strangers and Nonstrangers." Bureau of Justice Statistics, Special Report, U.S. Department of Justice, Washington, D.C., January 1987.

VELAZQUEZ, LORETA JANETA. *The Woman in Battle: A Narrative of the Exploits, Adventures and Travels of Madame Loreta Janeta Velazquez.* New York: Arno Press, 1972.

VOGEL, RONALD E., and DEAN, CHARLES. "The Effectiveness of a Handgun Safety Education Program." *Journal of Police Science and Administration* 14, no. 3 (1986): 242–49.

WALKER, LENORE E. "Battered Women and Learned Helplessness." *Victimology* 2, nos. 3–4 (1978): 525–34.

WHEELER, CHARLES. "A School for Aspiring Bodyguards." *Insight,* December 22, 1986, pp. 22–23.

WHITEHEAD, JOHN T., and LANGWORTHY, ROBERT H. "Gun Ownership: Another Look." Unpublished paper. Department of Criminal Justice, University of Alabama at Birmingham, 1986.

WINTER, BILL, "Gun Control: ABA Is for Curbs, Not a Ban." *American Bar Association Journal* 69 (1983): 425.

WOLFGANG, M. *Patterns in Criminal Homicide.* Philadelphia: University of Pennsylvania Press, 1958.

WRIGHT, JAMES D., and ROSSI, PETER H. *Armed and Considered Dangerous.* New York: Aldine De Gruyter, 1986.

WRIGHT, JAMES D.; ROSSI, PETER H.; and DALY, KATHLEEN. *Under the Gun.* New York: Aldine Publishing Co., 1983.

YOUNG, ROBERT L. "Gender, Region of Socialization, and Ownership of Protective Firearms." *Rural Sociology* 5, no. 2 (1986): 169–82.

ZEDLEWSKI, EDWIN W. "Making Confinement Decisions." National Institute of Justice, Research in Brief, Washington, D.C., U.S. Department of Justice, July 1987.

ZIMRING, FRANKLIN E. "Handguns in the Twenty-first Century: Alternative Policy Futures." *Annals of the American Academy of Political and Social Science,* no. 455 (1981): 1–10.

————. "Violence and Firearms Policy." In *American Violence and Public Policy: An Update of the National Commission on the Causes and Prevention of Violence,* ed. L. A. Curtis. New Haven: Yale University Press, 1985.

ZIMRING, FRANKLIN E., and HAWKINS, GORDON J. *Deterrence: The Legal Threat in Crime Control.* Chicago: University of Chicago Press, 1973.

ZIMRING, FRANKLIN E., and ZUEHL, FRANK. "Victim Injury and Death in Urban Robbery: A Chicago Study." *Journal of Legal Studies* 1 (1986): 15 ff.

TACKLE LIFE'S PROBLEMS.

With Help From St. Martin's Paperbacks!

HOW TO LOVE A DIFFICULT MAN
Nancy Good
_____ 90963-2 $3.95 U.S. _____ 90964-0 $4.95 Can.

BEYOND CINDERELLA
Nita Tucker with Debra Feinstein
_____ 91161-0 $3.95 U.S. _____ 91162-9 $4.95 Can.

HOW TO GET A MAN TO MAKE A COMMITMENT
Bonnie Barnes & Tisha Clark
_____ 90189-5 $3.95 U.S. _____ 90190-9 $4.95 Can.

HAVE A LOVE AFFAIR WITH YOUR HUSBAND
Susan Kohl & Alice Bregman
_____ 91037-1 $3.50 U.S. _____ 91039-8 $4.50 Can.

WHEN YOUR CHILD DRIVES YOU CRAZY
Eda Le Shan
_____ 92930-7 $5.99 U.S./$6.99 Can.